Praise for Wildlife in th

"Reading this book may change your mind about almost everything. Important beyond compare, utterly engrossing, at once chilling and heartening."

– Dame Joanna Lumley

"This book arrives at an opportune time with an important message to humanity: protecting, restoring and regenerating animal species are crucial to our own existence. The book provides a key insight for mitigating that risk: Animals are our allies in this fight. They do so by interacting with fauna, green and blue, creating the biodiversity that maintains balance in nature. The book's call to action: to change our behaviour towards our fellow animals and nature before it is too late, should be heeded by all those truly interested in safeguarding our own existence."

– Ralph Chami, Assistant Director, International Monetary Fund

"We can't exist without wildlife and the time has come to make sure, WITHOUT FAIL, we don't lose them. This book shows how it can be done."

– Robyn Williams AO, ABC Science Show

"A single life is finite and mortal. But, Life, as such, continues exactly because the many lives do not and cannot just live for themselves. As Mustoe clearly explains, humans cannot live without 'wild'-life, for we are all subject to the same universal laws of dynamic interdependence and needing each other to survive ... isn't this true joy de vivre?!"

– Professor Richard Banati, University of Sydney

"This book makes it clear that we have to value and respect the role of animals in creating a habitable planet."

– Leif Cocks, The Orangutan Foundation

"You might love animals. You might want to take care of nature. But you might not know how important other animals are in shaping and maintaining the world, and in contributing to the dignity and well-being of the particular animals we call: Human. This crucially important book informs us of the many ways that other-than-human animals shape the planet and contribute to the quality of human life. Mustoe shows us how there is much more than meets the eye."

– Carl Safina, author of 'Becoming Wild' and 'Beyond Words'

"'Wildlife in the Balance' captures the science in a way never offered before, exposing stunning and critical revelations relevant to both the layman and learned scientists."

– David Casselman, Ecoflix Foundation

"This delightfully evocative yet sobering book is the strongest of clarion calls as to why, with the utmost urgency, we must nourish nature and change our destructive ways. For our very lives, and that of our sustaining planet, depends on we humans nourishing diversity. This book is a rich primer and wondrous feast of information and conceptual clarity that will help people fall in love with nature."

– Dr. Charles Massy best-selling author, 'Call of the Reed-Warbler'

"This is an important book to read and, more critically, respond to and act upon. Astutely pulling together a complex web of facts, theories and stories, Mustoe conveys just how critically important it is that all parts of the wonderous ecosystems on which we, and all planetary species depend, are able to thrive. We, humans, must embrace the call to action so ably represented by 'Wildlife in the Balance'."

– Ian Dunn, CEO Plantlife International, The Wild Plant Conservation Charity

"'Wildlife in the Balance' pulls together thousands of threads into a dizzying but utterly coherent narrative that explains in terms even the most ardent industrialist will understand how animals are critical, not just to their own survival, but to our survival too."

– Charlie Moores, Unleashed Podcast

"What would our planet be like without animals? This lively and passionate book highlights the extent to which wildlife drive ecological processes—indeed, how animals, birds and insects create and maintain a livable world. Through research and reminiscence he shows how wildlife are essential to the cycling and conveying of energy, nutrients, and information, and why a vibrant future depends on thriving, abundant fauna."

– Judith Schwartz, author of 'The Reindeer Chronicles'

"Visionary, insightful, and full of original observations, 'Wildlife in the Balance' provides an utterly compelling overview of the importance of animals. I've been a conservation scientist for 25 years but this has helped me see nature in new ways. This is a hugely important book, and the more widely it is read the better our futures will be!"

– Dr Charlie Gardner, Durrell Institute of Conservation and Ecology

"A fascinating insight into the critical inter-dependencies of humans and nature, taking the long view and reflecting on the millennia of evolutionary processes. Our world is way out of balance and Mustoe puts forward a better way of appreciating and respecting nature, that would extend our time on Earth. Read the book, grasp the ideas and change our future."

– Professor David Hill CBE, Environment Bank

"Wildlife in the balance brings together a kaleidoscope of facts around the importance of wildlife to our survival, all amalgamated in a beautifully understandable fashion at a time more urgent than ever for us all to heed the words in these pages."

Greg Irons, Bonorong Sanctuary

"Captivating from page one. This is a story of our place on Earth and the important role we play in rebuilding a habitable world for all life. It is ultimately a book about our connection to nature, humanity and hope. Wildlife in the Balance is beautifully written and enlightens the reader with a powerful message – that Earth's wildlife and wild places are essential for our survival and we must act urgently and ambitiously to look after them."

– Dr Anika Molesworth, author of 'Our Sunburnt Country'

WILDLIFE
IN THE BALANCE

Why animals are humanity's best hope

SIMON MUSTOE
simonmustoe.blog

First published 2022 by Wildiaries

Melbourne, Australia.

ISBN 978-0-6454535-0-8 TBP

Cover art by Nicholas Girling, Girling Design, 2022

Design and layout by Jarrett Skinner, Objetda Design, 2022

For Charlie, Sadie and all the people and other animals helping us to survive.

With special thanks to

Scan this code to try for FREE.

I am convinced that man has suffered in his separation from the soil and from the other living creatures of the world; the evolution of his intellect has outrun his needs as an animal, and as yet he must still, for security, look long at some portion of the earth as it was before he tampered with it.

– Gavin Maxwell, *Ring of Bright Water* (1960)

Otters are joined by migratory birds to feast on seasonal riches fuelled by marine plants and kickstarted by the summer sun. Life started in the sea, and the powerful Scottish coastlines where Gavin Maxwell lived are still a stark reminder about how much we depend on wildlife for healthy ecosystems.

Contents

Foreword

You know how when looking at an optical illusion, you can look and look and then suddenly, with the same visual input, you see it - or when you are shown a camouflaged gecko on bark and see only bark until you notice the eye, then suddenly it becomes clear and you wonder why you couldn't see it before?

Reading *Wildlife in the Balance* is like seeing one gecko after another as patterns of life fall into place. Not only is it a readable romp through diverse areas of natural history, physics and philosophy, it strings together theories and facts with a rare clarity.

The reader emerges with an understanding of nature and the forces that shape the biosphere, our only home, and how we are a part of it and dependent on it.

Conservation of animals cannot just be about preventing extinction - our future depends on wild animals thriving, not just surviving, eventually recovering in number to provide the ecosystem services on which we depend.

Wildlife in the Balance is perhaps the most important book of our time.

Ian Redmond OBE

Co-founder, Rebalance Earth.
Ambassador for the UN Convention on the Conservation of Migratory Species of Wild Animals.

Introduction

People and other animals make our world habitable

Hundreds of millions of years of evolution led to human existence. We are among the last in a long line of animals that were the likeliest to survive. Strangely, the traits that make us one of the most destructive animals on the planet, are also the same ones that allowed us to create a habitable Earth in the first place. Two thousand years ago, our species had already modified most of the land, leading to the incredible diversity of wildlife you see today.[1] Our animality is our power to make individual, everyday choices, and this has always made the difference between life and death on a planetary scale. This means you and I are among the most powerful creatures ever to exist in the known universe.

Australia's lyrebirds are the closest living relatives of the ancestors of all the world's songbirds, and in their native forests each bird ploughs 350 tonnes of leaf litter and soil every year. This keeps the ecosystem intact, absorbs moisture from the ocean and means Melbourne residents are gravity-fed clean and fresh mineral water from their taps.

Things only started to go wrong for us in the last few decades. In that time, we've pushed three-quarters of animals out of existence. What we haven't realised yet is how much our future depends on them. We have lost touch with the systems of culture that connected us with nature to the point where we now face an uncertain future as a species.

The question you might ask is: what can I do about this? First, it helps to understand your role in ecosystems and how the planet fits together. Next, you can become part of a movement that inspires change.

There are three concepts that will help start making a positive difference.

- The first is that you are an animal like any other;
- The second is that every small action you take is potentially the most powerful contribution any creature can ever make; and
- The third is that you can't do this unless you surround yourself with wildlife.

This book is about the importance of animals, including humans. It's about why we need a diversity and abundance of wildlife working with us to recreate a habitable planet, to rebalance ecosystems. This is why your importance on Earth is no more or less than any other creature. It is about why we need a global change in human values – a change in attitudes towards wildlife – if we are to survive as a species. Over the next few decades, humans face a choice: re-find our place within nature, or succumb to a force that is unstoppable and unimaginably powerful.

This is the story of your place on Earth and the impact we all have on rebuilding a habitable world. It is a story of hope, in which all the world's animals have a role to play. Yours may just be among the greatest.

The urgency to protect nature is obvious but forests, grasslands and oceans aren't enough on their own without wildlife. Did you know Earth has more tree cover now than it did thirty-five years ago?[2] How can that be, I hear you ask, when the land and sea are clearly malfunctioning? What about climate change? Isn't that because we're cutting the forests down? All good questions.

Why do you think animals exist? What purpose do they serve, and why do we need them?

The answer is simple. Animals are not a by-product of our world. Our coexistence with animals is the key to how ecosystems have remained stable long enough for humans to exist. But ecosystems may not be what you think. Ecosystems are a dynamic community of animals, plants, fungi and micro-organisms where the maximum diversity and abundance of animals can coexist. For ecosystems to remain habitable, animals constantly adapt and rebuild them in an ever-changing way. They say it takes a village to raise a child. It took a community comprising trillions of animals to raise humans, and we are as dependent as ever on their nurturing influence. We live among animals, on their ecological plane, sharing the same basic needs. If we want to live in a world of plants, we can't, unless there are animals too. We animals can't survive without each other.

Today, we're deforesting primary wildlife-rich ecosystems faster than ever, and they are being replaced with regrowth and empty seas and vegetation. Without wildlife, the science simply doesn't add up – we just haven't worked this out yet.

This is ultimately a book about science. I hope you'll enjoy reading it as much as I did researching and writing, as it renewed my hope for our future, and my determination to appreciate and protect wildlife.

It does take a new perspective, a dose of cynicism and the preparation to rethink what you may have learnt about concepts like natural selection, evolution, ecosystems and conservation. Things don't quite work like we were taught. It's all at once more complex but also simpler than we imagine. I have tried to write it like a detective novel instead of a typical science book. The 'whodunnit' isn't revealed until you have had the chance to understand all the characters and their roles.

However, because this subject has hardly ever been written about before, it's inevitable that you'll need to grasp some new theories. The concepts I cover in Part 2 may be unfamiliar and have hardly ever been applied to conservation. Hence I've explained them in ways that relate to our everyday behaviour. This means you don't need to fully comprehend the science – you are the living embodiment of how animals interact with our world and that understanding will sink in as you read on.

Part 3 and Part 4 take these ideas and look at them in the context of the unimaginable power of wildlife to influence our planet's ecosystems. This is the heart and soul of the book. It's about how epic wildlife-driven patterns of existence from movement and feeding, to language and culture, deliver food, water, health and a fair climate for all.

In the last third of the book the mystery comes to a close. It brings this kaleidoscope of ideas into focus around our individual and collective power to change our world for the better.

My children were reading about ecosystem science in school. They said to me, 'Everything is about trees, plants and forests … none of the policy we're reading mentions animals.' We can't achieve any of our Earth-saving ambitions unless we prioritise repopulating wildlife. We need to start seeing ourselves as one member of a team of animals that make Earth function for the survival of all wildlife and humans.

Humanity's best chance is a global change in human values, one by which we treat animals equally, because all animals have to work together equally in building a habitable world and future for each other. Animals aren't commodities; they are the sole mechanism that delivers human life support. Conservation can't succeed until we've had this conversation, until everyone learns this. It is perhaps the greatest, yet unknown, challenge of our generation. This is what this book is about.

Join me to learn about the impact animals have on our survival and learn a new way to see wildlife.

PART 1–

Why do animals matter?

The unanswered question

It took a lifetime and career as an ecologist until, aboard a small wooden sailing ship in eastern Indonesia, in a place where wildlife abounds like nowhere else on our planet,[4,5] a non-scientist asked me this most challenging question of all: What is the point of an animal?

To be honest I'd not given it enough thought before then, but it had been nagging in my head for about twenty years. What surprised me was how much I have had to relearn, how much scientific practice has been drilled into me that I've since come to question. And how much I learnt from simply immersing myself back into nature for a few years, where I realised a new clarity, before I delved back into the detailed research with fresh eyes.

As I find now, the importance of wildlife isn't a fanciful notion at all. Animals do matter … a lot. Discovering this has forced me into a different way of thinking. It's altered everything I've learnt before.

I'll take you back to the moment when the idea for this book came into sharp focus – the first time I've ever felt an ecosystem close to fully functioning. It was exhilarating.

A Bryde's whale lunges out of the water, its tail as wide as a small aircraft. Thrown upwards, it powers through the ocean at breakneck speed, gulping mouthfuls of small fish and filtering them through coarse baleen. Moments later, calm resumes. A whale calf appears, its mother feeding underwater, leaving her infant unattended for a few minutes. Further out, the surface is occasionally sliced by the fin of an exploratory predator as the shallower embayment here provides protection from the sharks that inhabit deeper waters. The whales, the sharks and the schools of vivid fish they're intent on devouring demonstrate the connections that underpin our blue planet. We're in Raja Ampat. It forms the heart of the Coral Triangle, which is a magical reef-world encompassing the Philippines, Indonesia, Papua New Guinea, Timor Leste and the Solomon Islands, where it's still possible to see the action of healthy ecosystems with abundant wildlife.

You begin to feel miniscule after you dip into the otherworldly mysteries of Raja Ampat. It's like diving inside a gigantic living organism; navigating through its nervous system, riding the rush of currents passing down networks of ancient channels, highways for cells and plankton that feed its organs: reefs and ocean fronts where miniature forces combine on a massive scale, giving and supporting life. Immersed in the ocean here, you begin to appreciate a new sensory landscape and acknowledge an entire realm that exists mostly beyond our imagining. To float among this melee of life, disconnected from technology and simply at one with it all, is both intoxicating and incredibly emotional.

It was lunchtime, just after we returned from a snorkel, a guest asked me the ultimate question as, 'What is the point of a turtle?'

I'd not heard the question before in so few words. I contemplated answering immediately but struggled, so I deferred for time to think. I realised soon after that it wasn't going to be easy, and the thought process from that moment was one of the sparks for this book.

Surrounded by such intense animal activity, it's reasonable to ask such questions. But what do we really mean?

In everyday life, we're more likely to be surrounded by concrete walls, and more people and vehicles will attract our attention each day than birds or animals. When you're immersed in an immaculate wilderness, primal curiosities resurface and hit you like a massive slap in the face.

For many, experiences with wildlife are overwhelming and for others, unfathomable. Rather than asking 'why' an animal exists, the question surely has to be, 'Does it matter?'

Does it matter what an animal does? Aren't we really asking the question about ourselves? Aren't we asking, 'Why does it matter to me?'

Animals don't appear to be aware of having a role, which, in any case, would imply something preordained. Animals instinctively follow their needs to feed and reproduce, somehow making decisions along the way and surviving as species.

So should we ask – and care about the answer to – the question, 'Does it matter to us if animals do contribute to the way our world works?' We should.

Landscape ecologist Oliver Rackham noted that plants and animals are like actors in a play, each with its own character that we tend to regard individually rather than as performers in a bigger story.[6]

The idea that animals might serve an important function for human life is hardly talked about. To imply creatures have use-value can be unpopular among animal lovers, and that's fair enough. The problem is that a classical education makes you think of animals as resources. And you look for explanations outside yourself, when the truth was staring at you in the bathroom mirror every morning: that you are one of the animals with a value of your own. When you start to look at all the impact animals have on the world and how we connect with them to make ecosystems work, it stops becoming about what use they are to us and more about what use we are to each other.

For an animal enthusiast like me, the experiences I have in nature are more vivid and spectacular for knowing this. The essence of what it is to be human, our place in the world and even (dare I say it) a certain spiritual meaningfulness for the life we live comes out of watching and understanding animals at work in ecosystems and knowing I'm part of that. It makes me think twice about disturbing an animal going about its business. Animals aren't there just for our benefit. They are functioning parts of an ecosystem in which we too are embedded. We all depend on the processes they provide to all life on Earth. Most of the time we don't even notice the scale and importance of animals and what they do.

Fifteen years ago I was working on a ship monitoring the impact of noise on whales during seismic surveys for oil companies. The ships tow ten kilometres of heavy cabling containing thousands of hydrophones (underwater microphones) and, immediately behind, a noise source called an airgun. The sudden release of extremely high-pressure air creates a 'bang', and the behaviour of sound reflected off layers of rock deep below the seabed and received along the cables paints a three-dimensional picture of where there are possible pockets of oil and gas. Seismic surveys are renowned for their negative impact on the acoustic geography of whole regions and can often be heard hundreds of miles away.

A sperm whale popped up way ahead of the vessel, and I'd instructed the operator to stop work, but the ship, weighing tens of thousands of tonnes, remained at full power due to the immense drag caused by towing heavy cables. The sperm whale was facing away from me, replenishing its blood oxygen at the surface, breathing deeply after an exhausting hour chasing squid. As we approached, it was clear the whale was not going to move – it had no idea we were there, despite the ship's intense underwater noise. I called the captain, and we managed to steer to one side. Out on the bridge wings, the sperm whale dived directly below me, calmly and vertically raising its tulip-shaped tail skyward and sinking into the abyss. It never even noticed us.

That evening in the mess, the captain asked 'Why didn't the sperm whale move?' There was some joking and exclamations by others: 'No wonder they're going extinct!'

Weeks earlier we'd been out on aerial surveys and found a sperm whale lying dead on its side in the same area. There were lacerations down the length of its body, the imprint from a ship's propeller that had gouged the life out of the majestic creature. It had been struck by one of the many boats that pass our coastline every day and, sadly for the animal, no-one was looking out for its welfare that day. So, why can't a sperm whale hear a 200,000-tonne supertanker coming up behind it?

Sperm whales eat almost a tonne of prey every day. They do this using incredible sensory adaptations combined with an ability to know exactly where squid occur, and contributing to the health of supporting ecosystems. These social and cultural connections to the ocean have developed over many thousands of years and are a large part of the puzzle of how animals like sperm whales can catch 350–700 squid a day.

Sperm whales are as alien as any creature you will ever encounter. They are wonderful and gentle animals that exhibit an almost blundering nonchalance regarding what's around them. Like you'd expect from the largest toothed predator that ever lived, they transcend any notion of ego and just exist as they always have. But a sperm whale can't hear behind itself, just like you and I can't see out of the backs of our heads, and they are quite nervy. I watched a video recently in which a filmmaker got excited when, after he swam towards a sperm whale, it ejected a massive cloud of pungent oily faeces. What I saw was the whale react, almost in slow motion, as it spotted something out of the corner of its eye and turned slightly to be surprised by swimmers at the surface. The whale panicked in a way only sperm whales can ... slowly. It tensed its body, arched its back and did what its kind have always done as a reaction to predators: it concealed itself behind the whale-sized smokescreen and made its escape.

Nothing happens quickly or without purpose in the sperm whale's world. They don't immediately leave an area of noisy boat traffic because they think they might be harmed. Where else would they go? This doesn't make them stupid or unintelligent; it makes them exquisitely adapted to what they do best.

The sharp beam of sound that a sperm whale emits every second or so allows the whale to scan the environment in front of it. The reflections received through its dense jawbone are processed with the largest brain of any animal on Earth. It's packed full of glia, non-neural cells that are thought to be essential for data processing. It's probably how the whale can interpret all that sound energy into a picture. We have no idea what a sperm whale actually 'sees', but it's a good enough image to catch small squid. With a mouth slung far beneath a bus-shaped head, it would be like us trying to catch bugs using the loose flap beneath the sole of a shoe … while blindfolded!

A supertanker doesn't matter to a sperm whale as it's a species already far more successful on Earth than humans. Their kind have existed for over ten million years. To the best of our knowledge, no animal except a human has ever pondered the meaning of its own existence, and even if it did, what difference would that make to us? The main thing that matters to a sperm whale is catching squid. A sperm whale is unlikely to ask, 'What is the role of a supertanker?'

We are mostly curious about the importance of animals when it might affect us, not because we have any real interest in whether they matter in any general sense. Like the sperm whales, we only exist in our own realm of thinking. The sperm whale is doing what it's meant to do without thinking about it, or else the sperm whale might consider taking a holiday now and again, or feeding somewhere without supertankers or seismic surveys.

The reason we haven't considered why sperm whales or any reasonably abundant animals are important for a functioning planet is because it's never mattered to us before. Now we are thinking about global ecological collapse we've started to ask whether animals do exist for a reason after all. I can tell you they do: it's because ecosystems don't exist without them, and it is ecosystems that we need to survive. The impact of sperm whales is huge, on a planetary scale, but we're only just finding out. We'll discover more about that in Part 2 of the book.

If animals are so abundant, and so are we, why don't they destroy the Earth like we do? The short answer is that individually they do but as a group their collective behaviour has evolved an alignment and co-dependence with ecosystem stability. You might never notice the species matters because its impact isn't negative; it's benign, silent, unnoticeable like an ordinarily dressed person wandering down a high street.

For this reason, we are ignorant about the sheer scale, magnitude and intensity of animals' impact and wildlife's sole responsibility for building habitable ecosystems. We have formed an opinion that they don't do very much, and that is the very opposite of what we need for human survival.

The impact of only a small handful of animals can have a huge effect. It only took a few wolves introduced into Yellowstone National Park to alter the behaviour of grazing animals.[7] Willow trees recovered and beavers created dams, altering the course of rivers. If a few animals can breathe life back into a local landscape, imagine what the birds are doing in your local park. Imagine that on a global scale with abundant wildlife.

The wolf studies sparked debate among scientists. Was it true? Were the wolves really changing the course of rivers? In fact all of this is true, but humans like to look for simple cause-effect in nature, when the reality is always more complicated than that. We'd like to say that we can introduce animals in order to create a certain outcome, but it's unpredictable. We can't 'manage' animals. Indeed, the opposite is true: we need animals to recreate the life support systems around us, while we concentrate on our own behaviour.

Consider how often you hear scientists and conservationists talk about 'managing' wildlife, 'managing' fisheries and 'managing' forests. The opposite view, the one that matters, is rarely heard. Marine mammal biologist Dr Heike Vester once told me off for even suggesting that we 'manage' animals. It never actually occurred to me before … yet it seems so obvious now, but it took someone to say it bluntly before I realised I'd been thinking about it wrong for years. Even the inconvenience animals create for us is the result of us mismanaging our own environment. It's our fault, not theirs. All animals are doing is stepping in to reset the imbalance. Whether its wolves, butterflies, soil springtails, sperm whales or songbirds, small numbers of wild animals have a huge effect and are the driving force behind everything that is good for our survival.

Our first challenge will be to accept a shared identity and need to coexist with animals and understand that we hold no 'dominion' over animals – an attitude that seems to endure in thought and deed today. The idea that human and beast are disjoined pervades public policy and science worldwide. Political scientist and environmental policy expert Frank Biermann[8] says that this mainstream view is outdated and incompatible with the kind of innovative approaches we are going to need if we're to address environmental problems today.

The very assumptions we base our decisions on, which have contributed to the wholesale collapse of wild animal populations, are leading us into the greatest existential crisis of our age. And we don't even know it yet, because the true story of animal impact is still largely missing from the global conservation narrative. I am hoping we can change that, with this book.

Your power to make a difference

It's inevitable that someone will one day say to me: 'Why are you making animal conservation all about humans?' I sympathise with this view.

When I see suffering inflicted on wildlife I feel like the world might be better off without us. But that would be the most selfish view of all, and it won't help because we are all animals and our destiny is interconnected.

If we try to preserve animals for their own sake we inevitably make them into victims, which is a principal reason why our species doesn't take animal conservation seriously enough. Think about gender equality. That's not only achieved by supplementing pay; it's reached by creating conditions for equal opportunity. That's what leads to a stronger and more resilient society. Similarly, conservation can never just be about protection and support for threatened species – which is tantamount to control. It must be about respect for animals and giving them equal opportunity to survive. That is what makes for the strongest ecosystems.

What if we did give animals equal opportunity to survive? Where can we start? How can we each make a difference?

We would first need to believe they have equality – I'm not strictly talking about animal rights. If we lord it over animals as their 'protectors' we are still exerting dominion over them, and it misses the point that the world can't function without them, that we can't survive without wildlife. The only perspective we can ever have is centred on ourselves, but – as conservationists – when we regard people as supreme and separate, we risk being as anthropocentric as those who care little at all.

Today we face one of our species' worst ever existential crises – climate change. We dig up and burn about the same amount of fossilised carbon as the Earth produces every day. The second, more serious problem, we don't even recognise yet. Even if we stopped our pollution tomorrow we don't have enough wildlife left on land and in our oceans to maintain our food security, let alone the planet-cooling ecosystems that we live among. We need animals to survive and deliver sustainable life support, and a single species like ours can't do this alone.

Homo sapiens was the latest in a long line of animals that was likeliest to survive because that was the outcome that stabilised our planet's biosphere at the time. We have had great success as a species in the past, but our animality can also explain our current failures. Behaving in absurd and seemingly destructive ways is actually very predictable and animal-like, because that is how nature hedges its bets.

This is the paradox that creates our feeling of helplessness. There is discomfort around accepting that we are capable of destroying ourselves, while also knowing we have the ability to create a better world, but one where we're still only just surviving because 'nature' is far stronger than ourselves. But that's the point. Survival only comes from the collective power we have with other animals.

Before we can accept these truths, we are going to need a global change in human values – a new conservation narrative – one that challenges old-fashioned, rusted-on beliefs about wildlife. We need to understand and accept that animals have an equal role in our existence.

Equal because, if we allow them to go extinct, we are likely to go extinct too.

Equal because they are as dependent on our actions as we are on theirs.

Knowing that you might be driven by forces beyond your control is quite cathartic. What sets us apart, however, is having a brain and collective consciousness that's capable of realising we are now making things worse for ourselves. We've disconnected from our knowledge of how to survive, but we still very much depend on the stability of Earth's biosphere and, therefore, depend on wildlife in equal measure.

The internet has become an incredible knowledge base about how the world works and we live among billions of animals that we can observe to learn how to behave better. We can also talk among ourselves about our actions and their consequences, run scientific experiments, create change-making television shows and vote for better leadership. Our ability to act collectively makes us a truly remarkable species.

Maybe we do have the chance to correct our path and achieve a different destiny for all of nature. Knowing we can do something certainly gives me some hope.

Some of you might think this is overly optimistic, but one way or the other we will be forced to work out our mistakes, because we are the embodiment of a system that will correct itself with or without us. We have the opportunity to reinterpret our behaviour and safely reconnect with the world if we observe and live alongside wildlife. It's no different to how our ancestors lived.

In Tom Huth and Mike Keighley's book *True Tales of an Outback Guide or Why Kangaroos Go Boing, Boing, Boing*, they explain how Indigenous Australians used wildlife to indicate changes in season, enabling them to balance their food, vitamin and protein intake. If you've ever been to Kakadu National Park in the dry season, you'll have seen the bright yellow flowers of the Kapok tree, whose flowering signifies that crocodiles are laying their eggs. Observing nature allowed people to move seasonally between hunting grounds, which enabled other animals to recover and maintain the balance in these life-supporting ecosystems.

Like many of the world's surviving Indigenous cultures teach us, empathy, respect and coexistence with animals can once again become an extension of our survival instinct. That's a lovely thing to think we can achieve. But we're also running out of time, and the world is just too complex to describe in full; and it's unnecessary. We can afford to take some educated risks and do what we know is needed to rebuild wildlife populations.

You have to remember only one thing. It doesn't matter whether it's climate change, decline in soil fertility, disease, clean water, healthy oceans, war or famine, the key to solving all our problems, saving our planet for humanity's sake (after all, what other reason would our species have to) is to *rebuild a world rich with a diversity of vibrant and abundant wildlife*.

My hope is that, after reading this book, you will believe this. And you will feel more enlightened and positive about your contribution to the world and perhaps a little less guilty because you know you can be part of a solution and not just the problem. Rather than thinking that your lone voice and your actions count for little, you should know that your individual connectedness to ecosystems makes you the most powerful force there is in nature. This means you're not alone.

You are among the most recent (if not the most intelligent) animal on the planet, the last in a long line of advanced creatures to evolve over billions of years, and your species was placed here to make a difference, alongside the rest of animality. You only get to vote once every few years, but when it comes to nature and wildlife we all act continuously, and our individual decisions provide the greatest impact we can ever have on anything in the universe.

PART 2-

How animals combat chaos

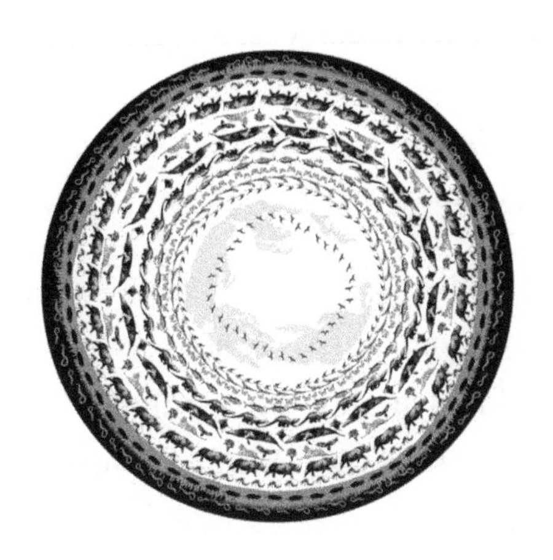

The chaos that would exist without animals

Everything descends into chaos under the influence of an invisible force that physicists call 'entropy'. Entropy is the framework for all life; it connects everything, and it's the reason animals – including humans – exist.

Without wildlife this universal law of nature would mean Earth could never stabilise sufficiently to support human life because animals control the disorder. The world can be blanketed with forest and farmland but without animals, ecosystems will collapse and we won't

---

Animals are often viewed as the final step in a pyramid of life, whereas in fact they are the fabric that binds everything together. Animals work for each other by taking what plants make and manufacturing it into something useful for all. Our world view of wildlife and our place in it needs to change if we're to have any chance of surviving as one of them.

be able to feed ourselves. Accepting that wildlife is the harbinger of stability means we can start to protect ourselves against the threat of climate and food security chaos.

Luckily, because we're all animals, we still exhibit the traits of wildlife trying to stabilise our world, and our own everyday behaviour is the perfect and simplest demonstration of how entropy and ecosystems work, as well as how they couldn't work without animals like us.

Each week we gather food. Many of us visit supermarkets in droves, supplied by thousands of businesses, farmers, factories and truck drivers. The wares are housed in buildings with structures that create order. Like ecosystems, a supermarket maximises its revenue by creating an internal order and minimising the amount of energy an animal like us needs to exert to find food. None of this would be possible if a whole population of human (animal) employees weren't busy at work maintaining the essential functions. We drive our cars into parking spaces that maximise throughput, and chaos is minimised by placing food in aisles, grouped in familiar ways. Trolleys are collected and placed where we can find them. Regular stocktakes are done and new food ordered. We know that in aisle four there are tinned tomatoes and tacos, aisle seven has everything we need to make a cake, the vegetables are all stacked together, as are the frozen desserts.

With this chaos minimised, the supermarket can convert an optimal amount of produce with as little waste as possible and support lots of employees. Meanwhile, customers can shop efficiently without wasting valuable energy critical for reproduction and survival. While entropy is an unfamiliar term to many of us, it's also a simple concept once you realise we live under its influence every day. Supermarkets and ecosystems work exactly the same way against entropy, and as soon as you remove the animals that maintain order, or disrupt existing patterns of behaviour, chaos ensues.

How much energy would you waste if the milk, eggs and bread were no longer where you expect? What if they were placed in obscure locations rather than at the shops? How much longer would it take you to find your food? How would it make you feel? Then consider the impact on your life if this became permanently unpredictable. In between your job, driving to work, sleeping, socialising and eating, you would need to find the ingredients for breakfast most mornings by door-knocking, in the hope that someone could spare basic ingredients.

Koalas can coexist with farming but only if they are able to reliably find food. When we damage ecosystem processes we put unnecessary pressure on animals. Koalas, though, are as much a part of the fabric of the landscape as its trees, so protecting their welfare is essential if we are to have healthy and sustainable farmland ecosystems.

You would feel the same as any animal that has had its ecosystem disrupted. Scientists in Paraguay found that stress hormones in the fur of small mammals were higher in individuals living in degraded forest fragments.[9] The authors assumed this was to do with the higher risk of predation, but it's more likely the overall effect of uncertainty: not knowing where your next meal is going to come from creates anxiety. In wild koalas, the level of stress hormone of animals living in areas of land clearance was fifteen times higher than the average levels in healthy koalas. It was even higher than in animals that had been burnt, attacked by dogs or were suffering kidney failure.[10] While we tend to notice more obvious causes of stress, you can't often see the outside symptoms of chronic conditions, even though they're deadlier. And if habitat destruction and collapse of ecosystems is contributing to the rise in diseases in animals like this, it must also be affecting humans too.

These are the laws of nature that describe order in the universe, and our health suffers when chaos ensues and we disconnect from it.

German scientist Rudolf Clausius coined the term 'entropy' in 1854, but it was Einstein's work from 1902 to 1904 that clinched its importance, when he published his second law of thermodynamics. It is simple to understand. Energy always moves towards a state of greater chaos. The discovery of this natural law was so important and definitive that it led Einstein to say:

> It is the only physical theory of universal content which I am convinced that, within the framework of applicability of its basic concepts, will never be overthrown.

Entropy is how energy flows through the universe. It's the reason why time can't run backwards and why, when you break an egg for breakfast, the egg remains broken rather than turning back into an egg, and why a dead animal doesn't come back to life. Likewise, the food in a supermarket will be bought and dispersed into the pantries of thousands of houses spread across the suburbs. It doesn't magically reappear on supermarket shelves – we have to put it there. What Einstein proved was that all energy in the universe, the energy we are all made from, constantly flows towards its most chaotic form. What shoppers prove is the tendency of animals to counteract this process. We regather food and establish patterns of order among the chaos. Humans have a complex society that continuously grows more food and centralises it to feed a whole population. This behaviour underpins our entire global economy.

Likewise, if you degrade an ecosystem by removing wildlife, chemical energy that is processed through the bodies of animals and plants will escape to become so chaotic and widespread that it can no longer be restocked by wildlife. This is what we are doing to farmland soil fertility. Every year we kill wildlife through misuse of fertilisers and pesticides, the soil's organic layer (its energy-laden nutrients) escapes and becomes 'free energy' – in other words, energy that isn't stored in some form of logical order and can leach out into our atmosphere and oceans, where it causes havoc. At the one end, we lose a source of food and at the other, we create more planetary instability. Learning to think in terms of free surplus energy is surprisingly liberating … there is a lot that goes on in the world that makes more sense when it is framed this way.

For example, in 2020 three thousand tonnes of fertiliser exploded in Beirut, tragically killing over two hundred people and flattening the entire central business district. It wouldn't look like much in a warehouse, but the pure pile of nitrogen, hydrogen and oxygen was like a balloon ready to burst. If we assessed the danger of stockpiling fertiliser based on the potential risk of huge amounts of free energy suddenly escaping, we would never store it in a built-up area. That stockpile was enough to fertilise one-twentieth of the entire agricultural land of the United Kingdom and indeed, chemical fertiliser originates from science used to make bombs and poison gas used during world wars. We release vastly greater amounts of chemical energy from ecosystems each time we degrade them by killing animals or cutting down habitat. We're creating tiny and invisible explosions of energy that add up to all the environmental chaos we see in the world today.

When Al Gore published *An Inconvenient Truth* in 2007, it created a decade of reference to 'global warming' even though the Independent Panel on Climate Change was barely using the term, instead referring to 'climate change'. The threat to human civilisation isn't only from a warming planet but from the chaos that this free energy creates in our climate and food security systems. Later in this book we'll return to the subject of climate and see how the collapse of wildlife and escape of energy from ecosystems is contributing to climate chaos in ways we aren't even aware of.

If you shake a bowl full of water you are introducing free energy, which destabilises the surface, but the greatest changes in level are at the sides where the water oscillates above and below the average. The amount of water hasn't changed, but the distribution of the effect varies as you move away from the bowl's centre. If you're unlucky enough to live at the extremes you'll be more seriously affected. This is why Texas got freezing weather in 2021 but Australia and California, on the other side of the 'bowl', ended up with catastrophic bushfires in 2019–2020. Introducing surplus energy results in a bigger climate gradient and more extremes of hot *and* cold. Burning fossil fuels blows more free energy into the atmosphere.

Ecosystems work in much the same way but I don't want you to worry too much about understanding the science behind entropy. All we need to think about is how safely energy is distributed within our biosphere – and whether our actions create a *change from a state of order to a state of chaos.* Or, putting it another way, the movement of energy from where it's useful to where it's not.

We can't survive if chaos exceeds habitable levels. An ecosystem that swings unpredictably between one extreme state and another doesn't support enough life. We can't survive without wildlife because, as we're about to find out, their collective action is the only thing able to keep this under control, keeping the whole world habitable for us.

The power of animals to stabilise ecosystems

If the universe is continuously trying to break things down then you might ask, How can either ecosystems or animals still exist today? You're not the first person to think this. It's a paradox that caused debate between Austrian-Irish physicist Erwin Schrödinger and Albert Einstein in the early 1900s. Schrödinger argued with Einstein, asking him how he could explain the order and function of nature.

Chaos-inducing entropy is an all-powerful universal force of nature that we can't turn off or build defences against. But we now know that it has a weakness, an Achilles heel that slows the progress of natural decay to a crawl and makes our biosphere liveable. These are the structures we call ecosystems, but they couldn't exist unless there was a way to extract free energy and then rebuild it into something more benign and stable.

This is where wildlife comes in. Animals like you and me extract energy from the food we eat or the air we breathe, because entropy enables energy to flow in one direction through us, like a current passing down a wire or fuel being syphoned through a hose. The gradient between negative and positive entropy is just enough to keep it flowing constantly, and as it passes through us, our cells can extract it. This is the magic that sparks life into us all.

Only then can we start to trade energy with other lifeforms and form working ecosystems in which every animal has a specific role. When you eat pizza you are consuming energy made for you by animals and plants that turned it into chemical energy. The heat you emit from eating pizza (the more chaotic form that represents the positive end of the gradient) can be felt by rubbing your hands together; you're currently breathing molecules that are the waste energy emitted in the same way by plants outside. There's no escaping it: you are irrevocably connected to everything else in the world. You are part and parcel of ecosystems, these networks of energy-transfer pathways we live among, invisible to the human eye, that result in the awe-inspiring complexity of everything we see in rainforests to coral reefs, oceans to deserts.

As Columbia University's Ruth DeFries, author of *What Would Nature Do?*[11] explains, ecosystems are incredibly complex, and while diversification was beset with the risk of self-destruction, wildlife was able to develop strategies to overcome change and survive. Just how much has the system done to overcome chaos?

While I was drafting this book, my son said to me, 'Dad, do you know there are more permutations of a deck of cards than there are atoms on Earth?' It seems a fitting analogy to demonstrate the complexity of ecosystems.

The sheer diversity of possible arrangements of particles, even from fifty-two cards, is staggering. If every human shuffled a deck of cards every five seconds since the beginning of time, it would still be possible to have never repeated the cards in the same order. A pack of three cards (king, queen, ace) has six permutations:

AKQ AQK KAQ KQA QKA QAK

Number of cards	All the possible permutations after shuffling
1	1
3	6
4	24
7	5,040
10	3,628,800
13	6,227,020,800
16	20,922,789,888,000
19	121,645,100,408,832,000
22	1,124,000,727,777,610,000,000
25	15,511,210,043,331,000,000,000,000
28	304,888,344,611,714,000,000,000,000,000
31	8,222,838,654,177,920,000,000,000,000,000,000
34	295,232,799,039,604,000,000,000,000,000,000,000,000
37	13,763,753,091,226,300,000,000,000,000,000,000,000,000
40	815,915,283,247,898,000,000,000,000,000,000,000,000,000,000
43	60,415,263,063,373,800,000,000,000,000,000,000,000,000,000,000,000
46	5,502,622,159,812,090,000,000,000,000,000,000,000,000,000,000,000,000
49	608,281,864,034,268,000,000,000,000,000,000,000,000,000,000,000,000,000,000
52	80,658,175,170,943,900,000,000,000,000,000,000,000,000,000,000,000,000,000,000,000

The permutations of all the cards in a 52-card deck exceeds the number of atoms on Earth, which, according to the US Department of Energy's Jefferson Lab, is approximately 133,000,000,000,000,000,000,000,000,000,000,000,000,000,000,000,000 (equivalent to the permutations of between 41–42 cards).

Add one more card and the number is twenty-four. Additional cards grow this number exponentially until fifty-two cards is six hundred thousand billion more than all the atoms on Earth.

As you can see, it may be quite simple to arrange a deck of cards in order, but left to blow in the wind, universal laws quickly take over and chaos can ensue on a scale that's unimaginable to humans.

Reduce a normal fifty-two-card deck by ten cards and the number of possible patterns reduces by a hundred thousand billion times. Reduce the number of animals in an ecosystem and the number of possible connections reduces exponentially.

Earth has lost two-thirds of its wildlife in the last fifty years.[3] Imagine the number of connection points that have been lost and the amount of free energy that's now circulating in our atmosphere and oceans. Imagine the short-tailed shearwater, a species that may have numbered over 200 million birds before Australia was settled by Europeans and today numbers only a few million. Every one of those birds was connected every day throughout the year to processes that span the globe from the Antarctic coastline to the north Pacific Ocean.

Biodiversity is a term that has become bastardised over the years, crowbarred into policies to justify an intent that was never meant to be. It is often misunderstood. The 1992 United Nations Convention on Biological Diversity definition was never written to mean the number of species of animal, or even the number of individuals, although that is how most people commonly interpret it. Biodiversity is the product of all interactions between animals and the mechanisms that stabilise the biosphere's energy so it's habitable for all lifeforms including humans. It's more to do with the abundance of animals in the right proportion, regardless of species richness.

If the connections we refer to above become our definition of biodiversity, what impact do you think a global decline in the number of animals could have on Earth's life support systems? A study in 2018 found that a decline and breakdown in the relationships between animal and plant life could accelerate environmental change, even before an abundant species had gone extinct.[12]

The loss of abundant animal life is a huge existential threat to humanity because losing the biodiversity that is delivered by the ecosystems they build, even at moderate rates, means we race towards tipping points. Adding carbon to our atmosphere is a linear process, but even small amounts of biodiversity collapse, as indicated by a deck of cards, can rapidly and exponentially ascend into a spectacular degree of significance for human survival as we create a world of greater carbon-energy chaos.

From the moment of the big bang, the deck has been truly stacked in favour of the universe, as Einstein discovered. All matter marches

---

Long-tailed ducks congregate in the Baltic Sea but populations have more than halved. They were consuming over a million tonnes of prey per year, selectively eating animals that have now become invasive and are destroying mussel beds. This imbalance has led to declining fish habitat and now threatens the region's fisheries.

inexorably towards chaos. Time is non-reversible and everything will eventually erode into its simplest parts. All else being equal, you'd expect Earth to become a gallimaufry of matter draining into the abyss, with chemical energy distributed so evenly it would be featureless and obscure, presenting no horizon for life.

But that's not the case. The reason we can survive on Earth is because the ecosystems we were born into were transformed into stable structures by animals absorbing dangerous free energy, giving us a planet suitable to live on. Biodiversity is a poorly understood and massively under-valued function of global life support. A free energy explanation of how ecosystems work is the missing piece in the story of why animals exist and how wildlife is essential to a habitable Earth.

The scale and intensity of the ecosystems that animals have been able to create defies imagination, but they weren't even built by exerting power; instead they were able to yield to the greatest of universal forces – entropy – and use that power to build stabilising structures. Entropy is like the renewable power of ecosystems, and wildlife is like solar panels that capture it and turn it into something that helps animals to survive.

Years ago, I was on an Antarctic yacht in the Southern Ocean captained by an explorer called David Pryce. David wouldn't have non-stick mats in his galley and I asked why. He explained: no matter how good your non-stick mats are, eventually a wave will strike that's big enough to throw your hot bowl of soup across the room and scald someone. His yacht had twice fallen off the back of waves in the Antarctic and done a full three-hundred-and-sixty-degree roll before settling back on course. Sailors know how to yield to the wind, to make headway without breaking a mast or worse.

A yielding force can't be beaten because it will use its mighty energy against you until you are broken or die of exhaustion. Nature is immovable, and if we try to combat it, we apply our own force against this inexorable power and stable ecosystems break apart. This lessens our chance to survive because we create more chaos. As any sailor knows, to make headway against the strongest storm, you sometimes have to drop sails and lay back for a while, or perhaps change tack altogether. Instead, you have to find your own shape to fit in among the waves, to ride with them.

The most ancient pyramids of all

Triangles are everywhere in nature. From the molecular structure of methane to entire mountains, any construction with a base wider than its summit is strongest in design. It's the same structure we use to reinforce human-made bridges, and it's how the roofs of our houses are held together.

Triangles built of energy also lie invisibly in the heart of all ecosystems. At its base, about one one-billionth of the heat released by the sun reaches our planet, and every square metre of the atmosphere receives enough energy to warm a cup of hot chocolate every minute – but that adds up to a lot. This makes our planet a heat engine that we survive inside, only as long as surplus, volatile, molecular free energy that's charged by the sun remains locked inside the most stable biological processes driven by animals.

But with a human population of eight billion people altering every part of Earth's landscape, if we allocated everyone an equal share, the twenty-five football fields' worth of space we each have left to share with wildlife is under stress. A pyramid of animal life needs to share this space with us if we're to have any chance of moderating the waste energy extracted from the sun by continuously pumping solar-powered plants.

The energy that flows into ecosystems starts with super-abundant primary-energy-producing plants (trees, grass, algae, bacteria, etc.) at the base and dilutes each step up the food chain. At first, plants consume about ninety-nine per cent of energy by living, building their bodies and reproducing,[13] and what remains is emitted as waste or is eaten by animals above. That single per cent of waste is a huge amount of energy. Every subsequent step through the animal food chain uses about ninety per cent of the energy on that step, with the remainder being waste.

On the first step, herbivores eat the plants, then those are eaten by other animals who also dilute the available energy and so on and so on. By about five steps up, when you get to top predators like lions and sharks, the energy is diluted about one hundred thousand times. Ecologists call this a trophic pyramid, from the Greek *trophikos*, meaning nourishment.[14] These patterns can be found in the Amazon rainforest, the Great Barrier Reef and even your garden pond. For example, a healthy pond might have one frog but thousands of algae.

Ecosystems can only counteract the potential destructive power of entropy while the architects – the animals – are in the right proportion of abundance and distribution. This energy distribution of animals in any functioning ecosystem[14] is remarkably similar to the arrangement of particle sizes in the strongest concrete. Lots of small particles are too brittle, so the optimum for strength and endurance is where there is a mix of several large particles and an increasing number of smaller and smaller ones.[15] Likewise, in ecosystems, bigger animals that have a slower turnover of energy, such as elephants, are naturally far less abundant than plants … but if you remove the elephants, you reduce the strength of the system to stay stable, and it becomes brittle.

Because these are the most stable patterns, they are the ones that hold their shape longest, and that is the secret to how ecosystems remained habitable for millions of years. When you get a perfect arrangement, any 'free energy' that's flowing out of one lifeform is almost immediately passing into another lifeform, and everything becomes more predictable as a consequence. The system has reached a steady stable state … not equilibrium. Equilibrium suggests a state of permanent balance but that would be impossible, because there are always some gaps in the structure and everything is prone to changes in conditions outside – just like Earth is prone to changes in the sun's activity. It's this tendency for ecosystems to always shift and change that makes wildlife an imperative for our existence. Animals adapt and act together, to adjust the situation, so every species retains the greatest likelihood of survival – but the shapes stay the same.

Big creatures like us live on a higher plane, balanced on the shoulders of other animals. We rely on all other wildlife for the structure's stability.

Some animals have managed to leap the trophic steps and specialise in eating high-energy food a few trophic steps below. Baleen whales feeding on plankton are an example, but they are also among the least numerous animals on the planet and highly specialised, only able to survive by concentrating on areas of extraordinarily high prey density, such as seasonal patches of krill. They also do more than their fair share of heavy lifting, massively concentrating critical nutrients that stabilise climate and food security.

All animals including humans and even whales exist in a narrow energy corridor, or 'niche', so we depend on one another to deliver us the energy we need and ensure balance isn't upset. How easily this can change is nicely illustrated by a study of gannets off South Africa in 2005.[16]

Gannets are a fish-eating seabird that dive into waves to catch food. On the Atlantic coast of South Africa, there are raucous colonies numbering thousands. The adults are elegant, long-necked aerial gymnasts that manoeuvre on slender, ink-tipped white wings, flying in skeins, searching with forward-looking eyes for fish, spiralling above the shoals and plummeting face-down at speeds of ninety kilometres per hour to plunge dagger-first onto unsuspecting prey below.

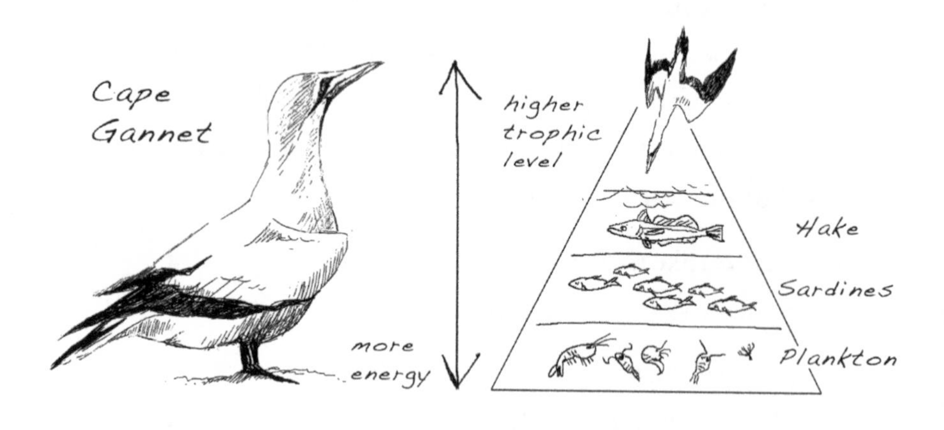

Gannets are one of dozens of species of seabird that form part of a trophic pyramid that maximises energy in food chains. Maintaining the structure and distribution of animals in the right proportions of abundance is one of the things we need to do in order to stabilise ecosystems.

After studying these supremely adapted birds for many years, scientists began to get concerned when they started to see a generation of chicks fail to survive. The explanation was both extraordinary and worrying.

Gannets evolved to give their offspring the best chance at life by targeting filter-feeding fish, sardines and anchovies, during the chick-rearing season. These fish are small, abundant and near the base of the food chain, so they are numerous but far, far richer in energy. The recommended daily energy intake for a human is about 8,700 kilojoules. The average human weighs twenty-seven times more than a gannet, but an adult gannet needs as much as 4,700 kilojoules during chick-rearing. For their size, the gannet's energy needs are more than ten times greater than ours.

Generally speaking, smaller or more numerous animals tend to have higher energy demands than larger ones. Gannets are also more active, diving into the frigid water and flying, so they have to burn way more energy than we do sitting around most of the day. Gannets have little choice but to target high-energy food.

It turns out, fisheries had begun to plunder many of the most energy-rich sardines and anchovies that gannets traditionally fed on. That itself wasn't enough to seal the chicks' fate. In a further twist, vessels were discarding unwanted fish into the sea that, for one reason or another, were either not economic to keep or not licensed to be caught. Seeing a source of free food gannets started consuming these bigger fish, hake.

Because hake is a predator and feeds on sardines and anchovies, it is higher up the trophic pyramid, so it contains a lot less energy, and the colony started to collapse because there was no longer sufficient sustenance for the gannets' chicks. The authors referred to this as a 'junk-food hypothesis'. The chicks were eating the equivalent of fatty hamburgers, depleted in nutrients despite being easier to find in greater volume. It simply wasn't enough energy for the chicks to survive.

Small adjustments we make to energy flow are like placing a dam on a river. Animals suffer downriver and the surplus energy pools behind the dam walls, putting pressure on the structure. The animals respond instinctively. We can't stop them, because it's what they've evolved to do. Once a tipping point is reached, the collapse of the structure might be inevitable, and this is how the gannets had reacted.

When energy is released from ecosystems or redistributed in a less-than-efficient way, it threatens to topple the whole pyramid, but often the imbalance can be reset. Studies have shown that reintroduction of European beavers in Scotland has an overwhelmingly positive influence on biodiversity, leading to healthier, more structurally complex woodlands.[17]

The killing of Alaska's sea otters in North America for the fur trade impacted fisheries, birds and coastlines. By the 1970s, the near-extinct populations had recovered, and by chance researchers noticed that where they lived, there were healthy kelp forests, even though the otters don't eat kelp. Otters love to eat sea urchins and, in their absence, these spiny kelp-eating predators had been responsible for wiping out whole undersea forests. It was only after the otters' return that urchin numbers were suppressed just enough to allow the ecosystem to bounce back. Their recovery meant it was transformed back from a two to a three trophic-level system and in doing so, helped tackle coastal erosion[18] and increased the number of mussels, fish and even bald eagles.[19] The otters' reintroduction affected species both above and below them in the food chain. Their return benefited local recreational and commercial fisheries and restored systems protecting the coast against erosion.

Ecologists are known to refer to species like sea otters, European beavers and cape gannets as 'keystone species', but I am not a fan of that definition. If you remove any large animal from an ecosystem and then return it, the impact is going to be significant. My leg is a keystone part of my body, but it's not much use on its own, and I'm quite sure if I lost it I'd notice and want to have it back. There is another dimension to the value animals create, and that is their ability

---

While it may be argued on purely academic levels, that parts of an ecosystem will survive perfectly well without animals like sea otters, this imbalance results in 'pests' like sea urchins. The word pest has no ecological meaning other than a massive inconvenience to humans. The point is ecosystems aren't habitable for people without animals like sea otters.

to deliver nutrients to us in the right time and place. This critical role they play is vastly underestimated, and an understanding of its importance is lacking.

Nature trades energy in much the same way our society trades money, except no animal, including us, can centrally manipulate the markets or broker power. In either a financial or ecosystem sense, there can be no monopolies because any sustainable system will always depend on a pyramid structure and a diversity of players with different roles and skills.

Pyramids are one of the structures that resist the power of entropy. This is why water forms waves and sand settles into triangular dunes. They are able to absorb lots of free energy without falling over. Pyramids of life that can support humans need to be built by animals and become an infinitely complex network of interlocking and overlapping energy pathways, even though they operate on a relatively simple structural principle. This is happening at a whole-of-planet scale and pervading every living space in a way that humans alone can never hope to replicate.

While there is a degree of flexibility in animal behaviour that allows the world to maintain a steady stable state, as we begin to lose animals we wear down this mechanism and suppress Earth's ability to respond in a calculated and measured way; we remove the resilience of the system that maintains a liveable environment for all but the most fortunate species.

At this point most conservationists don't think in terms of chaos and the role of animal-driven structures in creating order, or suppressing the collapse of ecosystems. Neither do we tend to consider human beings as one of many animals that exist because of it and that without all animals, we cannot create the ecosystem complexity necessary to withstand this all-consuming force of nature. When you do realise it's important, it becomes pointless thinking we can 'manage' wildlife. As animals, we were born into a system that is full of animals like us, because that was less likely to collapse. It delivers us a habitable planet only because of the role we all play together.

This may be the most important and humbling thing you'll ever know about why animals are essential for a habitable Earth. It's even more so when you realise how it can explain why you exist and we come perhaps the closest we've ever been to a meaning of life. But first, you are probably thinking, 'What about plants?'

Battle of the plants

It's always with a sense of guilt that I start to explain the sinister side of plants, but they do warrant a cautious level of respect as they are immensely powerful lifeforms and represent a great danger to ecosystem stability that only animals can control. In the book *Ring of Bright Water,* Gavin Maxwell described a dissonance between the ancient, unyielding Atlantic coastline and the profligate activity of spring plants, referring to them as a 'stifling … green stain' and 'depraved'. This statement reveals a genius that exceeds that of almost anyone else I have ever read. Maxwell knew the significance of wildlife, observed and described the connections between migration and plant energy abundance before any popular concepts of biodiversity, rewilding or indeed the majority of the science that underpins conservation today, had been written.

Plants are so powerful that physicist Brian Cox, Robin Ince and Alexandra Feachem's book *How to Build a Universe*[20] contains a section titled 'Life, Death and Strawberries'. During their podcast several scholars argued about whether a strawberry was alive or dead. It was argued that a strawberry, due to its complexity, is one of the most formidable lifeforms in the universe and remains connected to its surroundings long after it splits off the stem. As a plant it drew energy from the sun but as a fruit, its energy can bear more life, all of which accelerates universal disorder through the amount of waste it contributes back to the biosphere.

This is what Einstein was talking about, and it is exactly why strawberries taste so good! We think of strawberries as something that animals eat. But the strawberry couldn't exist if the animals didn't consume some of that energy. If the strawberry's energy goes to waste, its kind is less likely to survive, because the free energy it creates can pollute its own environment. Humans are part of the blueprint to moderate plant waste and bring the system back into order. Plants aren't in an arms race with animals at all; they are in a dance, each partner pushing and pulling in turn, to maintain consonance with the laws of nature. If either party leans too hard on the other, both fall down. When animals and plants move in synchrony, it creates some of the most beautiful landscapes on Earth.

This is why it makes no sense for us to plant forests to combat climate change while simultaneously killing all the animals around us. As they say, it takes two to tango.

I'd never say plants aren't important. They are incredibly beautiful, and life without them wouldn't be worth living. We can't exist without plants either, but Earth's ecosystems weren't able to reach a steady stable state with plants alone.

I've always been taught that conservation is about habitat and that forests are ecosystems. Both these statements are correct but for one missing part. Habitat is for animals, and forests aren't ecosystems without wildlife. Ecosystems are habitats that animals enhance so they can survive in them, and because we are animals a world of only plants is uninhabitable and not much use to us. Planting trees alone doesn't deliver clean water, fertile soil, food and a stable climate; those things depend on a cooperative outcome that only animals can build for each other. It's the deadly one percent of waste energy that plants create[13] when using the sun to convert carbon dioxide and water into sugars (photosynthesis), that poses a risk. This is why – from the moment the first people learnt to make fire, to the combustion engines of today – we have been in a battle of life and death to control the release of energy from vegetation.

Every time you start your car, fiddle with the air-conditioning, put on a pullover, rub your hands together or light a fire, you're manipulating energy from plants. This all-consuming activity defines what we are. We are an animal, and without us plants would destabilise Earth's chemistry with consequences worse than climate change.

Before the rise of land animals about 470 million years ago, the slow march of plants across the world contributed to a mass extinction.[21] All of the animals back then lived in the ocean, and most disappeared forever. At that time, the sea was teeming with life of all shapes and sizes. In 2013, scientists discovered the fossil of *Edenopteron*, a crocodile-sized predatory sea fish that lived 360 million years ago. The

Devonian rocks it was found in are a deep purplish-red and folded into sea-cliffs in southern New South Wales, Australia. About this time, ancestors of present-day lungfish had struggled onto land, amphibians had started to evolve and there were inch-long bugs like millipedes and scorpions. Fossilised footprints from a quarry in Poland suggest even some four-legged animals existed by then,[22] but on the whole there were few land animals. There were ten-metre-long predatory sharks and fish the size of buses and everywhere there were coral reefs. The ocean had become enriched by the flow of energy through food chains, creating an opportunity for new animals to evolve and to feed on each other's surplus.

Earth's climate was warm, humid and perfectly poised for the first land plants that had evolved to use photosynthesis to build their bodies. Horsetails and cycad ferns were among the earliest to appear, and some ended up growing to thirty metres or more. Flowering plants came much, much later.

Plants benefited from the carbon dioxide–rich atmosphere, and this made them so successful at putting down roots that they eroded the rocks they lived on and made deep soil from their own leaf and branch-fall. However, unlike today, animal life on land was scarce, so there was nothing substantial to absorb the decay.[21] Atmospheric oxygen increased enormously because there were no abundant animals to breathe it, and this reacted strongly with other volatile elements in the soil, creating waste that washed into the sea, combining with the ocean's oxygen and choking the then-abundant ocean megafauna to death.

The rise of plants changed Earth's chemistry too suddenly, triggering an extinction event that wiped out most life in the oceans.

Almost all the bizarre sea fauna that had come before were razed from existence. Soft-bodied Ediacaran animals variously described as quilt-like, mud-filled and tubular would be no more. No modern-day animal even resembles them, and they left only traces in rocks, to be discovered by humans hundreds of millions of years later.

Earth's self-regulating process snapped back like elastic, resisting changes, converting one impact back into another, looking for a way to rebalance a system thrown into chaos by the sudden success of an entirely new biologically driven world that was releasing free energy back into the oceans and atmosphere at an intolerable rate. Between about 383–359 million years ago (the Devonian era) over three-quarters of the world's species, including almost all the animals living in the ocean, went extinct.

Given a few million more years of animal evolution, the chance of this event happening again became slim, because by then wildlife had diversified sufficiently to create the more permanent stable structures needed to absorb the free energy and bring ecosystem chaos under control. This is why today there are 500 more known species of animal in the world than there are species of land plants.

Most individual trees have a couple of hundred types of animal living among their leaves and branches, but what plants lack in diversity is made up for in the energy they capture and store – a staggering eighty-three per cent of living carbon is in the world's plants, and a fifth of this is as trees.[23] Plants are super-abundant because they are first in line to absorb the sun's energy, and that makes them the foundation for ecosystem building and the base of the supply that energises the entire food chain. Captured inside their carbon mesh are other elements, and together they contain energy as electrons that whirl around the various molecules and flow like a fuel. Such is the power of plants' energy that we can heat almost anything made of wood to about 250°C and it ignites, creating a runaway thermal reaction. House fires and bushfires are all the release of plant energy back into the atmosphere.

As long as this energy lives on inside plants and animals, it isn't free to dangerously react with our atmosphere or oceans. But being at the frontline of trapping the sun's energy, plants naturally produce a lot of waste, which you can see lying around below or next to any tree, shrub or grass verge. It's this gargantuan quantity of surplus energy that unsettles ecosystems if animals are not present. It's also why it's so dangerous to be digging up the energy plants stored millions of years ago, which subsequently turned into coal, because the animals that were present to regulate matter in those days went extinct long ago.

Plants are so ridiculously powerful at absorbing energy they can colonise anywhere, almost instantly.

As a consultant in the 1990s I surveyed derelict industrial land on the Thames in London, opposite Millennium Dome. The glass towers of Canary Wharf provided a backdrop to charms of goldfinches swinging from the pendulous dead heads of thistles. The occasional call of a black redstart echoed off broken glass against soot-blackened, red-brick factory walls covered with red valerian flowers, like hanging baskets on the walls of an East End pub. Rapacious Japanese knotweed plants were claiming the land, their steel-like stems able to lift concrete slabs, push over houses and climb through every crevice and crack in concrete. And there were purple-flowering snap-dragons and feathery grasses.

On Australia's Atherton Tablelands homeowner Sue Gregory once told me that, 'Within a very short time, the rainforest would eat my house, if we let it'. On the island of Nosy Be in Madagascar, there are ancient temples covered in the asphyxiating tendrils of strangler figs. These are often the first trees to colonise ruins, climbing like the mythical beanstalk, racing towards the sunlight. Once they breach the canopy, they strengthen their natural scaffolding and spread their limbs out like opening an umbrella, catching the sun's rays while carefully channelling rainfall, leaf over leaf, and scattering it to the ground over the plant's root-line. In a natural setting the figs scale the tallest rainforest trees and can outlive their arboreal partner, which dies and rots away inside, feeding the fig nutrients and leaving its intricate exterior latticework standing on its own.

Sundews, pitcher plants, bladderworts and Venus fly traps are extreme examples of the power of plants to occupy the world's emptiest mixing-bowls and fill them with ingredients. Carnivorous plants have turned the tables on animals and become predator, not prey. In Indonesia's Raja Ampat archipelago, pitcher plants grow densely from limestone rocks far above the sea. Weathered by salt air, baked by the sun and washed clean by tropical storms, the rocks offer little footing yet the plants succeed against all odds by creating their own soil. These foundations of karst ecosystems are some of the most diverse in the world,[24] despite having little or no nutrients. From the heathlands of southern England to the forests of southern Australia, sundews do the same, trapping insects on sticky fronds and absorbing their protein with potent enzymes.

There are few places more inhospitable and nutrient-poor than tropical sun-drenched Pacific sand islands in the middle of the Coral Sea, yet the shallow depression of a turtle nest and a few seabird droppings are enough for thintail grass to take root. Before long, it sends out underground runners, tapping the soil for the minutest resources, spilling them out as next season's leaf-fall, turning the sand grey and giving their successor, another species of grass, a place to take root.

Their success comes down to their ability to photosynthesise: to make food from basic elements. And they do this by drinking water and inhaling carbon dioxide, using solar-powered leaves and the sun's radiation to build cellulose, a network of sugar molecules stitched together and made from carbon, oxygen (used in rocket fuel), nitrogen (used in bomb-making) and hydrogen (the reason behind the disaster that befell the German airship Hindenburg). The cotton you wear is almost entirely made from cellulose, and today's plants produce about 220 billion tonnes of the stuff every year.[25]

These raw ingredients create a powerful transfer of energy and allow plants to build their bodies into massive structures. In turn, animals eat them and extract amino acids, of which there are only about twenty-two types that make up every living thing on the planet. When you put these simple molecules together like bricks, you can make eyes, hearts, legs and even brains that think for themselves.

Plants continuously absorb and convert endless amounts of sunlight, and if enough of the energy-filled chemicals they make escapes into the oceans and atmosphere, they could still contribute to a mass extinction of animal life.

On Earth today, increasing atmospheric carbon is causing an acceleration in the rate of natural vegetation cover, and we are also pouring huge quantities of artificial nutrient into the ocean. There are two-thousand-kilometre-long dead zones in the Gulf of Mexico today that mimic the Devonian extinction processes. A massive surplus of agricultural fertiliser runs down the Mississippi River, creating huge algal blooms that suck the oxygen from the water and kill everything from surface to seabed.[26] The Great Barrier Reef is becoming similarly affected by the nutrient runoff from coastal farming.

What do you think will be the consequence of this increase in plant abundance while we've simultaneously killed most of the world's wild animals?

There's a good chance we are facing a problem worse than climate change. How we choose to treat animals in the coming years could determine how likely our species will be to survive on Earth.

The meaning of life and why animals exist

You are an animal, and you don't exist because plants evolved. You were the likeliest to survive because you were the last in a long line of animals that balanced Earth's energy surplus and brought ecosystems under control. The origins of our universe, solar system and life itself can all be traced back to these same complex processes. Knowing how and why life exists gives us the humility we need to understand our place among other animals and their importance to our mutual survival.

There was a time Earth rained molten iron and there was no life at all. The shock waves from rocks travelling at high speed and colliding like missiles with Earth's surface would vaporise the metal and generate clouds of ferrous gas, which condensed into liquid and rained over the planet's fiery surface.[27] Before that there was just space. Across this vastness formed plumes of mostly hydrogen and some helium, the first primary elements. Gravity and shock waves from exploding stars stirred the cosmic ecosystem and, much like the way patterns form in our oceans today, generated some patches of more concentrated, high-density matter and energy.

Gravity, the literal bending of space-time around objects with mass, formed around these patches, drawing them together into clumps in which gravity increased even more. The elemental fog began to spiral like water sucked into a washbasin, and the outer arms of its celestial dance were drawn towards the body with increasing force and speed. It flattened into a disc and created such pressure at its centre that hydrogen nuclei fused to make helium and release enormous light and heat.

Emerging as a bright light from the gravitational centre of one of these systems was our sun. Glowing with enough nuclear fuel to shine for several billion years it spewed solar winds powerful enough to blow away anything less than already planet-sized.

From modest origins only 10–100 million years earlier, our solar system accumulated matter and clumps of different sizes started to collide and merge. What would become planet Earth was a rock ferociously bombarded by meteorites and beginning to fatten by absorbing nuggets of mostly iron and nickel that had been scattered across galaxies billions of years before.

In 2003, Stanley Salthe in the *Journal of Ecology and Society*[28] described how iron-rich matter first clumped together. As more clumps formed it became less likely they would be destroyed. They formed patterns, so the probability of large clumps colliding or being obliterated by smaller clumps was now low enough for new planetoids to coexist. This ability to create stable patterns of combined matter and ordered energy – a result of the same laws of nature Einstein described – would become the defining feature for the evolution of all life on Earth.

The first organisms appeared about four billion years ago and were most likely archaea, which were discovered by Dr Carl Woese and George E Fox in 1977 after the invention of modern DNA fingerprinting techniques. Scientists have since found them living everywhere throughout nature. There are methane-producing archaea happily living in your guts right now and others on your mouth and skin. They contain a primitive chromosome called ribonucleic acid or RNA, which contains the ability to make copies of itself – to take charge of replicating oneself is a fundamental for life.

What Earth probably looked like a billion years ago before there were animals or plants. It was warm and the skies were clear, except for smoke from erupting volcanoes. Cyanobacteria had started to invade the shallows, forming mushroom-shaped stromatolites.

But which came first, the RNA or the ability to self-replicate? How did an organism evolve to make enzymes and develop processes to build complex self-replicating proteins, if it wasn't already self-replicating?

In 2013, Jeremy England[29] revealed a formula in theoretical physics that explains how living things are better at energy capture than simple clusters of matter like carbon. His theory has led to the interesting possibility that self-replication might simply be a sophisticated extension of stable pattern-forming entropy behaviour by molecules.

As early as 1964, James Lovelock proposed to colleagues in NASA that measuring entropy could allow us to detect alien life on other planets.[30] Stable entropy processes are represented as breathtaking patterns that can be seen throughout nature. Scientists Armando Azua and Cristian Antonio Vega-Martínez[31] have measured entropy complexity using fractal geometry, a field of maths from the 1970s invented by Benoit Mandelbrot. The simplest example of a fractal pattern is a tree that branches by continually dividing into two. Fractal patterns can be seen everywhere from snowflakes to leaves, snail shells, river beds and cloud formations. The same approximate shapes – a central thick spine and soft perpendicular fronds – can be found in a tiny bird feather and in the velocity flow streams of the Laniakea superstructure of galaxies spanning 500 million light-years.

Natural systems are underpinned by a few relatively simple rules that work to create complexity and strength. The authors suggested that even at the furthest reaches of space, simple rules emulating complex natural patterns could indicate a degree of order and therefore life on a distant planet.

In his book *Every Life Is on Fire: How Thermodynamics Explains the Origins of Living Things*[32] England describes how the rhythm and form of many physically interacting particles will cause them to settle into these patterns. It's not the composition of matter that creates life; it's the continual repetition of the most likely shapes that appear lifelike.

Take a grain of salt, for example, which is made up of lots and lots of sodium and chlorine atoms. Like a little magnet, each has a positive end (Na^{+}) and a negative end (Cl^{-}) so when you put lots of them together, they stick to each other. The most stable structure for a salt molecule is a lattice of 3 x 3 x 3, which forms an almost perfect cube. Rather than arrange themselves in an atomically thin layer of dust, the molecules are so eager to make this cube shape, this formation is scaled to billions of atoms in size, without breaking the pattern. This you can see in every kitchen of the world.

Go and grab a few grains of salt and if you have a pair of binoculars or a magnifying glass, get them too. You can look backwards down binoculars and use them as a powerful magnifier. Some of the salt will be ground up, but you should be able to find a grain that is close to a perfect cube. What you're seeing is the optimal and most stable arrangement of salt molecules; so stable that 10 billion billion atoms still decided to arrange themselves in a square, even though they could remain as molecular dust. This propensity to settle into repeatable patterns is how Jeremy England[29] believes complex life evolved.

Once a simple pattern is replicated, it sets up conditions for another pattern that is slightly more sophisticated and more likely to occur. This chain reaction means anything from molecules, planetoids or even herds of animals have to create predictable physiology and behaviour in order to 'fit in' and be more likely to survive.

Dugongs are a marine mammal in the Sirenian family, and their grazing helps ecosystems resist chaos-inducing entropy by increasing the amount of energy that seagrass beds can absorb. Otherwise known as sea cows, they forage on seagrasses, flowering plants that form lush lawns across vast areas of submerged sand flat. Dugongs will swim hundreds of kilometres between patches and have a profound impact on their environment, even reducing seagrass growth by half.[33] Is that impact good or bad? As lawn owners, many of us might think a reduction in the grass is unappealing, but that's because we don't think in terms of free energy.

Dugongs, along with grazing green turtles, increase the complexity of seagrass beds by selecting certain species over others. Grazers, whether on African plains or in the sea, will show a preference for returning to the same places over and over despite their actions reducing the amount of food in the short term. It's about quality over quantity, about getting more bang for your buck, being able to consume the most energy for the least effort.

It's been shown that a large enough herd of dugongs forms a mosaic of feeding trails criss-crossing vast areas and maximising the growth of new grasses, and although there is less grass, it becomes far richer in energy-giving nutrients. The dugongs, like any animal, are maximising the amount of energy that can pass through the ecosystem to their own advantage. Scientists call this 'cultivation grazing'. In one study in Indonesia[34] dugongs removed ninety-three per cent of seagrass shoots and three-quarters of growth from four centimetres below ground, but it only took five months to recover and the consequence was more carbon stored overall. The grasses bounced back stronger, thicker and more diverse.

This way, the evolution of all life and behaviours, and hence of ecosystems, has been a progression towards a steady stable state driven by animals. Stable patterns can even be seen repeated in crystals forged from the earliest chemistry of our solar system right through to the bodies of animals, such as one unique deep-sea snail that exists around hydrothermal vents.

Golden-haired snails were described in 2015,[35] the same year George RR Martin was writing his fourth instalment in his *Game of Thrones* book. Their shell is clothed in hundreds of iron-imbued overlapping scales resembling the series' infamous iron throne with its adornment of swords, and they have been dubbed by some the 'Game of Thrones' snail.

Harking back to a time when Earth had little oxygen, as far as we know it is the only species of its kind. It lives in the vents' iron-rich

The golden-haired snail gives us insight into the inextricable link between animals and Earth's processes. The snail's shell is armoured with scales and is imbued with iron pyrite or 'fools gold', a common crystalline structure found in the first fragments from the birth of our solar system.

waters by forming a bond with extremophile (an animal that lives in extreme environments) bacteria, which it hosts inside its body. In the absence of sunlight, they oxidise iron compounds and hydrogen sulphide as a way to convert carbon-containing molecules into living matter. The bacteria provide all the snail's nutrition, so it doesn't feed … ever. Its mouthparts are massively reduced, and for its size it has one of the largest hearts in the animal kingdom,[36] because it has to breathe for itself and its bacterial passengers.

Some of the potential waste iron that's absorbed by the snail is deposited in its mineral-rich shell-casing and arranged as threads of glittering golden pyrite crystals, or 'fool's gold', a crystal commonly found in rocks all over the world.

The same crystal arrangements are found in the 4.5-billion-year-old Imilac asteroid, a fragment found in the Atacama Desert that's now housed at the London Natural History Museum. Made of iron, nickel and a magnesium silicate, it combines into a brilliant, glittering green-gold crystal array. The pyrite takes on a familiar shape, emulating the tessellation patterns of its atomic particles. The heavier compounds sank to the centre of the meteorite, eventually growing resilient to the immense heat and pressure from collisions with competing particles. The meteorite is thought to have been part of the process that formed the first steps in the appearance of our solar system's planets.

From the earliest formation of our solar system to today's most complex lifeforms, pyrite crystals have retained their structure and this blueprint for existence. The most stable patterns repeat themselves in nature, as determined by the surrounding environment. Crystals, whole ecosystems and even the way we speak to each other in a common tongue are examples of stable structures. People who speak the same language, for example, are more likely to congregate together. Their offspring don't suddenly create a new language.

Basic molecules also congregate and react differently if they are similar. The amino acids that make up your body come in two mirror-image forms. The ones in nature are all 'left-handed', and this means the double helix that forms your DNA only spirals in a right-hand direction. In the same way as you can't put a right-handed glove on your left hand, neither can you bind proteins to your DNA unless they are the right way around.

If you produce simple amino acids in a lab, you can get both versions in roughly equal proportions, but in nature, half of them are redundant, so they went extinct. Even the way you respond to food is determined by the shape of molecules. Your tongue's taste receptors are extraordinarily sensitive to the amino acid asparagine in both its sweet and tasteless or slightly bitter forms. Your food preferences, and hence the impact you have had on plant evolution, is determined by the most dominant ancient molecular pattern that first emerged from the primordial soup.

In the same way as you can't put a right-handed glove on your left hand, the natural selection of self-replicating life, as England describes, is likely to be driven by pattern formation as opposed to any preordained energy-driven process. This way, the destructive influence of entropy is turned on its head and is not only able to build the most incredible resistant structures, it can create life itself. This means we can trace the origins of life back beyond our ancestral primates, past the first archaea to two source molecules that combined at some point in our universe, to set off our entire history. The most stable and fitting structures are always those more likely to be able to combine with others, to succeed in the current environment and will replicate by proxy and behave 'like' life, or go extinct.

This brings us closer than ever to a theory for the origins of all animals and their role on planet Earth. Those first clumps of matter that drifted together in our solar system eventually led to the diversity of living organisms we see today. This is also the reason why survival is about creating stability, peace and cooperation with other lifeforms and how the opposite, where energy is relentlessly forced into systems, leads to chaos, collapse and extinction.

When Earth became dominated by wildlife

When we try to recreate even the simplest biological chemistry in a lab we tend to heat things to extraordinary temperatures, but that's not how life was created. Life was formed through a dance, not a fight.

Animals exist and behave in ways that yield to the most stable strategy (pattern) for the current ecosystem. The sperm whale can't hear behind it because that wouldn't help it survive in the open ocean. The golden-haired snail didn't choose to stop feeding; it came into being that way, because its adaptations were the most likely to survive in its hydrothermal vent environment. The bacteria it hosts and its behaviour are intimately woven into the world around it. Our common perception of animals, or ourselves, as benefiting from fighting has to be turned on its head to make any sense. Likewise we have to stop thinking we can impose our control on nature. Instead we have to let nature take its course.

Most famously Darwin described the principle of natural selection as a 'law' of nature, saying:

> I think it inevitably follows, that as new species in the course of time are formed through natural selection, others will become rarer and rarer, and finally extinct. The forms which stand in closest competition with those undergoing modification and improvement will naturally suffer most.
>
> – *On the Origin of Species (1859)*

Animals are the product of their parents' environment, bound to a local system by laws, natural or otherwise. In a fully functioning natural world, animals are born into a pattern that is already the most likely for their species' survival. Survival is not of the fittest, as many of us may have been taught or learnt. Natural selection is not caused by competition. Evolution may be more properly defined as 'survival of the likeliest',[37] or the state that nature selects as the most likely befits the species that are adapted for it, and, as Darwin stated, 'the forms which stand in closest competition … will naturally suffer most'.

Evolutionary biologist Suzanne Sadedin points this out in an article in *Forbes Magazine*,[38] saying that humans are mostly nice to each other and we are disappointed when we act selfishly. The fittest of a lineage is the most cooperative, and this trait has been very successful for our species. While ultimately no animal has control over the origin or fate of its species – that is defined by chance – finding your place peacefully among others is an overwhelmingly beneficial strategy.

A recent study of marine fish by a manifold collection of scientists from all around the world and published in the journal *Nature*[39] discovered that species evolve more than twice as fast at the poles than they do at the equator. The theory is that polar freezing and thawing puts pressure on ecosystems, constantly altering conditions, randomly closing some areas down and opening new ones.

When an ecosystem reaches a tipping point, the patterns that came before are all of a sudden smashed to pieces. Animals trapped in rapidly changing environments have to race to change their behaviour, and the most likely patterns to survive in this new normal will be the ones that absorb the most energy. This is what creates the pressure for natural selection. Fighting happens on the margins, where the change is most extreme, and this is due to a breakdown in the information structure, the inherent knowledge that animals have built over generations. Conflict arises from the anxiety and stress of not knowing where to find food. Natural disasters and human-induced climate change are common factors that create disruption and cause fighting and famine among humans today.

However, the rate at which Earth can diversify animal life to bring ecosystem collapse under control is when there is least pressure from heat, meaning the resilience of ecosystems is greatest in colder climes[39] and why the overall warming of our biosphere today makes it harder for us to get a grip on climate change.

Frigidity is among the most powerful and nurturing of Earth's creative influences because it creates unequivocal change fast and with great brutality. Warming, on the other hand, is degenerating and degrades species richness by providing a more uniform and less challenging environment.[40] It's almost the opposite process to what we think happens. Today we are seeing a drift of invasive species away from the equator, but it's not warming that is causing it: it's the abatement of annual freezes that releases animals from the grip of winter and allows them to journey outside their normal range.[41] It's this lack of cooling that jeopardises the rate at which the Earth can rebuild its tolerance to climate change.

An event known as 'snowball earth', about 750 million years ago, may have been the first ice age to befall our planet since the dawn of time. It lasted for 120 million years and pre-empted an explosion of animal life like never before. What was once an ocean of single-celled animals became the domain of many bizarre creatures.

Until that point, bacteria had only managed to transform air and water into sugars and discarded waste full of carbon and nitrogen products. Much of this sank to the seabed and the rest drifted around as new free energy, repeatedly upsetting the ocean's chemistry. Iron was still the dominant element in the seas, but for the first time the ocean and atmosphere were being flooded with oxygen. Oxygen and iron are at opposite ends of the scale as they combine creating orange-coloured rust, stripping iron from the oceans and depositing it on the seabed. Later we will discover how we remain slaves to the legacy of our iron-rich world and how the scarcity of this once abundant element makes us more dependent than ever on animal impact.

Oxygen was a powerful-enough fuel, though, to make a new wave of creatures: scavengers that could consume the waste rained down on them from above and burn it to fuel their internal engines, rather than making it themselves. For this to happen, something extraordinary had to happen.

From the humblest of beginnings and over a few billion years, it was a cooperation between two bacteria that laid the path to what would eventually become humans. Two of these lifeforms successfully formed a union, and the offspring of that first marriage of convenience still exist in every cell of your body today, and in the cells of every other animal on Earth, as mitochondria. They are the very creatures that connect us to our world, by channelling ecosystem energy into our bodies.

One bacteria climbed into the body of another, and they assumed different roles. One became dependent on the other bacteria's ability to survive and generate fuel. The other would feed and both would reproduce. The relationship, though entirely mutual, was driven by each other's individual needs to survive, but they became more and more reliant on the partnership to grow, divide, reproduce and spread. The new alliance was so powerful that when presented with an atmosphere dense with carbon dioxide and coastal wetlands full of freshwater, they would eventually become the key to creating lifeforms that could launch into the air and colonise the land. But that would take millions more years.

It remains remarkable that, to this day, we owe our existence to the relationship we have with primitive animals like bacteria and viruses, originating in the world's earliest oceans, without which our ancestral species would never have been able to manipulate oxygen and iron and use it to process enough energy to conquer land. This meant that about half a billion years ago, Ediacaran fauna appeared. These included soft-bodied jelly-like and rice-sized ikaria preserved in rocks in Australia's Flinders Ranges.[42] These tiny worms fed like today's earthworms in the oxygen-rich sediments below the seafloor. With a rudimentary gut for processing organic material rained down by myriad plankton, chemical energy that once upset the ecosystem was starting to be absorbed into food chains and recycled.

Still, during this period there were no land animals and few land plants, other than perhaps lichens – the flaky growths you see on stone walls or roof tiles. Atmospheric oxygen (O_2) was only a quarter of what it is today, but enough for an ozone layer (O_3) to begin forming, that could protect early animals from the sun's searing radiation. Oxygen levels weren't high enough yet to power muscles needed to lift bodies above the surface or create skeletons to help keep them there.

By about half a billion years ago, sea animals were combining their destinies by trading off each other's energy use and waste production. An ecosystem was forming with these patterns, each part in balance with the other, every component reordering matter to serve the function of stabilisation. The chemical pendulum that had swung so wildly for so long, that had caused repeated mass extinctions in the past, was beginning to slow. Single-celled animals were able to flourish in a more moderate way, and the ocean was beginning to leak oxygen into the atmosphere at greater rates. Animals were starting to be successful, not alone but as a tribe, as an unwitting alliance that was reshaping Earth's chemistry and creating a great new opportunity for conquering the land.

As in animals, the first plants – primitive algae – also formed around a symbiosis between bacteria, where one was able to synthesise sugars from sunlight, carbon dioxide and water, while its host performed tasks of survival and replication. Unlike animal mitochondria, where there is only one form of the union, plants have three types,[43] and they became known as chloroplasts – the microscopic organelles that live inside cells and allow the plant to extract its energy from the sun.

These stowaway bacteria, found in all animals and plants today, have managed to leapfrog extinction. Bacterial chromosomes were so driven to self-replicate and succeed, they gave up their freedom to behave as independent entities, instead embedding themselves into each other and subsequently into the cells of every animal and plant that has ever lived since. Surely, if we were to measure any lifeform's success by its ability to replicate itself for as long as possible, these primitive bacterial protein chains have managed better than any other.

With their new super-powered cells, plants became the first lifeforms to appear on land, their chloroplasts providing the energy needed to suck water from the ground, transport sugars from leaves and compete for sunlight. The plants were then able to create a structure strong and fibrous enough to rise above the Earth's surface by mining air for its carbon. With four bonds emanating from its atomic nucleus, carbon can be constructed into a bewildering and beautiful array of patterned compounds, providing strength, flexibility and diversity. It was the perfect element with which to grow biological structures. Little more than thirty centimetres tall and with shallow roots, the first plants and their bacterial passengers quickly colonised vast landmasses. For the first time ever, the continental coastlines turned green.

That is when the Devonian mass extinction happened. There were too few land animals to eat the waste made by plants. This polluted the ocean and contributed to the extinction of sea life. It was only after this event that land animals were finally able to diversify enough to build defences against the damaging effect plants could have on Earth's stability – to absorb the new free energy into food chains. The sustainable rewilding of continents occurred after the first fish (ancestors of present-day lungfish) struggled from the sea. Having secured the partnership with bacteria that animals needed to extract phenomenal quantities of energy from ecosystems, they were finally able to start lifting themselves into the thin air. Oxygen levels had to climb further before the evolution of amphibians, then reptiles, insects and finally gigantic dinosaurs, could be completed sufficiently. They needed the rocket-like oxygen fuel to drive muscles, build their skeletons and stride across the new animal empire.

Our blue planet's landmass back then was a single supercontinent, covering about one-fifth of its surface and, for the first time, functioning animal-based ecosystems were formed that would begin to resemble the planet we're familiar with today. The Devonian mass extinction was the final event that would lead to the rise of animals. Earth's chemistry had reached a point where it was more or less balanced for plants and animals to coexist, because wildlife had made it that way for themselves – not plants. Plants provided the basis for life, but it was animals building ecosystems, using the energy from plants, that allowed other wildlife to thrive.

Over the ensuing few million years, with the exception of a few ice ages and one catastrophic asteroid strike that wiped out the dinosaurs about 66 million years ago, things were beginning to calm down. Initially, plants were bathed in atmospheric carbon levels far higher than today. The air was humid and warm, and during the aptly named Carboniferous period, vast peat swamps developed from the deposition and decay of dead wood and leaves – and there was an abundance of animal life to recycle surplus plant waste. As the supercontinent began to break apart and pieces drifted into one another, jagged mountains rose where they collided and, luckily, valleys between were filled with the dead matter. Under great pressure and millions of years later, it became fossilised coal, a vast and potentially ravaging energy store safely locked away underground and away from Earth's atmosphere and oceans.

Leaf-fall adds soil depth at rates of between about 150–300 millimetres every thousand years,[44] as you can see just by wandering through a forest. Archaeologists uncover Roman roads buried beneath a metre of soil, mostly made from the organic matter that plants lay down. This surplus, which at first caused a mass extinction, is dealt with through decomposition by super-abundant fungi and the resulting energy consumed by a trophic pyramid of millions of microbes, wriggling worms, insects, birds and mammals, serving to recycle chemical waste, safeguarding Earth's finely tuned chemistry and keeping ecosystems habitable.

On the whole, the last couple of hundred million years have been relatively stable as animals reached a diversity and abundance attuned with all the waste surplus created by others. The golden-haired snail in the deep-ocean thermal vents lived on despite losing their ability to eat. The snails somehow help remove the build-up of toxic chemicals that could otherwise collapse the bacterial population with which they coexist. It never is just about the animal; it's the diversity of the ecosystem and all its players that contribute to the regulation of heat and energy that passes around fragile and volatile habitats. Animals are the final pieces, the adjustment that brings the planet's ecosystems into a sharp habitable focus.

We, and everything that came before us, are a consequence of these processes. Life that first appeared in the oceans would create ever-more-complex animal designs and, by extension, the way they behaved and arranged themselves on Earth would also be in the patterns most likely to survive. Through natural selection, elegant structures would evolve in which maximum energy could be absorbed and every species increased its mutual likelihood of reproducing and lasting as long as possible.

For decades, we've been trying to create life in test tubes mixing chemicals with heat. Likewise we try to impose our will on ecosystems through management and wonder why the outcomes are always impossible or disappointing. It's obvious. If we set out to create a salt crystal by assembling a billion billion molecules into a perfect cube, it would take years. The way to create a salt crystal is simply to allow salty water to cool and the molecules will appear as if by magic. The law of nature that created life and allowed it to flourish is powered by a different and altogether more powerful force.

The system isn't perfect and change is inevitable, as is extinction, but it led to the diversity of animal life as we know it today, because this was the most likely outcome all along, the one that avoided chaos. These structures had formed into something that could balance the energy consumption puzzle at every available scale and location, maintaining patterns that large-bodied animals needed to exist. It was the first time in our planet's several-billion-year history. All of this eventually led to the first humans appearing on Earth about two million years ago.

PART 3 -

The magnitude of animal impact

Abundance

In Brazil, there are interconnected termite mounds comprising billions of tonnes of soil. Originating from a single source colony over 3,820 years ago, these insect super-cities cover an area the size of Great Britain.[45] Termites enlist a wide variety of breeding strategies so successful they have been able to create a fertile network of adjoining passages below 200 million conical termite mounds.[46]

Below, they construct an air-conditioned hypogeum with the perfect climatic conditions to sow, grow and reap mushroom spores

---

The common wallaroo is among the largest of seventy species of kangaroo. Today forty million of these types of marsupial roam Australia. This makes it the only country in the world with more megafauna than its human population. The animals make it ideally suited to rewilding a continent and reaping huge economic benefits from soil replenishment.

and help break down leaves and deadwood. They coexist with their fungal partners, collecting vast quantities of tree waste and reordering the energy from within, optimising its consumption and recycling it back into the system. This is carbon-laden soil that would otherwise wash into the ocean. Earth is a network of ecosystems like this at every spatial scale. From the most minute rock to the whole planet, animals relentlessly go about their business day in, day out, moving energy from place to place.

The sheer abundance of animals is testament to their significance, and it's what they do, at what scale and in what proportions, that makes them critical to our survival.

The animals we connect with most closely are the birds, mammals and invertebrates we see every day in our gardens, on our farms and in fisheries. What should matter most to us is ensuring they survive, because they are our tribe, the animals that regulate and concentrate energy and supplies at the right level of significance to assist the survival of a large-brained and complex primate like us.

Animals are everywhere, delivering infinitely overlapping processes: trillions of croupiers, each reordering a deck of millions of cards, continuously restacked in our favour, ensuring for as long as possible that we can all survive. Luscious landscapes need to be grazed and verdant grasslands fertilised, but that's only half the story. There have to be animals to consume and recycle, otherwise the waste and decay from plants and microorganisms would overwhelm our planet, as it did during the Devonian mass extinction.

Forests and plants need animals to germinate seeds and spread pollen from male to female flower, but that's the by-product of a partnership animals have with the world, driven by the universal laws of nature, a system that could only stabilise with them. Where once we imagined an arms race between predator and prey or herbivore and plant, we now know these are idle contests. The sword-billed hummingbird has an unfeasibly long beak used to pillage nectar, elongated in unison with the long-fluted tacsonia flowers on which it feeds. Without animals, the flowers' sweet nectar would be spent candy, free energy lost to our atmosphere and oceans. The flower would disappear and the hummingbird wouldn't exist if it hadn't helped alter the flower's structure.

The race between the springbok and cheetah is a life and death contest for both animals, for if either species fails, the other will too. Without abundant wildlife, Earth's cards are cast into the wind to create a world of chaos that few animals can survive within.

The most abundant species we have left are a timely reminder of the significance they have in holding our world together.

Short-tailed shearwaters are an unassuming brown seabird that appears on the southern Australian coastline and builds nests at night, hollowed deep underground. As the last rays of sun fade away and Venus appears in the night sky, they appear as traces of wings in the twilight before silence gives way to thuds and cracking vegetation as they collide with the ground, followed by riotous, staccato voices and wailing moans. On the ground, the birds look stunned for a moment, as they orientate using weak night vision, then flutter and tumble, frantically scurrying on tiny legs towards the familiar calls of their burrowed offspring. Within an hour, the sand dunes are full of their voices and there are birds in every square metre, some resting in the open, others busying themselves below ground.

For millions of years short-tailed shearwaters and their ancestors have been arriving at breeding grounds. There were an estimated 23 million of them in southeast Australia in the 1980s.[47] In the late 1970s off New South Wales, birdwatchers reported 60,000 flying past every hour.[48] Most breed in Tasmania where ice-age Aboriginal people were able to cross what is now the shallow Bass Strait by land, following the ridgeline of islands between present-day Wilsons Promontory, Flinders Island and Cape Portland. Bass Strait is the corridor between two oceans, and these birds are traces of a powerful ecosystem. Legend has it, you could once walk across the backs of right whales in the mouth of the Derwent River. There were thriving colonies of southern elephant seals, New Zealand and Australian fur seals, abundant little penguins, white-faced storm petrels and fairy prions. Today blue whales still migrate here from Indonesia, sperm whales forage in the nearby Bass Canyon, and shy albatrosses nest on rock stacks with views of the Southern and Pacific oceans in opposite directions.

Archaeological evidence suggests shearwaters made up a small proportion of early Aboriginal diet,[49] but it wasn't until the collapse of the seal industry in the nineteenth and twentieth centuries that 'muttonbirds' became a mainstay of European colonial settlers' diet. This did lessen, though: between 1930 and 1990, annual catch declined from about one million birds to only 300,000 a year, with chicks making up ninety per cent of a heavily commercialised harvest.[50]

Before the Europeans, bird numbers were huge. The following account is from the diary entry of Captain Matthew Flinders.[51]

> A large flock of gannets was observed at daylight, to issue out

> of the great bight to the southward; and they were followed by such a number of the sooty petrels [short-tailed shearwaters] as we had never seen equalled. There was a stream of from fifty to eighty yards in depth, and of three hundred yards, or more, in breadth; the birds were not scattered, but flying as compactly as a free movement of their wings seemed to allow; and during a full hour and a half, this stream of petrels continued to pass without interruption, at a rate little inferior to the swiftness of the pigeon. On the lowest computation, I think the number could not have been less than a hundred millions; and we were thence led to believe, that there must be, in the large bight, one or more uninhabited islands of considerable size.
>
> Taking the stream to have been fifty yards deep by three hundred in width, and that it moved at the rate of thirty miles an hour, and allowing nine cubic yards of space to each bird, the number would amount to 151,500,000. The burrows required to lodge this quantity of birds would be 75,750,000; and allowing a square yard to each burrow, they would cover something more than 18½ geographic square miles of ground.
>
> – *Captain Matthew Flinders, 9th of December, 1798*

The population in 1803, when European sealers first arrived at the islands, could have been over 250 million. Recent scientific literature rarely reports declines for more than the last twenty-five to fifty years or so, which in this case is about forty-five per cent,[52] but we may have lost ninety-five per cent of the original population since Flinders sailed through Bass Strait.

For as long as we have had records, the entire short-tailed shearwater population has arrived to breed in Australia after a 12,500-kilometre migration from the Arctic, no more than a day or two either side of 24 September. That was until 2019 when, for the first time, the colonies were mainly empty by the end of October, a signal that things on our planet were going very wrong.

The top few metres of the sea is a constant commotion of protein and energy, absorbed and repatriated into the sunlit surface, where it's consumed again and the process goes on and on. There are large patches, some small, some predictable, some regular, some rare. Animals didn't evolve to exploit these riches; they are part of its richness, a result not only of the sea's bounty but natural laws that bind them to the whole system. This is how populations of these birds or those like them have lasted on Earth for sixty times longer than humans: 15 million years.[53]

Where seabirds feed, there are myriad tiny particles that fall like snow to the abyssal plain 4,000 or more metres deep, and the process starts again with tiny animals on the seabed, until one day a thousand years later a stray current might sweep them back up, reviving and re-energising the process all over. Much of this material is locked into sediments, a huge oceanic carbon storage system that keeps our weather and climate under control. Imagine that process long-term and focused on the very places in the ocean where the concentration of life is magnificent, where the greatest oceanographic events once occurred and where the sea boiled with every conceivable size and shape of animal.

Each year short-tailed shearwaters journey from the Bering Sea off Alaska to Antarctica, following the places where sunlight shines for up to 24 hours a day, and melting sea ice delivers a pulse of freshwater nutrients onto the ocean, so algae bloom and set up a vital food chain. Oily waterproof feathers and webbed feet placed well back on the body make shearwaters efficient underwater predators. In flight they are like aerial surfers, cutting elegant arcs over and between wave troughs.

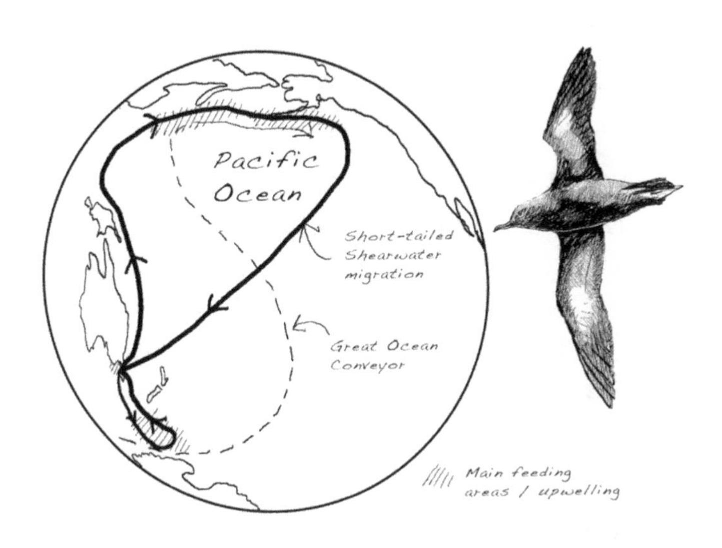

Plunging underwater, they wing powerfully downwards with athletic stamina, barrelling and twisting as they pursue fish and krill to depths of forty metres. During the breeding season in Tasmania, when chicks are young and need nourishing with the highest-energy food, adult birds fly to the Antarctic ice-edge to feed in this permanently sunlit nutrient zone – 4,500 kilometres in a single foraging trip[54] – an absurdly long way to travel for a meal, especially when most is regurgitated for their chick on return to the nest.

Short-tailed shearwaters migrate in a figure-of-eight around the Pacific. They feed over areas where the Great Ocean Conveyor surfaces and amplify nutrient processes.

The birds follow the path of the Great Ocean Conveyor, a current so large it continually circulates water around the world every 1,000 years.[55] It forms through the rotation of the Earth and slithers about the continents, rising and falling with changes in ocean temperature and salinity. Cold, salty water sinks and flows east along the Antarctic shelf edge, where it scours the seabed, and shearing waves displace its density upwards, resuspending nutrients at the surface. This nourishes the sea with food for the shearwaters and helps absorb a quarter of the planet's atmospheric heat: the energy the sun pummels Earth with every day that would overheat us otherwise. The birds feed in a surprisingly small and highly focused area.[56]

Before Europeans arrived in Australia, the whole short-tailed shearwater population would have weighed the equivalent of about 2.6 million people – about the population of Chicago (US), Birmingham (UK) or Brisbane (Australia). We plunder the sea with mechanised vehicles and trawl nets, consuming seafood in vast quantities and putting nothing back. In 2018 Australians ate 340,000 tonnes of seafood. Two hundred years ago, short-tailed shearwaters may have consumed as much as seventeen million tonnes a year but with no negative impact on ocean processes; in fact, quite the opposite. They are as vital as music is to the words of a song, because they fertilise the ocean, recycle its waste and remove its surplus energy. Even today, seabirds rival human consumption of seafood each year. The annual consumption by all seabirds is estimated to be almost seventy million tonnes compared to human global marine fisheries landings of eighty million tonnes.[57] Seabirds' total consumption before industrialisation may have been more like hundreds of millions of tonnes.

It's not just the amount of food animals eat that matters though; it's the patterns of connectivity and behaviour that millions of birds and other wildlife create, the innumerable pathways and processes, stacked up to a practically infinite level of resilience to the destabilising effects of the sun's energy and the unmitigable power of photosynthesising plants.

Ecosystems collapse and reach tipping points because animal populations decline, and this creates an exponential loss in the structure, process and connectivity between animals and the habitat they occupy. During the COVID-19 outbreaks in 2020, we learnt about exponential change and how a continual doubling of a chaos-forming factor can quickly lead to massive global destabilisation. Animal extinction works the same way, translating into a vast and cumulative excess of free energy that quickly throws ecosystems into chaos. If you think the COVID outbreak was destabilising, it's just a blip compared to ecosystem breakdown.

Declines in abundant species are of greatest concern to humanity. The story of the short-tailed shearwater is repeated in all the world's top twenty most numerous seabirds[57] that have declined overall by seventy per cent since 1950.[58]

There are enormous multiplier effects of hundreds of millions of seabirds cycling nutrients in marine fisheries hotspots and redistributing these across entire ocean basins and continents, and this is the reason we have fisheries in the first place. It's a point rarely acknowledged, and we often think of them as competitors to our fisheries. It's madness.

What supermarket could survive by sacking all its workers, stripping out the shelves and just tipping the food delivery into a big pile in the middle of the warehouse? When you next hear stories in the media about the competition of seemingly abundant wildlife with fisheries or farming, think carefully what that means. Animals were here long before us, and unlike us they didn't choose to exploit nature but are the end product of an ecologically sustainable system on which we evolved. If we are to have a future with fish in the sea, stable climate and food to eat, we need their services.

Species richness

A single litre of seawater can contain 20,000 species[59] amounting to billions of microbes (archaea, viruses and bacteria) all invisible to us, each modifying Earth's chemistry just as they have always done. Put like this it's easier to imagine a planet four billion years ago dominated by only these species, microscopic sludges clinging to the glowing walls of deep-ocean hydrothermal smokers, invisible layers on surfaces distributed through water columns, conducting vast chemical experiments that caused massive fluctuations in Earth's climate.

But we humans don't only live among the bacteria. The kingdom of animals, the animals we live among, make up only 7.3 per cent of all species and only 0.37 per cent of biological carbon, but their size, sheer diversity and ability to mobilise large quantities of material make for a rich tapestry and one that tells a very different story of life on Earth compared to when plants and bacteria ruled alone.

Until recently the best estimates for the total number of species in the animal kingdom were between 1.5 and 11 million. New studies have smashed this assumption as now we believe there may be 164 million. This means there are about 500 species of animal for every type of tree, shrub or flower that we know about in the world. If you throw in everything else – plants, fungi, microbes, the lot – there may be up to six billion species of lifeform on Earth.[60] Without this diversity of animals working together, the ecosystems we know, the ones that cradle animals like us, would fall apart.

But we can't live among just bacteria. Desert soils are crammed with microbes that reduce moisture loss and seal in nutrients, but that's still not much use for farmers. Deserts don't have the density and abundance of animals that equate to our nutrient needs – the resources are too finely distributed. Meanwhile, in the most suitably productive areas, where animals have tilled and mulched a deep, rich soil layer for thousands of years, we've turned this land into desert, losing billions of tonnes of soil carbon since the industrial revolution.[61]

The elements we need to live, the currency on which the whole natural world turns, take not only a diversity of plants to extract, but animals to build it into something of use to us and to stop the system falling into chaos. It is what animals do with this energy that makes our world liveable. This is what you feel when you walk into a functioning landscape at dawn and hear the flourish of birdsong.

Mangrove forests are great examples of ecosystem powerhouses that help store carbon at phenomenal rates, far higher than tropical rainforests. These feats of ecological engineering are driven by their animal tenants who can mobilise nutrients, from leaf to leaf and tree to tree, forcing the ecosystem to diversify and grabbing every last drop of energy possible. One mangrove tree can't dominate because insects consume a third of the trees' leaves, and crabs, over two-thirds of seedlings.[62] The interlocking canopies of different trees and their subtly hued greenery are crafted by foliage specialists. Like an inverse bonsai, the tiniest of creatures go about manicuring giants.

A quarter of the species living in a mangrove system are leaf-eating insects such as caterpillars that consume vegetation at such a rate that newborn individuals can increase their body mass by a thousand times or more. By suppressing a monoculture, they maintain tree species diversity and ecosystem function to its full extent, meaning they can absorb and reorder the powerful energy contained in elements like carbon and lock this away in processes before it becomes pollution.

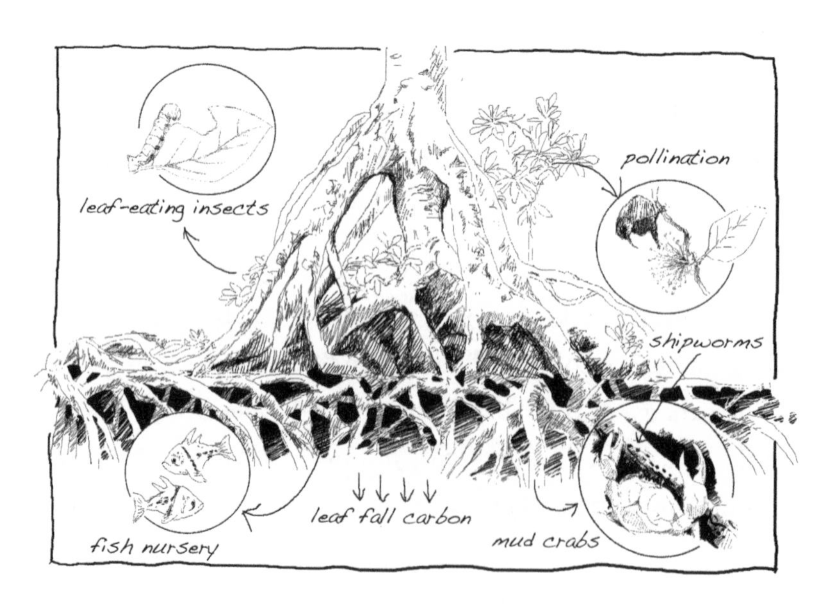

Mangroves are a living city of animals. Almost any tree, shrub or grass carries numerous animals that maximise the turnover of energy, maintaining diversity and keeping waste under control. We tend to think of animals depending on forests, but from a functioning ecosystem perspective it's the other way around.

If you've ever stepped among mangroves the environment seems fairly simple and is often dark and silent, but it's a complex habitat brimming with animal activity, most of which happens out of sight. You can hear it though, and smell it. A sweet, rank, damp odour hangs in the still air, and the silence is fractured by sudden loud bursting from air-filled roots, the occasional creak and crack of a structure under great strain and stress from a weight of animals and constant decay. The canopy is full of bright green waxy leaves that tilt to capture as much of the sun's energy as possible.

The physical structure of mangroves is augmented by the actions of animals and its functions enriched by the processes they create by just living and feeding. Carbon is locked into the oxygen-deprived sediments at such intensity that it's thought deforestation of mangroves releases more than ten times more carbon than tropical forest.[63] The reason why mangroves can store so much energy is because their animal workforce fastidiously processes it at far greater rates than their land-dwelling cousins.

It takes four years for the wood to decompose, and most of this is done by shipworms, a type of clam that forms colonies inside the timber. A tangle of white, calcified tunnels is the giveaway on the timber surface. They were a notorious pest infiltrating the hulls of wooden vessels in the 1700s. These termites of the sea crunch and munch the dead wood like Swiss cheese, leaving it spongy and porous, dropping the waste onto the sediment for the crabs and snails. These processes release important nutrients back into the ecosystem, with remaining sediment exported on tides, washed back into the mangrove systems where the soil layer is three metres deep. The rate these processes occur is critical. If the trees or animals generate waste too fast, that surplus becomes pollution.

If animal-rich mangrove forests didn't exist, the sediment trapped there would have nowhere to go. A mangrove without animals would create a huge quantity of carbon that would seep back into the atmosphere, upsetting Earth's chemistry. There would be many fewer species of tree and sediments from the physical breakdown of leaf matter, and branches would pollute coastlines. This can't naturally happen because plants allied with wildlife long ago, and while individual plants can survive, ecosystems like mangroves that provide biodiversity services could never have succeeded on Earth without animals. They are bound to each other by the forces that stabilise ecosystems and allow them to endure.

Yet we too often consider animals to be non-essential. One reason for this may be that we learn about ecosystems through our destruction of them. We *measure* their value once the animals are gone, when they are worth far less. Our preoccupation with measuring impacts is a reason we fail to recognise the role of animals at all, so when we talk about the function of mangroves, it's important we recognise their value in terms of the services they provide – the value we get from nature. Mangroves might exist fine without us, but if we want them to provide a habitable place, they and their animal residents are coincidentally important to our future.

Mangroves protect shorelines from hurricanes, storm surges and cyclones. They rebuild themselves and adapt to sea level changes and tidal surge. Each time we cut them down or kill off insects, birds and crabs through pollution, we don't just slow down their repair, we reduce connectivity at an exponential rate. What can take a few weeks to destroy could take thousands or millions of years to come back to normal, and meanwhile we risk having to engineer paid-for alternatives that are less than satisfactory.

Mangroves are already being destroyed at a rate several times greater than average forest loss, yet it is estimated the ecosystem services they provide are worth US$33,000–57,000 per hectare per year, and global carbon emissions from annual deforestation are costing up to US$42 billion in damage every year.[64] The value of mangroves cannot be overstated. They filter our pollution and store monumental amounts of carbon, offsetting the effects of climate change, and are nursery grounds for fisheries.[65] Over a quarter of the world's mangroves are found in the Coral Triangle, an area of South-East Asia essential for the future of all coral reefs. The region provides more than ten per cent of global fisheries production[66] yet almost half the mangrove forests have been destroyed already,[67] and food security for 250 million people is dependent on these healthy functioning coastal ecosystems.

What started with a story about birds, crabs and snails ends with animals securing the structures that defend fragile coastal communities from flooding, supporting global food security and maintaining climate stability – all a consequence of controlling the release of free surplus energy, whether it's in the form of water pollution, climate, wave or tidal energy. In many parts of the world where mangroves have been cut down, sudden catastrophic flooding and coastal erosion have inspired efforts to replant. But whenever habitats are replaced, they will only be a fraction of the value of what came before.

This is because newly replanted habitat can take thousands of years to return to its former glory – it takes that long to reassemble the animal communities and trophic structures that support its complex latticework. When mangroves are replanted, each year seasonal floods wash away freshly exposed and destabilised soil, making it difficult for new saplings to take hold (another consequence of free energy, this time in wave form). Meanwhile, without the structure to support their livelihoods, animal populations may have disappeared in a single generation. Getting animals back is harder than reseeding trees. If important species have gone locally extinct – many of which may not even be known about – that can tip the balance towards recovery periods way beyond a human lifetime.

Next time you're outside, stop to look at a tree, inspect the leaves and look for telltale signs of damage from insects. You might see strange nodules or galls caused by parasitic wasps, chew marks from caterpillars or sap-sucking aphids. Birds might be feeding and mammals nesting among the branches. Then look on the ground and spread the damp leaf litter to see what insects leap about in the fray. These processes are scaled up to every piece of vegetation on Earth and even happening in every square millimetre beneath your feet.

When we stare at a tree, we don't tend to notice the number of animals. We might even be misled into thinking there are no animals present, but we'd be wrong. Studies on mangroves have found between 66 and 128 leaf-eating species per tree, and in one study from the Andaman Islands and Nicobar an overall total of 276 types of insect.[68] Entomologist Douglas Tallamy has identified 897 caterpillar species dependent on oak trees in the US, with single trees capable of producing three million acorns in a lifetime and dropping 700,000 leaves each year.[69] Ecologist Rob Wolton in Devon, UK, started recording all the animals he could see with the naked eye living in an eighty-five-metre-long hedge next to his house. In the first two years, he recorded 2,000 species, and he believes the total might end up at about 3,000.[70] When you strip back a tree's leaves and wood, you reveal a dynamic machine that is continuously absorbing and emitting energy, connected to everything around it, and helped to stabilise by hundreds of animals.

If we lose animals, the impact they have on maintaining the integrity of Earth's processes becomes harder to fathom, and reversing the loss would be impossible. We already know where some of the most important places are because it is mostly where we already live and commercially value wildlife: our timber forests, agricultural food bowls and fisheries hotspots. They are also in the places where the greatest concentrations of animals occur, not just the species-rich rainforests and coral reefs but also the open plains where breathtaking animal migrations happen all the time. The process by which mangrove crabs and insects lock carbon and nitrogen into sediments is the same as how worms create fertile farmland and shoals of anchovies and feeding gannets create fisheries.

What makes these places so important is not just how much we rely on them but also how intensely energy, in the form of nutrients, has been concentrated there by animals over millions of years.

Nutrient transfer and migration

Migration is happening everywhere all of the time. It's the mobility of animals – from a billion caterpillars' daily walk from shade to sunlit leaf, or the Arctic tern's seasonal 30,000-kilometre migration – that allows them to stabilise Earth's ecosystems on a planetary scale. Migrations follow the sun, making invisible patterns of energy that flood our world and set in motion rhythms, actions and patterns that have lasted for millions of years.

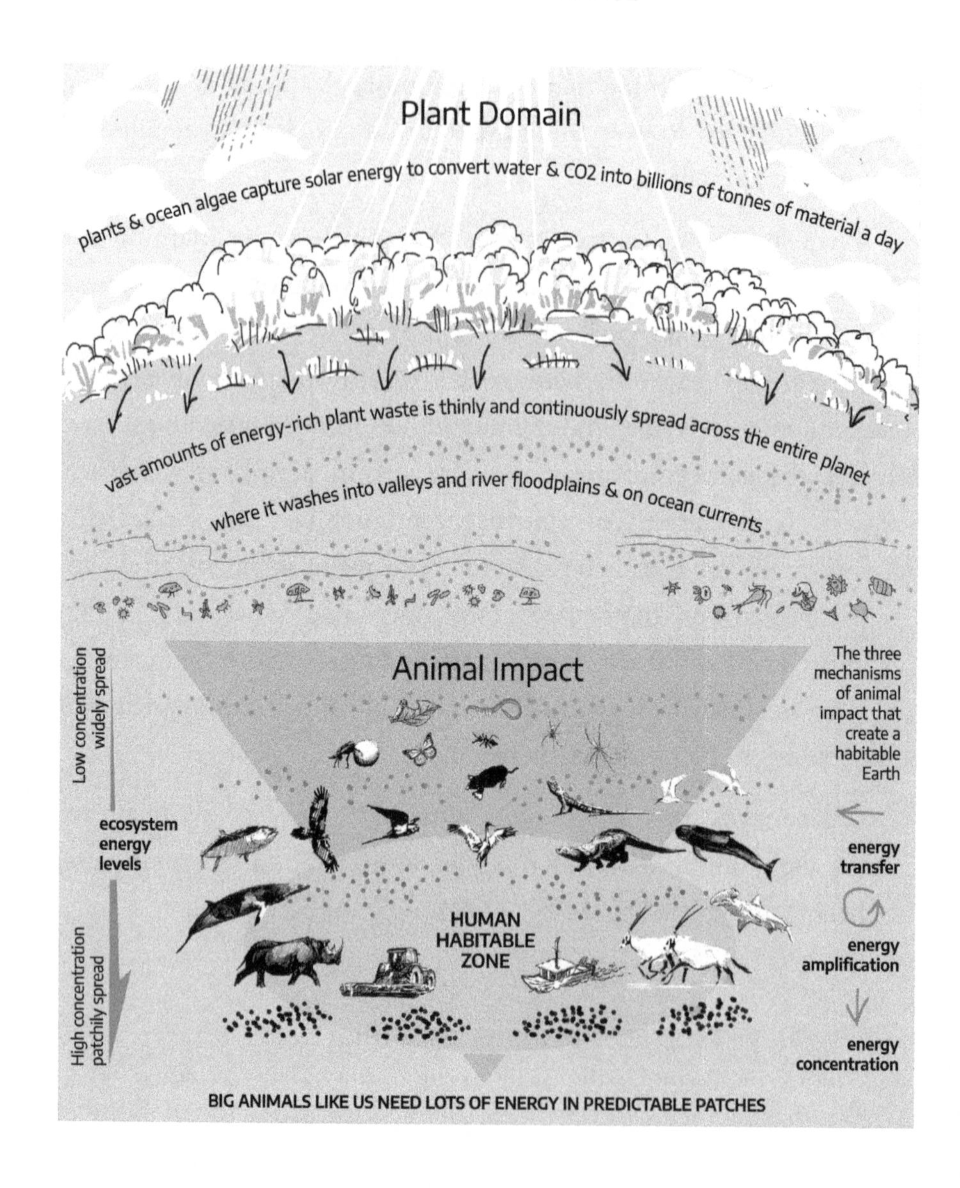

Earth is divided into two domains. Before there were animals only plants existed, and our planet was chaotic. Once animals evolved, free energy was able to be controlled. Evolution has enabled the creation of a network of wildlife that interconnects to ensure energy (particularly carbon) is kept under control. We call these ecosystems. For our primary agriculture, farming and fisheries, we still depend on animals to transfer, amplify and concentrate energy in reliable patches.

Photosynthesising ocean microorganisms struggle to move independent of Earth's physical processes, and plants are rooted where they stand. Most of the energy they create drops where it is and is not concentrated enough for a human or other large animal. Even the nutrient value of our vegetable diet depends on animals making it that way. Every fruit and leaf we eat is a tiny ecosystem in its own right, constantly cultivated by herds of insects and mammals, in the same way as our bodies function because we have an ecosystem of bacteria more numerous than stars in the whole Milky Way living inside our guts.

Plants are Earth's frontline factory workers, converting the sun's renewable power and pumping out energy continuously. They pile it up on a huge scale and need animals to stop it spilling over and becoming unstable and chaotic.

Ecosystems are at their most energetic where the greatest physical forces on Earth collide, where the strongest ocean currents smash into continents or the greatest tropical rivers divide over towering mountain ranges and pour into vast floodplains. You find an abundance of plant life in the awe-inspiring Amazon rainforest and Pantanal, the Himalayas and Indus River, the Great Dividing Range of Australia and Great Barrier Reef, the Coral Triangle, the Bering Sea, the Gulf of Mexico, the plains of Africa and the Antarctic Peninsula, but these places are also where you go to see the greatest seasonal animal exoduses, which have a huge impact on our way of life.

Migration increases the transfer of nutrients from far-distant locations, amplifying the opportunities for more and more animals to congregate, and it is in these locations we find wildlife spectacles. These hotspots create the basis for our food and climate processes.[71]

The answer to why animals migrate and how they evolved to time their movements to maximum effect lies in the impact they have on the ecosystem they serve. Their behaviour evolved at the same time as continents slowly drifted apart, the climate shifted and whole ecosystems developed new patterns to stabilise energy. The most likely strategies that formed since the last mass extinction event favour migration and the biggest of these occurs between areas of most extraordinary productivity. It is in these places where there is both the greatest risk of catastrophe and the most uplifting opportunity for life: the deepest peat beds, the thickest ice sheets, the most abiding forests and the richest oceans brim with wildlife because this is their natural state, the most compact and elegant of nature's solutions, the one that harmonises most readily with the universe's destructive potential.

Animals do not migrate *into* the wealthiest food areas, rather they have evolved to migrate *between*, to preserve the riches in the long term. They stabilise disorder by transferring and concentrating energy at these places, reducing the risk of wild fluctuations in the environment while creating a nest egg for their own future. In the north Pacific, nutrients get transported in huge quantities upriver by spawning fish like salmon and eels. After they die, their bodies provide essential resources for forest growth,[72] which maintains the integrity of the river system and its clean crystal-flowing and oxygen-rich waters the fish larvae need to thrive.

A million wildebeest would soon deplete east African grasslands if all they did was feed voraciously year-round in one spot, yet their absence would also lower grassland productivity because they serve up an almighty amount of natural fertiliser. It is the combination of migration and grazing pressure that enables an ecosystem to diversify.[73] These light-footed megafauna, perfectly adapted to savannah grasslands, stimulate growth and selectively graze, which increases plant and animal diversity, amplifying the availability of energy. The mosaic of grazing lines that criss-cross the plains, the application of manure droppings and soft hoof depressions create niches to support countless other birds and animals. These smaller residents, in turn, amplify nutrient processes at ever-decreasing spatial scales, until every square millimetre has maximum energy order, right down to the tiniest microscopic lifeform. If the wildebeest didn't stride through ahead, the scene could not be set for other animals and insects to follow up, or for local African tribes to have survived for hundreds of thousands of years.

In 1937, Canadian scientist Duncan MacLulich described a relationship between a predator, the Canadian lynx, and its prey, the snowshoe hare. Their populations went up and down together. These boom-bust cycles, in which animals move in and out of an area, expand and contract geographically, are necessary to allow recovery of grasslands and animal populations in between. Fluctuations in both animals' movement and numbers balance the environment, making food predictable for all the other animals that depend on it.

Animals have a similar impact on vegetation on the Great Barrier Reef. There is a particularly successful tree that makes up the majority of forest cover. *Pisonia* is a fast-growing species often over ten metres high. Its bark is flaky, its core sponge-like and its tendril-like limbs terminate in a flourish of large, bright green leaves. Black noddies gather its fallen browning leaves and combine this with guano to construct their nests. Precariously balanced on thin branches inside the canopy, they are protected from the raging tropical sun and, worse, the torrential downpours.

While the tree offers shelter, there is a price to pay. *Pisonia* has evolved a macabre solution to surviving on the ocean fringe. It drops dense racemes of prickly seeds covered in a sticky mucus that attach to feathers. Any unfortunate chick or bird that falls into the seedbeds becomes engulfed and almost certainly dies.

While it's tempting to assume the tree might benefit from extra nutrients provided by dead birds, scientists have disproved that theory. Mortality is an unfortunate evolutionary by-product of the tree's need to disperse seeds widely from island to island. It's been shown that seeds do better when wetted occasionally but do no better on a dead bird than they would otherwise.[74] The pact between birds and trees simply serves both parties – it's an evolutionarily stable strategy in which they live in an involuntary embrace, even sometimes to the death.

Once seeds have germinated, however, they would not thrive without the nutrients the birds bring onto the island's ecosystem. This returns nitrogen in a form that is available for absorption into the food chain. Black noddies, bridled terns and wedge-tailed shearwaters constantly stream out to sea and back, transporting nutrients from the ocean back and forth[75] and amplifying their availability, playing their part in maintaining healthy fish stocks, whales, dolphins and turtles. Plants couldn't arrive, they couldn't survive and they couldn't disperse the fruits of their reproduction without the birds either. But they also couldn't maintain such a rich diversity of natural processes and wildlife. There isn't a square centimetre of the island that's untouched by animals.

Scientists in Australia's Shark Bay suggest that the seasonal migration of tiger sharks might influence dugongs to move away from seagrass beds, allowing the habitat to regenerate and come back stronger.[76] If these predator–prey relationships break down, the seagrass beds become less rich and animals need to move longer distances for food. Their efforts become more random and stressful, leading to disease and a decline in the scale and distribution of nutrient transfer around the world. In two-thirds of cases, today's animals are having to move seventy per cent further as a result of human disturbance.[77]

These examples of animal movement across planet Earth everywhere and at every scale imaginable underscore their importance on global nutrient processes. Scientists have only just begun studying this. Most migration is out of sight, invisible to us, either hundreds of metres above the Earth at night or in the sea. In Europe, during spring and autumn, you can hear the soft, nasal, drawn-out 'se-eeep' voice of migrating redwings, a type of thrush that calls throughout the night as they migrate

Dugongs will swim hundreds of kilometres between feeding patches, and their trails have a profound impact on seagrass health. In nature, dugongs, and indeed all animals, cultivate their own food. In this case, the seagrass bounces back richer and more abundant.

overhead under cover of darkness. Millions of birds secretly congregate using subtle acoustics to form loose aggregations and fly thousands of kilometres on the strength of a few grams of body fat.

Using supercomputers and data from modern weather radar networks, scientists can now spot the blobs and lines of insects and birds flying across entire continents. Among the biggest migrations on Earth are ones we're hardly aware of. In the UK, 3.5 trillion insects, amounting to 3,200 tonnes of biomass, migrate above the region annually.[78] This aerial plankton is fed upon by birds and bats, which concentrate, disperse and amplify nutrients at colonies or throughout forests and grasslands, where wild bison, wolves and herds of deer would once have concentrated it even further. The fertile food-bowl floodplains that provide market garden vegetables to your local supermarket today were built on animal activity, the transfer and laying down and storing of soil nutrients for millennia.

Sunlight gives animals like butterflies the chance for mobility through flight. As kids, we would associate dragonflies with warm summer days because they need to warm up their muscles to fly. Among the first winged insects to evolve 300 million years ago, they developed sophisticated strategies and super-charged sensory adaptations that not only enabled them to survive but to move from place to place. This represented a major power shift in animals' ability to influence global energy transfer.

Dragonflies have compound eyes, all-round vision and can see ultraviolet, giving them an amazing ability to detect shape and movement. Military experts have studied their behaviour to develop software for stealth aircraft because they hunt using active motion camouflage.[79] When a dragonfly hunts, it hovers still and positions itself between its prey and some shadow behind it cast by, say, a tree, concealing its position. It's a bit like creeping up on someone in a forest hiding behind branches you're carrying (but less comical and more intimidating for the fly). The dragonfly can continually change its position based on where its prey moves, to keep the tree and its prey lined up – a butterfly, fly or mosquito won't notice. The dragonfly gradually looms closer until it reaches striking distance.

This evolutionary adaptation has suited dragonflies well, and they have become super-successful energy distributors despite living short lives. Dragonflies live from two to six years underwater, breathing through their rectum and hunting using a terrifying hinged lower jaw, enabling them to impale victims from a distance. The adult form is more of a system to guarantee breeding but has enabled massive nutrient transfer. There is a species, aurora bluetail, common throughout Australasia, South-East and Central Asia that disperses as aerial plankton and can be found anywhere there is water. After mating they take flight high into the air and get caught in trade winds, eventually laying in lakes hundreds of miles away.[80] They are among the first to recolonise dried out wetlands after the first seasonal rainfall, and without them inland lakes would be less productive, because they are the megafauna of pondlife and do all the same things that rhinos, elephants and orangutans do, only at a smaller scale and in far greater numbers.

Able to reproduce much faster than mammals, insects are among the first to colonise any new habitat, or to respond to sudden increases in free energy – hence locust plagues. When there is lots of surplus nutrient produced on the soil, locusts grab it and move it vast distances.

They hoover up surplus energy to rebalance the ecosystem, so waste matter doesn't overflow and cause pollution and chaos.

Insect flight isn't limited to winged animals either. Spiders have been found ballooning four kilometres above the Earth using silk threads to gain lift. Previously it was thought they did this by simply catching passing wind currents, but research has shown they use electrostatic forces in the atmosphere – they fly by static electricity. The spiders can detect these minute electric fields and prepare for lift-off.[81]

Consequently, on a small scale, grasslands are thousands of times more species-rich than rainforests. A hectare of the Ecuadorian rainforest has about 950 species, but grasslands in the Czech Republic can have forty-four species for every 25 x 25 cm – that's 7,500 times more species-rich. Shrink down to this scale and spiders become the predatory megafauna, and it's no coincidence that ninety-five per cent of the 400 to 800 million tonnes of prey they consume each year is in forests and grasslands.[82] Think about that next time you are scared by one. Imagine how much nutrient is regulated by spiders and insects every day.

During torrential rainfall in eastern Australia, social media went mad after millions of otherwise invisible spiders were filmed ascending from their burrows, scurrying ahead of the floodwaters. Spiders are the megafauna of the insect world and part of a process that controls our weather systems and puts food on our tables. They are frontline top predators and the first wave of animals that move in to restore damaged ecosystems, feasting on animals below them in the food chain, recycling energy back into soil and boosting carbon absorption. The island of Guam in the central Pacific is like a haunted house for the ghosts of native birds wiped out by introduced brown tree snakes. The abandoned forests are eerily covered in spider webs, the animals moving in to fill the empty niche, part of the process of rebuilding the island's natural processes.

For the ability to transport nutrients over large distances and affect ecosystems in opposite corners of the world, flight is still the ultimate behaviour any animal can have. Birds and insects have evolved to modify their waste and excrete toxic ammonia as uric acid (the white centre in bird poo), which they will drop just before take-off. This means they are unencumbered by heavy quantities of water, which would make flying far more energy-intensive. Offloading this excess baggage contributes to both their flight ability and the stability of the ecosystem because where they congregate en masse, whether it be along hedgerows, on lakes, in parkland trees or at the top of fruiting rainforest trees, the nutrients they deposit are redistributed on a phenomenal scale worldwide.

This behaviour, the deposit of nutrients in certain places, the ability to fly, is a reaction to their environment. The most stable interaction with the world is their annual migration because this created the connection with climate and food that has enabled them to survive for millions of years.

In the tropical ocean, seabirds are particularly important, because nutrient levels are typically low and unavailable to other animals. Frigatebirds or man-of-war birds were named by early mariners for their superior navigating and flying ability, large size and habits of stealing food from other birds. The males of these rakish, gothic-looking wanderers inflate a large red balloon under their chin during courtship. They are animals of extremes, uniquely adapted to life in the tropics and with an ecology similar in many ways to the albatrosses of the Southern Ocean. They have the biggest wing surface area to weight ratio of any bird in the world, meaning they can glide one-hundred kilometres without a flap using the weakest of convection currents cast beneath scarce clouds. With elegant, sickle-shaped wings and a long, forked tail, they soar to 4,000 metres, where it's -10°C. From these heights, they can see the curvature of the Earth and detect telltale nutrient patches miles below using binocular vision, before dropping out of the sky to feed. At sea level, it's almost as though they appear from nowhere, and they are always conspicuous among flocks of birds in the most remote places.[83]

Migration is a response to the promise of a flourish in predictable and life-giving energy. Butterflies and other insects come out to feed when flowers open during the day. Songbirds migrate in their millions across the Sahara, chasing the warmer weather, insects and flowering plants. Arctic terns and humpback whales flee the perpetual darkness of polar winters for warmer climes. Domestic cattle even orientate themselves north to south, along the Earth's magnetic axis, no doubt a throwback to times when they munched their way seasonally in one direction and then the other. Australia's honeyeaters follow the patterns of flowering trees across the continent, only stopping to breed when and where it's most profitable.

In terms of biomass, the greatest migration on Earth happens every day in the ocean. Living in the depths must be a constant dogfight with other animals, manoeuvring in every way possible to outwit and defend against predation. At those depths there is no sunlight, so each night and day, the creatures of the deep ocean – squid, plankton, and billions of tonnes of thumb-sized lanternfish – migrate up and down, grabbing the leftovers from sunlit feasting by their diurnal counterparts at the surface. Lanternfish have such a twitchy and oversensitive way of being; they die from the mere vibrations of being contained inside an aquarium. They need to be paranoid, because they wear bioluminescent headlights to attract the plankton on which they feed, and this makes them vulnerable to animals like the strange strawberry squid, which have one massive yellow eye that looks up towards the sun or moonlight and can detect the passing shadows of animals above, and another tiny blue eye that looks for the telltale bioluminescence of prey, such as lanternfish, below.

Lanternfish are extraordinarily abundant and, by some estimates, the two hundred or so species make up over half the biomass of all the fish in the ocean, yet they surface rarely.[84] From time to time you can see them in the mid ocean and where they congregate to spawn. This provides sustenance for gentle, giant whale sharks. In the Southern Ocean south of Tasmania, lanternfish surface at night over invisible deep-sea mountains: volcanoes that have emerged from the seabed reaching thousands of metres tall but never quite breaking the surface. Currents that collide and shear off the side of the mountains' steep sides whip the ecosystem into a frenzy, wafting nutrients up from the deep and stimulating a smorgasbord of animal life.

A few years ago, I sailed to one of these mountains on an Antarctic expedition yacht in the middle of winter, three hundred kilometres south of Tasman Island. After a couple of days of gut-wrenching seas, escorted by light-mantled sooty albatrosses and sei whales, the seas calmed and for one night we drifted on a still, calm, pan-flat ocean in complete darkness with the lightest of misty rain falling. Among flocks of Antarctic prions and Buller's albatross attracted to the navigation lights, we watched lanternfish and other strange unidentifiable creatures pass below. There were chains of sticky fist-sized salps, looking like the product of a mad scientist's experiment zapping cells with a growth ray. They are gelatinous and glob-like, with a big dark nucleus in the centre. Closely related are the pyrosomes, another colonial sea-squirt that is cylinder-like and can grow to metres in length. Under light, they looked like pink, fluffy paint-rollers. At night, over the sea mount, they flash on and off luminous yellow in a spectacular natural light show. The strange thing about sea-squirts is we share a common ancestor. When they decide to breed, they produce an embryo that you'd be hard-pressed to tell apart from a human embryo. Both have a notochord, which in our case turns into a spine. In the case of sea-squirts, it's absorbed before it metamorphoses into one of many thousands of peculiar other forms of life, too weird and varied to describe here.

These daily events that shock and entertain us are going on all of the time on the land and coasts we live on, from the appearance of the first birds of spring, to the butterflies in our gardens and news reports of the season's first migrating whales. Only in the last few years has there been widespread recognition that migratory animals, including birds and insects, play a major role in maintaining Earth's ecosystems and biodiversity processes.

All animals are constrained by food and the availability of places to breed, but the process isn't random, and animals don't choose where to feed. The frigatebirds that live for thirty years or more have been selected to survive in locations where, over thousands of generations, they developed an instinctive flight plan and a bird-brain Google map to reach the richest and most reliable areas. The natural distribution of frigatebirds, and indeed most migratory animals, has long been determined by wind and rain patterns. With climate change, the pattern of distribution and intensity of meteorological events is becoming more chaotic and the way they distribute nutrients is also becoming less predictable. This leads to confusion among animals, who use their intelligence to find food based on the predefined patterns created by the behaviour of their counterparts.

Of the world's five species of frigatebird, the lesser frigatebird has a global range estimated at over 160 million square kilometres,[85] equivalent to about a half of Earth's ocean surface area. Right now, there are several hundred thousand birds plying the oceans, continuously finding and consuming matter, moving it around and placing it back onto the surface, amplifying the availability of nutrients and recharging a system that would otherwise pollute.

The greatest migrations on Earth are a visible and cultural reminder of our dependence on animals, but the greatest movements that occur are not over vast distances at all; they are the circadian rhythms that pervade the daily existence of all wildlife, driven by the power of sunlight and the constant need to combat the erosive power of its energy, to sustain a world in a stable, steady state where animals survive.

Plummeting insect numbers worldwide should be our biggest cause for concern, because at this microscale, insects are megafauna. Our use of insecticides is obliterating butterfly and honeybee numbers.[86] Traditional grasslands are like tiny rainforests, with a canopy of flowering plants, a sub-canopy of mosses and a dense rich soil layer deposited over centuries of industrious processing by billions of creatures, including insects and spiders. Agriculture and food security are built on these foundations, but as we remove whole layers from the food chain, we destabilise nutrient transfer at every scale, from planetary to our own backyards, leading to the kinds of environmental problems we have today.

Allowing migratory creatures – indeed all creatures – to go extinct, we may as well be cutting off our own legs, as we will no longer have the energy to walk far enough to find the food we need to look after the generations that come after us. In a habitable world, it's the animals that do the walking for us.

Amplification and concentration

There are two key nutrients that limit the ability of land animals to extract carbon, keep the Earth cool and make it habitable: nitrogen and phosphorus. A third, iron, is essential in the ocean.

We know that an excess of these energy-creating nutrients is dangerous as it causes pollution, reducing the habitability of ecosystems by inducing chaos. So it seems counterintuitive to suggest we need animals to amplify and concentrate them. That's until you realise that it takes a lot of animals (particularly big ones) to amplify these resources sufficiently in one place to allow all animals, including human beings, to access and use enough energy to thrive.

The diversification of ecosystems into structures with a maximum number of animals acts as the valve to regulate just the right amount of energy release for the optimum number of users. This could only have supported human beings once the system reached a certain biomass and complexity. That's a point worth taking a moment to think about. Our existence is balanced between having too much or too little of a good thing and, critically, it is wildlife that regulates this balance, and we evolved when things were just right.

Since the Great Oxidation Event 2.4 billion years ago, when iron was rusted into sediments and buried deep underground, biologically available iron (not the iron ore we dig out of the ground) has become so rare, it limits the magnitude of whole food chains. In the Antarctic, even in places where deep water resurfaces fast, photosynthetic microorganisms couldn't rely solely on iron in the ocean.

Being huge and abundant, whales and dolphins are superb examples of the magnitude of impact animals have on gathering scarce nutrients, particularly iron.[87] The goose-beaked or Cuvier's beaked whale is a strange and fantastic beast looking like a big dolphin suffering from middle-aged spread. It has ever-so-tiny fins that fit neatly into streamlined sockets, a sloping forehead, small eyes and a lower jaw that juts forward. On adult males, this is tipped with two upturned buck teeth used for mock combat, hence the many parallel rake-marks that cover their sensitive skin. The face is covered by sucker-marks from the razor-edged cups that line the tentacles of deep-sea squid, their favoured prey, which they catch at depths of several thousands of metres and where the pressure is equivalent to being stood on by 500 elephants. There are also pockmark lesions all over their bodies, the healed wounds from adventitious cookie-cutter sharks, which make a living sneaking about and biting the whales' live flesh, with jaws like a cigar-cutter.

One of the commonest of a suite of species that make up a quarter of all the world's whales and dolphins, these paunchy cetaceans hold the record for the longest mammalian breath-hold, a staggering three hours and forty-two minutes.[88] Supremely adapted to living underwater, they breathe anaerobically (without air), which isn't as odd as it sounds. We do it. Marathon runners draw on myoglobin, the iron-rich compound in muscles that colours them red. Myoglobin

---

In complete darkness at over 2,000 metres deep, a Cuvier's beaked whale digs in soft sediment using high-frequency echolocation to find its crab prey. The seafloor is a huge deposit for carbon. In places, the mud is a kilometre thick and took over 300 million years to settle.

releases oxygen slowly and steadily, enabling you to run much further than you could if you were just using your blood. Both myoglobin and haemoglobin are iron-based proteins essential for respiration. Iron is also the main ingredient in compounds essential for plant photosynthesis so there are no animals, and barely a square centimetre of planet Earth, that doesn't depend on iron. It remains super-important for cellular function in all living organisms.[89]

In whale faecal matter, iron concentrations have been recorded at up to 10 million times greater than in the surrounding seawater.[90] Sperm whales are among the world's biggest (also in terms of body size) amplifiers and transporters of nutrients in the oceans, but have declined by as much as eighty per cent from pre-whaling numbers of 1.1 million animals.[91] They are among the largest creatures to have ever lived and are the only animals that regard the whole of the world as their home range.[92] Before privately owned vehicles became commonplace sixty or so years ago, human home ranges were tiny.

By amplifying the amount of iron near the sunlit ocean surface where plants use it to photosynthesise, sperm whales make 200,000 tonnes of atmospheric carbon move down through the food chain to the deep ocean, every year. This also increases ocean productivity in their favour.[90] Before sperm whales were hunted this figure would have been close to 18 million tonnes – the one species could have been equivalent to the climate emissions budget of a small country like Slovenia.

Mobilising iron and other ecosystem-limiting nutrients to create a centralised trading environment – like a living stock exchange – is what animals like whales do. What matters is where and when they do it, plus having an entire supporting cast of other animals to absorb any excess and put it to good use.

In the US Gulf of Maine it's estimated whales are responsible for replenishing nitrogen at a rate of 23,000 tonnes per year, more than all river inputs combined. Much of this nutrient is re-released to spread out across the sunlit zone and the actions of feeding deep, defecating at the surface (which animals tend to do when they aren't swimming and feeding) and motoring through clouds of plankton, contribute to the upward pumping of material, delivering recycled nitrogen to the surface.[93] By congregating in certain places, these effects are amplified by fish, seabirds and other marine mammals, setting up multiple pathways, pumps and trophic cascades, before nutrients are transferred by other animals throughout the ocean and even into the coastal areas we rely on for our food.[94]

Animals operate on an unimaginable scale of *abundance,* supercharging Earth's ecosystems with life-giving *structures* and *diversity*, so we can get the energy we need. They reprocess, recycle and reshape things into bioavailable forms and at concentrations that we can use. And over about 30 million years they created stable patterns of behaviour, where energy was absorbed, and the structures powerful enough to counteract universal forces that would otherwise break everything down.

Because we tend to regard animals as separate to ecosystem function and overlook the magnitude of their impact on planetary energy, we still underestimate the significance of wildlife for climate regulation. The authors of 'Animating the Carbon Cycle' in the journal *Ecosystems* say that the animal-driven effects may rival any traditional carbon storage estimates.[95] We acknowledge how much carbon is locked up in plants every day but to re-coin a cliché, we can't often see the woodpeckers for the trees! It's the daily routines of animals making a living that drives this natural energy-based economy that we live in.

Buildings aren't just made to look at; they are like a landscape that houses an ecosystem, including a workforce, and are architecturally designed to accommodate people. The value of the Gherkin building in London's Canary Wharf isn't measured in glass and steel, or it would have been replaced years ago. It's measured in the amount of rent and the comings and goings of thousands of company employees and the tendril-like influence the building plays in the capital city's economy. The Guggenheim Museums use space and light to create artistic compositions that can be walked inside, providing an experience of contemporary creativity to foster ticket sales. Libraries are functional, with floors and shelving for catalogued books. The 'Green Building' in Melbourne, Australia, was built specifically to house conservation organisations and features its own water recycling garden. Economies and ecosystems are housed in buildings and landscapes but it's people and other animals coexisting that make them relevant – otherwise, nothing would be liveable.

This is the justification for celebrating animal life on Earth. It is to be in awe of everything they have done relentlessly, day in, day out, for millions of years among the architecture of the world we know today. It's to realise the complexity of a vast system that turns the mundane into a kaleidoscope of brilliance and has given us the chance to exist by concentrating and amplifying its effects to a point that we can afford to make our living among wildlife.

From habitat to habitable

The seeds of Bornean ironwood trees are the size of a fist, long and tapered, adapted to dropping from a great height and sinking into the soil beneath. The trees are rare because they are slow to grow, slow to reproduce and their wood is prized by people. These stubborn, slow-growing[96] and almost indestructible trees take nine to twelve months to germinate,[97] live for 1,000 years and until they finally burst through the canopy they often suppress their growth to an average of just half a millimetre a year.[98] Peter O'Reilly runs a historic eco-resort in the Australian Gold Coast Hinterland and has been doing conservation there for years. He once described an ironwood he had been monitoring for a decade. It was thirty centimetres tall. 'How fast does it grow?' I asked. 'We don't know,' said Peter. 'How tall last time you measured?' I asked. 'About three inches taller,' Peter said, and laughed.

Ironwood seedlings rarely die unless the parent tree is felled, as saplings seem especially sensitive to sunlight, so scientists assume that naturally regenerated trees only occur near the parents, but the truth is we don't know, because the animals that may have once transported their nutrient-packed seeds are long gone.

In Nepal, seedling growth in fruits of the false white teak is faster after passing through the gut of a rhino.[99] What if ironwood seeds were once grazed by South-East Asian hairy rhinos?[100] Hairy rhinos encountered our species of human in South-East Asia 100,000 years ago when they would have ranged all the way from the eastern Himalayas and the Indian subcontinent. There may have been 20,000 individuals back then, but today they number fewer than 200, and in Kalimantan (southern Borneo) they are close to extinction, exterminated by habitat loss, hunting and the ivory trade.[101]

The 20,000 Sumatran rhinos that existed before humans arrived would have been distributed throughout the island's entire forests, along with abundant orangutans. Unlike ocean-going creatures, these land animals have smaller territories, limited by the energy it takes to transport their large bodies from place to place. But animals all follow patterns of foraging, searching out food by repeatedly revisiting areas they expect to find it. As in the ocean, food can be hard to come by, and animals are critical to the patchwork mosaic of lowland rainforest peat layers, laid down through leaf-fall over millennia, farmed by insects and soil nematodes.

Tropical forest soils, peat beds and mangrove forests are packed full of nutrients and energy and contain immense levels of carbon dioxide and ammonia, both powerful greenhouse gases. On top of this, a fragile impermeable layer has to be carefully fertilised by animals such as rhinos, because too much release of nutrient damages its structure, and leads to collapse of local wildlife populations. Much in the same way you need a monthly salary to afford a week's shopping, animals need to consistently and reliably place nutrient currency into the seed bank and deposit energy in places from where a myriad of withdrawals are made by other animals, who redistribute the wealth among the ecosystem's many branches. If everyone withdraws all their money at once, the bank closes.

Pangkalan Bun is a city on the southern coast of Borneo, the world's third largest island. The region known as southern Kalimantan conjures romantic visions of old spice traders under the ancient rule of a divine sultan. The forest beneath is pan-flat and the mangrove edges meet the turquoise ocean, turned milky with stirred sediment. Here and there, the coastline's pastel fringe is cut by tannin-stained water from deep inside the forest, sharp incisions of the jet-black creeks that branch out into the brackish coastal estuaries.

This is one of the last strongholds of wild Bornean orangutans and the site of Dr Birutė Galdikas's Camp Leakey, where some of the world's longest-standing primate research is still being done. It's not a vast area. You can see the national park boundary from the air and at lower altitude ironwoods become visible, dotted emergent trees that tower over the primeval landscape. The northern border winds along the banks of the Sekonyer River, and elsewhere it is drawn in neat square blocks by surveyors, backing onto leases for palm oil production.

Palm oil plantations are slowly replacing the rainforest, and at the very edge the recently grown cash crops are fresh, lush and verdant. As you approach the city by air, you can see this forest of neatly lined trees with umbrella-like fronds become thinner, less healthy, exposing a sunburnt and red soil beneath. It's the first reminder how important rainforest animals are to avoiding ecological bankruptcy. When rainforest is slashed and burnt to make way for agriculture, the nutrients that were budgeted for the near future are released once only.

New palm oil plantations on the edges of rainforest are profitable only for as long as the energy stolen from the ecosystem can last. As for the people of Pangkalan Bun, the poorest now draw water from filthy rivers, heavy with dirt, sediment and agrochemicals. Ironically, the crystal, clear-flowing and clean black water rivers of the lowland forests are only a few kilometres away, threatened by the ever-increasing demand for a global palm oil industry that makes shampoo and chocolate.

There are currently about 120,000 orangutans in the wild, half the number there was a century ago, and with about 1.3 for every square kilometre,[102] the three-quarters of Borneo and Sumatra that was forested a hundred thousand years ago would have held a total orangutan population of over a million animals. Add another 75,000 rhinos into the mix and the scope for the transfer, amplification and concentration of nutrients would have been extraordinary. Orangutans eat hundreds of types of fruit and rhinos use a prehensile upper lip to selectively browse vegetation and munch the seeds of slow-growing forest goliaths like the ironwood tree. Both species are cultivation grazers that navigate verdurous laylines, criss-crossing vast tracts of forest, promoting health, diversity and the integrity of entire jungle districts.

Our world's animals contribute to an ecosystem order where portions of energy are packed to the hilt inside biological processes. The immense size of these animals, their mobility and abundance, would have influenced the architecture of some of the world's most magnificent forests. Now we have no idea what the future holds.

Everywhere you look in the world there is evidence of animal impact. The animals that make up coral reefs produce two and a half kilograms of carbon biomass a year per square metre, twice that of rainforests. In the Coral Triangle there are porous coral-bodies that on close inspection with a magnifying glass contain hundreds of holes, each filled with minute predatory mantid shrimps, punching at passing plankton and scooping it into their feathery mouthparts. Fifty-seven species occur in the region, over ten per cent of all the world's varieties, and some are up to a foot long. Kri Corner in Indonesia's Raja Ampat has a dive site where field guide author Gerry Allen recorded 374 types of fish in a 60-minute dive, about 7.5 per cent of all marine fish known in the world.

One of these, the bumphead parrotfish, crunches its way through coral, extracting its algal treats. They are formidable animals, taking twenty years to reach full size. Squarish and blue-grey, the traces of scales on their flanks catch the light when the sun is in the right place. They have beady, intelligent-looking eyes and fins that are a bit on the small side, like the forelimbs of a *Tyrannosaurus rex*.

Bumphead parrotfish perform a significant ecosystem function, acting like the elephants of coral reefs, selectively breaking off huge chunks of coral to digest the algae within. By doing this, each animal recycles about five tonnes of coral each year and helps create the complex patterns and structure of reef ecosystems.

The males are like a big swimming face, with a Frankenstein-like forehead that turns pink with age, and have a slightly ulcerous-looking indent in the centre, below which there is a massive protruding bone-coloured beak they use for crushing coral. They don't seem to spend much time in one place but pause periodically for a casual inspection, before slicing off chunks with their shear-like mandibles – the coral regrows surprisingly fast. An individual might consume five tonnes of algal-laden and nutrient-rich coral reef every year,[103] much of which passes through its gut, to be expelled as sand, the foundation of tropical island beaches.

Bumphead parrotfish are the elephants of the reef, doing the equivalent of pushing over trees, leaving the fine-scale pruning and vegetation management to the smaller fish and other animals. It is the total number of animals that live in these systems and the fastidiousness of their combined activity at every scale, from the whales that parade around deep-sea mountainsides to the crabs and clownfish that share the tendrils of colourful giant anemones, that makes the ecosystem so impressive, that diversifies its structure and creates homes for copious lifeforms. The abundance absorbs all the energy that is in constant flux, recycled and delivered precisely for all its animal residents, including local people who rely on the reef for their livelihoods and protein.

At nearby Manuk Island in Indonesia's Banda Sea, there is a remote volcano considered one of the most important seabird colonies in the whole South China Sea and Sulu Sea.[104] It's frequented by local fishers who often risk life and limb, travelling over one-hundred kilometres over open ocean in small boats to seek sustenance for their far-distant families, who they may not see for many weeks. The island rises 285 metres above the sea, then descends off its eastern flanks to a submarine area over 7,000 metres deep. Much of the perimeter is fringed with tropical dry forest dotted with red-footed booby and greater frigatebird nests. The boobies breed during periods of strong trade winds in the tropics, flying to nearby feeding locations at speeds of forty kilometres an hour.[104, 105] They make use of tailwinds to reach foraging grounds and tack north or south better than any ocean sailor, before finding crosswinds to return to their nest.

Breeding in trees on a mountainside gives the birds a vantage point from which to embark on their daily flight routines. Above Manuk's forest line there is a skirt of dense bushes grading into grassland interspersed with rocks and smoking-hot volcanic clays and seeps where common noddies and brown boobies nest on the ground. The mountain's summit is bisected by a saddle-shaped valley, and there is a breathy crater and sulphur vents that give off a pungent smell. Over millennia, the soil has grown deep and spongy, topped with dense grasses, rotting vegetation and full of bird guano. Standing in it, you can sink up to the knees – much like the thick friable soil Aboriginal people created in Australia. Early colonialists also described this as deep and spongy.[106] It's the kind of compost that would have any gardener drooling for a wheelbarrow-full, and the absence of this water-absorbing layer from landscapes all over the world now is causing unmitigated flood disasters.

Manuk's seabirds concentrate nutrients here on an epic scale and are essential to the whole region's processes. They nourish the surrounds, where gigantic tuna and hammerhead sharks run circuits between the islands. These act like motorway refuelling stops, between bouts of feeding at other hotspots on their migratory circuits.

The mountain creates a predictable flurry of nutrients – gradients that can be sensed by animals.[107] Seabirds evolved to breed during periods of *lowest* overall ocean production, because then everything has to gather around the breeding island, as there is nowhere else to find a reliable source of food. The birds' activity amplifies the effect, increasing the benefit for everyone, as transportation and concentration of nutrients by seabirds back to land is substantial.[108] It's the reason why local fishers depend on islands like this and even scuba-divers glory in the sheer abundance of marine life. But the island's seabirds are threatened by an infestation of introduced rats that kill their chicks, and this is almost halving fish populations. On rat-free coral islands, fish grow faster and are more abundant because there are more seabirds.[109]

On the tiny island nation of Nauru in the western Pacific, seabirds will have increased fish stocks and human survival, eventually forming a unique part of the islanders' culture. Nauru built its nation on the wings of seabirds. By the late 1960s, it was the second-wealthiest country in the world from mining guano deposits but descended into poverty once the resource was exhausted, by the early part of this century.

Catching frigatebirds is an ancestral tradition of the islanders that might date back tens of thousands of years. Locals lure them in with fish, put them in cages and tame them. Then they send them back out to sea where they meet other birds and bring them back to the island. Killing frigatebirds has always been taboo, as villages with the greatest number perched in front once had highest standing in the community. Villages with more birds would have had more fish, as a result of the nutrients brought back to the island by the birds. Villages with greater fish bounty would survive better. So the tradition of bird-catching became firmly embedded in their culture as a result. The effect that seabird abundance has on human health might be subtle, but multiplied over thousands of generations it becomes a significant driver for our survival.

Ironically, Nauru is now turning to fishing rights as a source of ongoing wealth, but for that to be economically viable in the long term, it will need to rebuild its seabird colonies.

Similarly, in Western Australia, survival and body condition of endangered dibblers – a type of marsupial mouse – are better in places where marine nutrients are brought back to land by seabirds because spider and beetle densities are far greater and soil nutrients up to eighteen times higher.[110] Everywhere you look, the legacy of animals concentrating and amplifying nutrients has led to rich and often economically important habitats.

Being able to consume, concentrate and reintroduce energy back into a system, amplifying its availability in the most important places and spreading the benefits out regionally, has enabled animal life on land and in the sea to persist for millions of years. Animals do this at every scale from microscopic to regional and some, like sperm whales, at an almost planetary scale. Whole ecosystems would effectively shut down if it wasn't for animals transferring, amplifying and concentrating energy, converting it into other forms, moving it around, placing it where and when it matters – and, most importantly, in sufficient bulk for our needs. Without wildlife, the world we need to survive would not exist.

Communication

Animals couldn't amplify, concentrate and transfer energy on such a bewildering scale if there wasn't a way for them to communicate with each other, but many of the sensory frameworks that animals use are invisible to us. The electrostatic field between the atmosphere and flowers, for example, can be sensed by bees, which gain a positive charge when flying through it and select flowers where static electricity gradients will aid in pollen transfer – like when you rub a balloon and stick it to the ceiling.[111] It's been discovered that birds have molecules inside their eyes triggered by light, releasing an arrangement of electrons that orientate depending on the magnetic field and can help them navigate.[112] Animals, from top predators like tigers to deer and moths, use strongly scented pheromones to communicate their location and mood. A stunning array of sensory adaptations means animals exist in a parallel dimension that human beings can often only vaguely understand.

It's beyond the scope of this book to describe all the weird and wonderful ways we connect with the environment. For that, Jackie Higgins' *Sentient*[113] is a wonderful introduction. It describes the interaction of many different senses and how this connects us to the world. Human perception is vastly superior to what we know but animal sentience, collectively, is beyond the most powerful thing we can imagine. Many of the senses animals possess are alien to us. Yet animals are responsible for building habitable ecosystems and it's their supreme collective ability to measure and alter the environment around them that makes our survival possible. Protecting the world's sensory ecology is a dimension to conservation that we hardly comprehend.

There is one invisible architecture, however, that is easily detectable by us. It plays a significant role in our culture and society, yet we have to be trained to notice its significance in ecosystems. Of all the senses we possess but don't use to maximum effect, or have yet to understand, sound is the one that affords us the greatest chance to learn a new way to see – or hear – the world. It is the sense we use to avoid other animals, and it's how we're able to spread out and avoid getting into fights.

Much of the sun's energy that reaches the Earth is absorbed, but it can also change from one form to another. Our atmosphere and ocean capture heat, and this turns into kinetic energy generating winds and ocean currents through the movement of air and water particles. You can't hear wind; what you're hearing are the vibrations of particles caused by friction against surfaces, objects colliding, falling or rolling around. The whoosh of the wind is a series of compression waves that bounce off things like mountainsides or forests, entering your ear and being amplified by three tiny bones that strike the membrane of your eardrum, displacing tiny hairs that your brain translates into something you interpret as sound.

There is no reason you should need to hear anything except, like most animals, hearing helps you connect to your place. Protecting our acoustic environment increases our likelihood of survival.

Your favourite café might be a noisy place, bombarded by sound. There may be thumping music, children joyfully playing, people's chatter amplified off tiled walls, the deep hum of fridges, the squeal of metal stools across polished concrete, the clinking of plates and rattle of cutlery dropped into dishwashers. This is a lo-fi soundscape. Urban. The more you concentrate, the more intense the noise becomes and the less you can discern a single sound through the chaos.

To survive in cities, we must consciously decouple ourselves from this noise, create an acoustic Chinese wall in our minds and continue as though normal. But it isn't normal. Animals like songbirds can't live a healthy life here.

Healthy soundscapes are also a prerequisite for human life, and despite being acutely aware of sound through music, we express poor judgement, concern or even awareness of noise on our lives, let alone its impact on wildlife. For many of us this is a sensory realm that remains unfamiliar.

Over time, animals adapted to create their own sound. The stridulating cricket, echolocating bat and guffawing human use wind, string or brass-style instrumentation to create noise. But why? Acoustic communication seems to have evolved independently in different groups of animals and has most notably driven speciation (the rate of species increase) in animals like birds and frogs.[114] What made amino acids combine in an ever-more sophisticated way until animals were able to make sound, sing, speak and finally form languages?

They say a picture paints a thousand words, but hearing is more powerful than any other sense because it conveys a density of information that, for the most part, is in our subconscious. We can't see through a forest, but when it comes to hearing we have superpowers. We can hear invisible things approaching and as soon as we are in the dark, we transform into listeners. We're so connected to birdsong that you could present almost anyone with a dawn chorus and they would be able to describe something about the structure of a forest without prior knowledge. If we know the calls of birds that live in the riverside forest, we can find water.

In the natural world, better sounding coral reefs, with their chirping fish and snapping shrimp, attract free-swimming coral and fish larvae.[115,116] Migratory bowhead whales use their calls to assess ice-thickness and push through thin areas to breathe.[117] Other cetaceans are likely to listen to their environment to navigate.[118,119] Ornithologists used to use birdsong to lure migrant birds into study traps by night, and it could be a strategy for night-migrating trans-Saharan birds to identify oases and land before the heat of dawn.

When you consider how much information sound conveys, its power should come as no surprise. Sound travels through walls and penetrates deeply into forests. From a kilometre away, you can hear someone whistle, but you can't make out words they hold up on a sign. In the ocean sound travels several times faster, and in three dimensions the quantity of information received over just a few kilometres is hundreds of times greater than on land.

Animals use sound in conjunction with the local environment, behaving in the way they are most likely to survive, which scientists call the 'soundtope hypothesis'.[120] Every ecosystem has its unique soundscape, which Bernie Krause in *The Great Animal Orchestra* calls its 'geophony'.[121] Animals have learnt to hear through this, adapted to fit inside but also taken the sugars created by plants, processed by insects and consumed, and reordered this into new molecules to build the muscles that allow them to reconvert it into sounds they produce themselves. Animals have extended the shape and patterns that create stable crystal and molecular energy structures and added noises to allow their behaviour to blend into the patterns of the world and other creatures around them.

Ours is a planet of creatures that actively produce sound, and many more that passively use the sound of others to comfortably fit in. Hearing-dependent species have evolved to process sound into a picture and have more than enough information to manipulate this for behavioural interests. Bats can use it to home in on the tiniest free-flying, zig-zagging moths. Dolphins even create signature whistles to 'name' themselves, and long-finned pilot whale families have identical and unique vocalisation where pods recorded twelve years apart can be told apart by their voice imprints.[122]

The most abundant and noticeable sound-producers in our lives are birds. Croajingolong National Park in Australia's southeast is one of the only accessible places in southeast Australia with intact rainforest outside the influence of human-made noise and traffic. An hour before dawn the sinister screech of a sooty owl rings across the valley, owlet-nightjars whistle and ring-tailed possums quietly chirrup. At the first hints of dawn eastern yellow robins begin to call … a sweet 'chup chup'. Then other birds join the chorus until there is an orchestra.

Shortly after dawn the loud chiming call of bell miners starts. This communal bird has developed a call that rings and drives other songbirds away from valuable nectar-rich trees by shouting over the top of them – annoying them out of the area. In suburbia, birdwatchers call them pests, since their unique audio-ecological advantage, combined with habitat loss, has made them so successful. Cicadas use the same technique to create a wall of sound. They advertise their presence, but by singing communally they can drive away birds that might eat them if they were calling alone. Farmers use scare-guns that mimic cicadas, as they are particularly effective at driving away songbirds from their crops.

In an unspoilt soundscape, the bell miner isn't so annoying. On top of a functioning and naturally structured forest, birds time their calls to occur in between each other, forming a sort of sound matrix in which there is mostly territorial balance.[123] This is the hi-fi version of environmental sound. Hi-fi, in a music sense, refers to high fidelity, which is the ability to record sound faithfully or exactly. In nature, it is used to describe a soundscape where noises are all heard and non-overlapping. It's the sound equivalent of an extremely energy-rich environment. The densest array of sound, supporting the largest number of species, is the most stable structure and allows the maximum number of animals to live alongside each other.

Compare this to industrial sound or modern music, which is layered and overlapping. A lo-fi environment is one with noise like a city or heavy machinery. Repetitive and loud sounds (think jackhammer) are almost universally annoying – it's a lot of 'free energy' that disrupts natural patterns, leading to chaos.

We can't easily ask an animal how it feels when it's subjected to loud noise, but we do know about ourselves. Offices, for example, are terrible places to concentrate ... the background din, repetitive sounds or voices destroy our concentration. While you may think nature sounds or even music could be more mentally stimulating, when it comes to work, silence is the only thing that increases productivity.[124] So if you want to maximise efficiency in the workplace you would place industrial noise protection on everyone's ears and completely block out sound, right? Wrong. We know enough about our psyche to realise that sonic isolation would be maddening. Indeed, studies have found that either too much or too little sound is unattractive. The most motivating level is somewhere between these two states.

Sound, unlike other pollutants, isn't something you clean up – that would be like removing an entire forest and its birds. There is nothing about offices that resembles normality, and this is why we escape to the local park for a quiet lunch where there is the breath of wind through leaves, the background chatter of songbirds and a peaceful throng of quiet voices. We tolerate the din of an office while working, but it is not the environment we would choose for survival.

Imagine a healthy acoustic soundscape like your house. The walls provide scaffolding for different acoustic scenarios. The sounds within the spaces (rooms) and the context in which you use them represent the diversity of different functions and processes you need to live alongside others. You tolerate the noisy television in the living room but seek peace in the bedroom and office. You will put up with din from the dishwasher in the kitchen but don't want that interfering while you're watching your favourite show. The time you do things is particularly important. You don't want the radio on loudly at night, or the microwave going 'ping' at three o'clock in the morning. Animals use acoustic space in a similarly diverse way. Loud sounds are fine, as long as they are the right noises at the right time and place.

In nature documentaries, adult penguins return from a week at sea to find their chicks among the cacophony of tens of thousands of avian colonists. Parents visiting primary schools know they can be well out of sight and hear their children easily over the throng of hundreds of excited shouting kids at pick-up time. It is an adaptation to survival. After all, if the penguin chick was silent, that wouldn't be much help, and it's almost certainly why we shout someone's name when we are desperate to find someone. As a community, we accept children's voices at higher volumes than other sounds because it's natural and part of our own species' survival strategy, but we don't accept adults shouting or a neighbour's dog continually barking, as that interferes with our mental and physical wellbeing. The same goes for animals.

Colour-shifting crabs on the shores of the United Kingdom were subjected to noise and failed to develop bright camouflage (and therefore became more prone to predation) when exposed to ship sounds but were unaffected by natural sounds at the same intensity.[125] These physical changes were caused by heightened metabolic rates and stress. Loud, repetitive, annoying and unnatural sounds also change our behaviour. In humans, urban rumble is strongly linked to increased anxiety, depression, hypertension, high blood pressure and heart disease.[126] It even reduces our children's rate of learning to speak.[127]

The context of noise changes our behaviour and mood. Once, when whale-watching off Melbourne, we encountered a southern right whale in rough sea conditions. On the days either side, when the weather was calm, the whale rubbed up against the boat, but this time it was spy-hopping to look at us (whales have very good vision) while maintaining a distance, even though we were stationary. Why would this be?

Because of their all-round hearing southern right whales seem acutely aware of vessels because the noise created by propeller-driven boats is very loud. This is unlike the sperm whales described in earlier chapters, which have very poor hearing from behind. When you go whale watching you may seem a distance away, but to the animals you are a looming and noisy threat. A study of killer whales in the Haro Strait off British Columbia found whale-watching boats could mask whale calls at a fourteen-kilometre range.[128] Sound travels at 1,480 metres per second underwater and only 343 metres per second in the air – this is because air is less dense.

The strong wind and choppy seas masked the southern right whale's hearing, which for us would be like turning the lights off. The whale became nervous about our approach and the danger we might pose in the same way as we might visit a 'haunted house' alone by day with little fear. But at night, when our primary sense (vision) is impaired, we can fear the creaks and groans of an old and unfamiliar building. We are less likely to walk confidently into a dark room with an uncertain noise than we were if the lights were on. The whale was doing the same. Birds do it too. They are more nervous about your approach on windy days because they can't hear you so well.

Sea creatures and nocturnal animals like bats and owls can be acutely aware of what is around them except their world has become one of human-made noise. In some places, the distance at which minke whales can hear each other has decreased from 114 kilometres to only 19 kilometres.[129] In oceans clear of artificial noise, scientists have been able to hear blue whales at distances of 1,600 kilometres,[130] but a hundred-fold increase in the background noise created by a crowd of increasingly large and numerous ships[131] is putting the recovery of this endangered species in peril. The blade-rate on a supertanker is about 7.5 revolutions per second, which means it is creating compression waves sending out noise at about 7.5 hertz (waves per second). Combined with all its other machinery, the noise from these ships is enormous and peaks at twenty hertz and below, which overlaps with the blue whales' voices.[132]

At a radius of 1,600 kilometres, a two-dimensional sea-surface area calculated by (πr^2) represents 8 million square kilometres over which they can sing and find a mate. That's been reduced to only 80,000 square

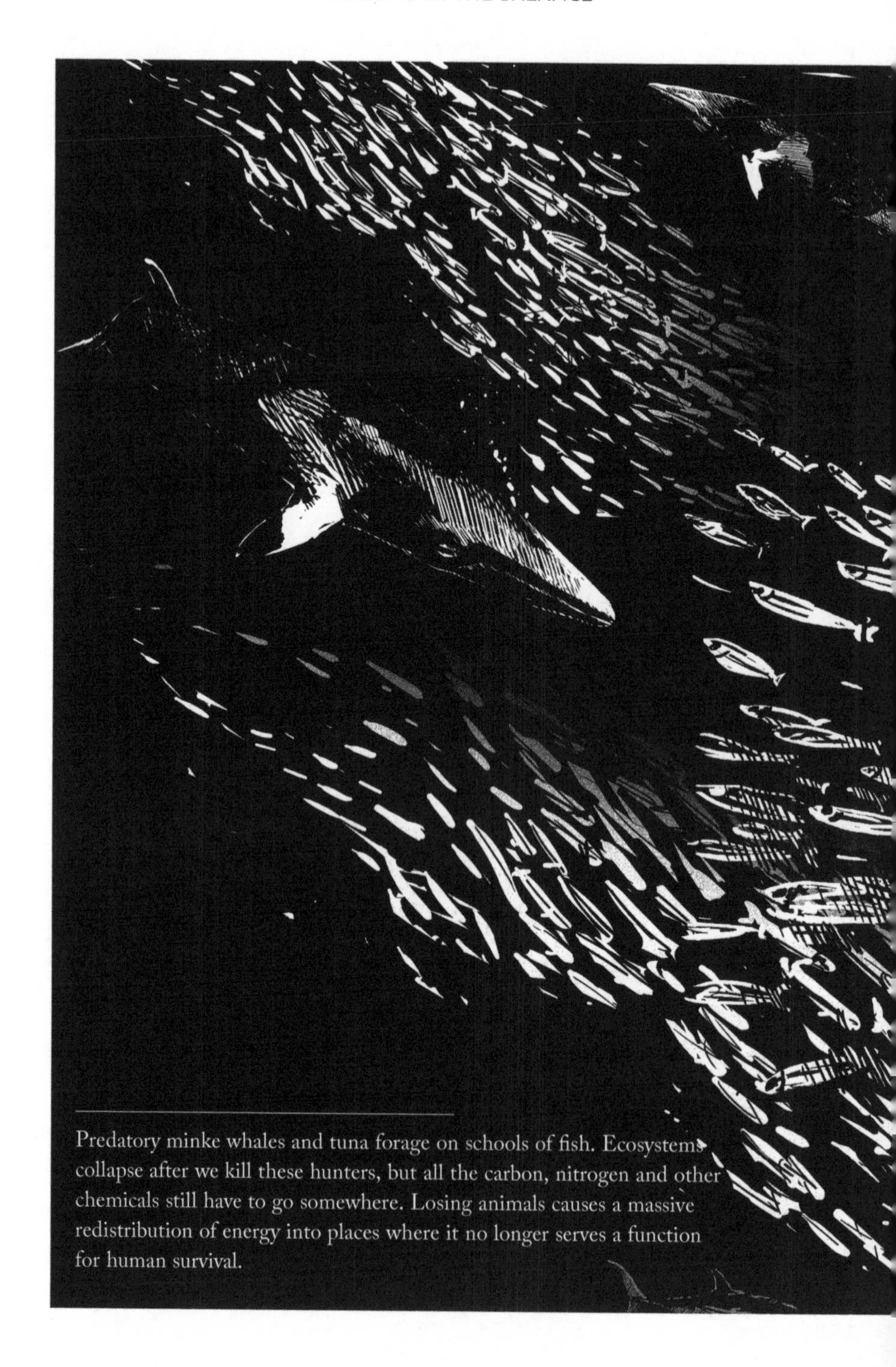

Predatory minke whales and tuna forage on schools of fish. Ecosystems collapse after we kill these hunters, but all the carbon, nitrogen and other chemicals still have to go somewhere. Losing animals causes a massive redistribution of energy into places where it no longer serves a function for human survival.

kilometres. For modern-day blue whales, life is like buying a ticket to the opera where only the theatre's first row can hear the singer.

Big whales like blue whales communicate at frequencies less than ten hertz, well below the level of interference from most natural sounds caused by wind and weather. This is an example of the soundtope hypothesis, where the animals have responded to the environment and adapted their aural signatures and sound production to fit around natural background noise.

Forest birds also adapt their calls to the environment. The eastern yellow robin emits a harsh 'chup chup' at dawn but changes it later in the day, because the quality of the dawn sound transmits easier in the cool dryness but not so well in the later humidity. It's the same reason why blackbirds sing before dawn and not at midday, and why the world-record-mimicking lyrebird breeds in winter, when the effect of its hoax calls is not diluted by genuine bird calls and the air is cooler. For the same reason, birds don't breed successfully along noisy main roads.

A vast array of animals, from insects to birds, fish, whales and dolphins use acoustics to create a living space around them.

If we threaten the structural integrity of the soundscape it's like moving the television into the office or the dishwasher into the living room. The complex acoustic scaffolding that wildlife produces is critical to ecosystem function. Animals are building rooms for themselves … we might call these 'territories'. These are places where they can live in peace, and if we upset this, we destroy the ambience, increase anxiety and create conflict.

A study of the bird known as the great tit found that increased ambient noise made for more territorial aggression. In short, increased noise turns urban tits into angry birds.[133] Noise pollution shaves the edge off the jigsaw pieces so fewer birds can fit in around each other. This isn't a sustainable strategy because it reduces the density and diversity of animals that can coexist in the space, leading to a decline in structure and ultimately the release of surplus free energy. By simply increasing environmental noise we destroy ecosystem structure and function.

From the sound of rainforest cicadas and songbirds to the din of snapping shrimp and singing fish or whales, animals make a sound to isolate themselves from others, to reduce the risk of competition. The trade-off is an easier life, one that maximises the chance of success for their species, and it is the one that makes a species more likely to survive. It is a more stable way to withstand the natural laws of Earth.

Think about it. If you were out today gathering berries, you wouldn't be looking to start a fight with a bear – you would be listening intently for bears and doing your utmost to avoid contact. You might even choose quiet windless days to forage, and you certainly wouldn't wander around singing at the top of your voice. However, if you see another human traipsing on your territory you might shout, to remind them this is your patch. Sound, particularly language, is an exquisitely robust yet harmless way to manipulate your environment and alter behaviours. This is how and why tribal customs and languages diversified in Australia and New Guinea in proportion to biodiversity.[134]

If we continue to allow our lo-fi existence to dominate, we risk our own health and we also destroy the invisible architecture that supports biodiversity on which our farming, fisheries and livelihoods depend. In a similar way, low frequency electromagnetic fields created by powerlines, home wi-fi and phone microwave networks have been shown to affect bee flight, foraging and feeding.[135,136] When we interfere with the flow of information between animals and disrupt their ability to communicate, we create a loss of clarity and understanding about how ecosystems are working.

There is nothing more beautiful than the sound of nature because it represents the ideal state for a habitable Earth. Information is the basis for all animal intelligence, and animals use sound like we access the daily news, to make the most important decisions for survival.

When humans became likely to survive

Before the first humans evolved from ape-like ancestors a few million years ago, our planet had been going through billions of years of evolution. Animal-driven ecosystems only happened relatively recently. By that point, Earth was stacked full of creatures with almost every piece of free energy soaked up like a sponge.

Modern humans are omnivores: we eat a mixture of plants and meat. The diversity of our diet means that we exist at different parts of the food chain. It doesn't make sense for an animal of such stature and sophistication to evolve and become so successful in Earth's late stage if it was to be a generalist from the start. Before *Homo sapiens* could become the next most likely animal to survive on Earth, there must have been a stepping stone. A recent study in the journal *Quaternary* may have the answer.[13]

Without energy to fuel a large brain and body, you can't exist. There had to be something providing a new and rich source of free energy, something that destabilised Earth's ecosystems, providing a gap in the market for a new type of primate. Ancestors of modern humans began hunting global megafauna two million years ago and human brain size changed with our ecology. The animals our Neolithic ancestors hunted, the Pleistocene megafauna, were the missing link, and the surplus energy-rich protein they provided was the imbalance needed to give rise to early humans.

Hunting big animals doesn't require a massive brain because it's easier to find and kill woolly mammoths than it is to chase small animals or grow food. Large animals do, however, have a very big footprint on the Earth (literally) so the average time before higher vertebrates go extinct is only between 200,000 and two million years.[138] Trampling the ground, ripping up vegetation and knocking over trees changes things. The very basis of your existence and how all animals behave is to alter one's living environment and behaviour, to bring the two into some kind of alignment. When you're on a planet covered in incredibly diverse and dense forests that become populated by huge animals, there comes a time when the animals themselves start to create disruption, and that opens up new evolutionary opportunities.

Animal brains are a computational storage device that lets us find food ... which explains why the researchers found brain size changed in humans over time (though that does not mean we were less intelligent). When we were spearing large, slow-moving and noisy animals that were easy to find, we only needed a relatively small storage device for the information about where and when to travel. As we hunted them to extinction (or cut down and burnt their forest habitat) we became dependent on chasing smaller, quieter animals that were harder to find (or hear), and our brains got bigger because they needed more capacity. Since we have invented agriculture, they've shrunk again – and most likely will get smaller still with the advent of supermarkets and fast-food restaurants!

Animal survival has always been a fine balance between disrupting the environment and maintaining stability. Ironically, the successful spread of large megafauna across the Earth might have compromised their own existence. While we always tend to look for physical explanations for evolution and ecology, such as the drying of the African continent, ice ages and so forth, we miss the obvious point that animals themselves have the most powerful influence on landscapes. The processes we depend on for a habitable Earth are created by the interaction of all animals, and we are part of those interactions. We are an animal, descended from the same processes.

It makes sense that human beings had to evolve at that time because we were the most likely to bring ecosystem effects under control. Megafauna are one obvious candidate for destabilisation. For hundreds of millions of years, the natural laws of our universe have conspired this way, time and again.

In high-functioning ecosystems, the likes of which would have existed two million years ago when we first evolved from ape-like ancestors, adaptation pressures were much greater because the energy was precisely distributed and advantaged only the most specialised. For humans to have even a slight chance would have required other very large animals to transfer, amplify and concentrate nutrients to an extreme level.

The megafauna became the concentrated source of nutrients that bore an entirely new human genus, *Homo*. Our prey was large and possibly herd-forming, the ideal centralised source of sustenance for a small-brained population of humans to become globally dominant.

Humans didn't begin as generalists; we became generalists after our ancestors wiped out megafauna and altered the landscape. We might think 'humans' appeared 300,000 years ago, but the concept of a species is subjective. Scientists made that decision based on certain genetic thresholds, but from a planetary evolution perspective the species concept is completely arbitrary and more of a continuum. What if we are simply the latest incarnation of a primate that had its stronghold a million years or more ago? What if the adaptation to an omnivorous lifestyle is the final stages in our species' decline from existence? Is it coincidence that the genus *Homo* appeared two million years ago, which is about the average maximum species lifespan of a higher vertebrate on Earth?

After all, we continue to alter the environment ourselves, to suit our new and ever-changing lifestyle. We're building cities, converting forests and grasslands to farmland and removing all the fish from the ocean. In a way, we continue to adapt to conditions of our own making, but lately this isn't good news. Like the megafauna, we may become victims of our own success, if we continue to force ecosystems into chaos.

The decline of megafauna and the short lifespan of species with a large footprint on the Earth should send the strongest message to humanity – disrupt things too much and Earth will find a way to bring your species to its natural conclusion. It's another example of how co-dependent we are on other animals to create a habitable Earth and why the conservation of endangered species, protection of unspoilt habitat and rewilding of broken landscapes is essential for all our futures.

Ancient human cultures made the most successful ecosystems by doing what any animal does best, which is modifying their world and adapting their behaviour first through trial and error and then storing that knowledge as culture. 'Ancient' probably isn't the best word at all, as there are still cultures alive today that maintain traditional low-impact lifestyles and live harmoniously alongside complex ecosystems.

Human impact and our animality

Bill Gammage's excellent book *The Biggest Estate on Earth: How Aborigines Made Australia* in large part tells the story of Aboriginal peoples' use of fire to create the landscape that Australia was before European settlement in 1788. In *Dark Emu* Bruce Pascoe describes the sophisticated land use of Australia's First Nations people, that enriched and cultivated the environment with their own food to eat.

This is not surprising at all. Humans have always done this. We create the conditions that befit our own survival. This is done within the limits of nature and alongside other animals doing the same thing.

The beauty of these books is in how they help us read the natural history of landscapes and our place in it. Oliver Rackham's *The Illustrated History of the Countryside* looks at the British landscape through the lens of human impact dating back to prehistoric times. You can walk through the Oxfordshire countryside and see ancient barrows from the Neolithic period, over 3,500 years old. Ridge and furrow fields created by ancient farmers can still be found, and they still create areas of wet and dry, enhancing the diversity of vegetation.

Of all the animals on Earth, humans have one of the most observable impacts over time.

I've learnt to look closely at landscapes and see the way animals interact with them and create the patterns that lead to critical processes: clean water, fertile soils and abundant food. It wasn't until I moved to Australia that I saw the remnants of wilderness that had been manipulated for many tens of thousands of years by *Homo sapiens*. For longer than there have been humans living in northern Europe, Australia has been occupied by a single successful group of people. When you grow up in Europe, you're seeing landscapes that have been intensively altered by many different civilisations of *sapiens*. It can be harder to understand Australia's landscape, because it's now shrouded in vegetation and mostly devoid of its animals and people. The human and animal-driven processes that kept the environment dynamic and habitable have been replaced by regrowth and this obscures our view. It's easier to spot blunt changes to landscapes we've cleared over a short time, like a recently felled forest, than it is to spot the hidden erosion of animal-driven ecosystems after tens of thousands of years of concealment behind regrowth.

I'm not commenting here on First Nation beliefs, as it is not my place. Suffice to say, though, that the concepts I discuss, which I came to through observing nature and animals, are comfortingly similar to the folklore, stories and traditional understanding of the world's oldest cultures. It's hardly surprising, as they were looking at the same things. If you want an enhanced understanding of their perspective, I'd suggest you might read *Sand Talk: How Indigenous Thinking Can Save the World* by Tyson Yunkaporta.

When Australia's First Nations people discovered Australia it was part of the land mass of Sahul, which included New Guinea and

Tasmania. The country was blanketed with rainforest and roamed by herds of megafauna. Hippo-sized *Diprotodon*, *Palorchestes* (the marsupial tapir), the three-metre-tall flightless bird *Dromornis*, a giant tortoise, huge monitor lizards (bigger than today's Komodo dragon) and the marsupial lion, *Thylacoleo*. Debate goes on about the cause of their extinction, but it seems obvious enough that Pleistocene megafauna were lost worldwide, coincident with the spread of *Homo sapiens* across the continents.

It wasn't as straightforward as simply hunting animals to extinction, though. There were concurrent changes in the climate and vegetation[138] because Aboriginal people were actively changing the environment, in just the same way early humans affected the Pleistocene megafauna in other parts of the world before. Within about 20,000 years Aboriginal people massively altered the Australian landscape with fire and cultivation, removing huge tracts of rainforest and creating extensive treed grassland. This combination of landscape-scale manipulation of ecosystems and, undoubtedly, hunting pressure, meant all of the continent's megafauna, apart from red kangaroos, emus and cassowaries, went extinct several tens of thousands of years ago.

Far from undermining Australia's fertility and clean water, though, Aboriginal activities created a new synergy with wildlife and the landscape, enough for early visiting colonialists to notice the orderliness of its ecosystem. Gammage quotes George Frankland, who observed 'an instance of the beautiful decoration of some of our scenery, for that park-like ground is entirely in a state of Nature', and John Oxley as recording that 'many hills and elevated flats were entirely clear of timber … the general quality of the soil excellent'. What they were seeing was the elegant patterns that Lovelock had encouraged colleagues at NASA to look for as evidence of life on other planets.

Aboriginal people managed to build an environment with deep, fertile soil and vast biomass and diversity of animals. But at first it must have been brutal. To change an entire landscape means sacrificing huge numbers of your own species, throwing the entire system into chaos – rather like we are doing to the world today. It's thought that extinction of megafauna was more to do with changes in vegetation and water,[139] which would also have had dire consequences for early settlers. Only the most well-suited cultures would have survived this traumatic period, and it must have taken about 25,000 years before it restabilised, as this was the time it took for the megafauna to disappear altogether.

Significantly, Europeans arrived in Australia in 1788, killed most of the wildlife, and forcibly removed Aboriginal people from their land. What our current generation now considers 'civilisation' is unstable. We may have a few thousand years to go, before we work out patterns of behaviour, in which ecosystems are habitable once more.

Over thousands of generations, Australian Aboriginal people have enshrined their hard-won survival into a culture that would eventually persist in harmony with surroundings for longer than any other human civilisation.

The characteristic land management of Indigenous people was not confined to Australia. Neither is it confined to ancient humans. All over the world, Indigenous people still have words to describe their own systems of historic laws and practice; their struggle for self-sufficiency that emerges via their culture and connection to the land. Among the Maluku Islanders of Indonesia it's *sasi*, and the Greek Vassilikiots call it *symferon*.

Neolithic Europe wasn't always blanketed in thick forest, either; it was grassy woodland plains and ancient trees, rather like pre-European Australia. In Europe, though, fire wasn't the driver, it was the huge biomass of herbivores that kept the vegetation pruned and healthy: elk, red deer, wild boar and predators like Eurasian lynx, wolf and brown bear, plus a smattering of humans. The same went for the US. This is an account from *Lumen Learning* on the settlement of Jamestown, Virginia:

> The English had not entered a wilderness but had arrived amid a people they called the Powhatan Confederacy ... They burned vast acreage to clear brush and create sprawling artificial park-like grasslands so that they could easily hunt deer, elk, and bison. The Powhatan raised corn, beans, squash, and possibly sunflowers, rotating acreage throughout the Chesapeake. Without plows, manure, or draft animals, the Powhatan achieved a remarkable number of calories cheaply and efficiently.[140]

Indigenous people of all nations were, up until European invasion, among the most successful and perhaps most likely to survive of all races of humans on Earth. Mostly because they had been unencumbered with the ravages of capitalism and the disruption, starvation and cultural disintegration that had affected Europe for so long.

Even in Europe, things were going okay. An ecologist studying in the UK will look at patchwork mosaics of ancient woodland and heathland, some of the richest habitat left in England. In western Europe some of the fertile flower-rich grasslands of the Picos de Europa in Spain are still hand-scythed. The small-scale farming of Indigenous Europeans created gorgeously rich environments adorned with colour, birdsong and even mammals like wolves and brown bears.

In the case of the Indigenous Greek Vassilikiots, they too were responsible for crafting a land full of sea turtles, woodchat shrikes and short-toed eagles but increasingly find themselves in conflict with conservationists, who might view their modification of the land today as counterproductive, despite centuries of care and control.

It's perhaps one of the harshest realities of our modern age that First Nations, whose ancestors built the ecosystems we are destroying today, might no longer be able to practise their traditional ways, as the scarcity of wildlife alone, can render the old ways unsustainable. Humans have fashioned new ecosystems and new behaviours based on modern living and industrialisation rather than wildlife.

So what can we learn from all this?

The incidental consequence of humans spreading out to colonise Earth tens of thousands of years ago was to build the incredibly biodiverse animal-driven ecological structures needed to support and sustain our species. In April 2021, a global team of scientists published a paper titled 'People have shaped most of terrestrial nature for at least 12,000 years',[1] establishing that human habitation had largely been beneficial and that only recent intensified use of ecosystems has changed that. Twelve-thousand years ago, over ninety per cent of temperate and tropical ecosystems may have been reshaped by our species.

This was a natural process that occurred because without diverse wildlife-driven ecosystems and stable landscapes, humans couldn't have survived for long, and indeed there are many civilisations that didn't, as described by Jared Diamond in his book *Collapse: How Societies Choose to Fail or Succeed*. Human animals cannot singularly create and maintain ecosystems, and that's why it's so tragic that wildlife has suffered such severe decline today. We persecute animals despite the essential role they play in recreating a habitable Earth. The pandemics, floods, fires and locust plagues are all predictable consequences of ecosystem collapse when you kill all the animals.

When it came to ecosystem stability, we effectively hit the restart button when industrialisation happened. Far from creating a liveable paradise, industrialised agriculture, the replacement of animals with machines and the creation of chemical fertilisers and pesticides have stripped bare our essential life support systems and left us with little soil with which to grow food and anoxic, fish-less rivers and wetlands, running thick with mud. Two hundred and fifty years ago, Australia's

---

When I was a child, I would ride my bike to this English valley where the landowner kept ancient livestock. There was remnant ancient grassland with orchids, lizards and dingy skipper butterflies. Migrant redstarts bred along the river, buzzards and barn owls hunted. Hedgerows provided habitat for tree sparrows and corn buntings. This is how farming had been for centuries. The land was healthier for its abundance and diversity of wild birds and animals.

rivers would have been crystal clear, overflowing with native fish life, grasslands brimming with dozens of marsupials, small and large, forests and skies filled with birds.

First Nations people all over the world settled on land with bountiful natural capital, a wealth they could afford to draw down and reinvest in, over thousands of years, to create the conditions for their own survival – but they did this slowly, without machines and chemicals. The rate at which they could afford to change things was limited by their own mortality. The megafauna that came before may have been the source of the opportunity, but the remaining wildlife that coexisted with Indigenous people for tens of thousands of years or more was a foundation for the continents' ongoing life support and couldn't be wiped out completely without the risk of taking human beings with them. By about 12,000 years ago, early humans had transformed three-quarters of Earth's land mass without a noticeable negative impact on its ecosystems – we were expressing the best of our animality.[1]

We are only decades into a new era of global environmental alteration by human animals, in which we've converted most of our land for agriculture and extracted more natural capital from the Earth than it can return to us for other forms of life support. We aren't anywhere near reaching the stability we need to survive because that's a process that took Indigenous cultures thousands of years of trial and error to perfect. Changes in the future are unknown, and science is only one tool we have to guide us. Research can't discover what takes thousands of years of culture to know for sure, especially when much of that traditional knowledge has been destroyed already. Aboriginal people changed the Australian landscape and developed the culture to live sustainably because this was a very natural process, and it represents a period of peak success for our species.

There are two questions we have to ask ourselves now, and these are:

1. Is there enough natural capital left in the Earth to allow us to start all over again?
2. Are there enough animals left to maintain our life support through the impending period of chaos, while we go through the trial and error of our ancestors but on a global scale and over just a few decades, rather than thousands of years?

Homo sapiens, with our relatively big brains, still needs ecosystems to function reliably. We are big-bodied animals, less mobile than birds and whales, long-lived and with the need to invest heavily in nurturing our offspring. It isn't enough to have energy abundant; we need to know where to find it and when. It has to be in the right concentrations and in the right places for us to survive. As a species, we need this availability to be seasonally predictable.

Our dependence on these patterns is so intrinsic that our hearts and minds rely on them. We create folklore, songs and religions to try to describe our interaction with the world, to maintain a semblance of order among something too complex to explain. We developed cultures based on landscapes and the plentiful wildlife that whirl around them.

Our emotional connection to animals is there. It remains ingrained in our everyday survival. Without even trying, animals have become the defining brand-value of whole nations. The kangaroo of Australia, the springbok of South Africa, the lion of England and the sacred cows of India. Yet somewhere along the way we've lost respect for animals, and we need to learn to behave better again if we are to survive.

PART 4 -

How animals affect humanity

Our animality, culture and intelligence

When I was at university it was still a bit taboo to be talking about wildlife culture and society. Ecologists are encouraged not to 'anthropomorphise' wild animals, which is to bestow human values onto them. Since then, science has uncovered many examples of knowledge transfer between animal societies, and we're realising wildlife, from whales to fish and even insects, have their own sophisticated cultures.[141]

Evidence for the link between wildlife and human survival can be found in thousands of years of culture. On Nauru there is the ancestral tradition of catching, taming and releasing frigatebirds. We now know that fish abundance increases around seabird colonies – as did the status of whole villages and their people's food security.

A paper in the journal *Science* compared the movements of real reintroduced, radio-collared bighorn sheep in North America to a computer-generated model they created.[142] They had one computerised herd doing random movement and another they called the 'omniscient' herd because they knew precisely where green vegetation occurred. The authors found that real and newly introduced sheep were no better at finding food than the theoretical random herd that wandered aimlessly. The only sheep that did better were those translocated into existing herds and able to pick up some of the existing cultural knowledge about where to find food. Existing flocks that had longstanding cultural experience performed almost as though they were omniscient.

Orangutans will climb into the giddying reaches of emergent forest trees to browse on fruits that come into season only once in a while. In the Australian bush, bright green little lorikeets appear as if by magic in patches of flowering eucalyptus trees, and disappear just as quickly once the blossom is exhausted. How do they know?

Animals follow reliable historic resource patterns, determined by seasons and predictable climate cycles over months, years, decades or longer. When an ecosystem has reached its peak, animals have had tens of thousands of years to cultivate the land. They've stored the least information they need to make survival decisions in their brains and minimised the distances they need to move to find the most energy and altogether create so little surplus that the environment remains in check. Some of the information is learnt and passed on, and some is hard-coded into brain function, such as the ability of migrant birds to know what direction to fly in different seasons.

This is the definition of instinctive behaviour. This is how the offspring of red-necked phalaropes know how to migrate halfway around the world, weeks after their parents headed south. The young are born in the tundra where they feed in freshwater pools, but by winter they turn into seabirds and group together in massive flocks in the tropical open ocean.

We try to study how migratory animals know where to go but that might not be the right question. A river runs through a valley not because the molecules know where to go but because the river itself created the path. Water flows in the direction it always has because it has always been part of the landscape's processes. Wildlife evolved in synchrony with ecosystems. Animals don't learn or choose where to go – they follow the patterns they created that meant their ancestors were the likeliest to survive.

Animals store knowledge about where and when to find the highest concentrations of food because they are coupled to its production and know those patterns. But they also organise themselves into social patterns to transfer this knowledge because groups of intelligent animals are less chaotic and more likely to have a positive impact on the population's survival. The newborn phalaropes have just enough knowledge to get them to where they need to go, then they learn how to behave, alongside others of their kind.

Complex society has long been studied in marine mammals.[143] Populations of sperm whales met at societal boundaries and transferred cultural knowledge of whaling, sufficient to avoid being killed.[144] These are rare examples of animals using a form of language, and it's not that different to how we communicate. It's certainly for the same reasons. Animal populations can rebuild their culture quite quickly, as was observed in herds of domestic cows in Chernobyl that have rediscovered their wildness and started behaving socially, developing hierarchies akin to the wild turs, a species of wild cow, to which they are distantly related.[145]

How animals act and shape their own living space delivers information to their brains so they know how to behave and, unsurprisingly, humans use exactly the same principles to deliver information through every piece of communication technology you own today from televisions to smartphones.

In 1948, Claude Shannon invented the 'bit', which means a binary decision: 1 or 0; yes or no; or the flip of a coin. It's the origin of the word megabit, the measure of bandwidth you frustratingly tell the phone company about when your internet keeps dropping out. His 'information theory' describes the way we can communicate with the least data possible. In computer language, the word 'yes' is made up of twenty-four bits as defined by binary coding.

If I exclaim 'Coffee?' and you say 'Yes!' we have exchanged very little information yet communicated quite clearly.

It could be said, in language terms, we have used one bit each … though your understanding of the question 'Coffee?' also depends on having learnt my language and understanding the questioning inflection in my voice. Otherwise I might need to say 'Would you like a coffee?' If I was in a foreign country, I might just wave a cup, point to a coffee tin and give you the thumbs up, but if I wanted to communicate anything more complicated, I'd probably waste a lot of energy.

If Shannon hadn't developed his theory, we wouldn't have the internet. A minimum number of bits determines how you watch videos on YouTube or how data is passed to you through your headphones. It's all zeros and ones, combined in increasing complexity to render imagery and sounds you can understand – the image of a face on video chat isn't real, it's the minimum information needed for you to recognise that person. It's an information ecosystem all of its own as the energy it takes to send electronic communications to you, the cost of your internet bills and efficiency of your bandwidth are all directly affected by the technology's ability to minimise information chaos.

In the infinite monkey theorem, an infinite number of monkeys given an infinite number of typewriters and an infinite amount of time will eventually complete the entire works of Shakespeare. The theory supposes that highly complex order could be created randomly with enough time and compositional complexity, but that's not how nature works.

The QWERTY keyboard minimises chaos because the effort it takes to type is somewhat based on human finger arrangements and the abundance of letters in the English language. Typewriters evolved from use by telegraph operators, who found an alphabetised keyboard to be inefficient.[146] In making the QWERTY keyboard, engineers changed the operators' brains and the physical environment so both would align, in the same way wildlife changes ecosystems to make communication more efficient – animals become more intelligent about their surroundings because they partly design them to be consistent with their own physiology and needs.

Monkeys' fingers are similar to humans, so if they are using a keyboard designed to spit out English words more efficiently than any other, it becomes infinitely more likely they will type a word we recognise. Could they write the entire works of Shakespeare? Unlikely.

But if monkeys began typing words they recognised when they felt a particular way and could learn to communicate that to other monkeys, they might form a language and then one day, a monkey might write a collection of plays *equivalent* to the entire works of Shakespeare.

After mass extinctions, Earth's ecosystems reform in a non-identical way but with similar function, because evolution is based on an *equivalent* set of rules. The point is, while evolution of life as we know it is serendipitous, the processes that led here weren't entirely down to chance. There was a set of criteria that, like the keyboard, maximised the likelihood that some cultural patterns would be more likely to occur than others. Just in the same way as the most likely to occur molecules and proteins evolved to survive and this set up a chain reaction for life as we know it today.

Binary choices determine whether an animal mates with another, informs decisions that lead to survival or extinction, even guide the series of steps that lead to duplication of DNA. You made a binary decision just then, when you decided to read this page.

Shannon's work helped set limits on signal processing in your mobile phone, and in recent times his equations have been used by ecologists quantifying ecosystem behaviour.[147] His theory simply describes how outcomes are achieved through basic decisions: a flip of a coin, whether to turn left or right, or whether an animal decides to fight, mate or look for a food in a certain place. To be useful, information, just like nutrients and energy, has to follow patterns that are easy and understandable. When it comes to survival, energy use and information go hand in hand.

The reason it takes so long to evolve stable ecosystems is that there is no specific blueprint or plan to follow; there is only the flow of entropy to channel energy between the animals' outside world, and stable behaviour can't occur until animals have had long enough to rebuild new cultures. This is the strongest evidence there is for important culture and intelligence in all wildlife.

The intelligence of animals is an undisputable facet of our planet's function. This organised ecosystem knowledge database has to permeate every living space as the organisation of societies requires sophisticated communication transfer to exist.[148] If it's in our society and we have the same role as all animals on Earth, it's another example of our animality: how similar we are to other animals, rather than how different they are from us. And while animals may not be able to speak our language, their ability to communicate is as sophisticated. It needs to be to make them the most likely to survive and therefore the most intelligent lifeforms on Earth.

This is all the more reason why we have to be very careful about disrupting our current environment, as it takes a long time to reform the complex relationships between animals and habitat. Even longer when there are few animals to work together. The more diverse and abundant wildlife is, the quicker ecosystems can recover from the impact we have had on them.

Richard Dawkins in *The Extended Phenotype*[149] talks about how a bowerbird uses the coloured fruits of its forest as an extension of its own DNA. He describes how strategies for wildlife to succeed at a genetic level involve connection between an environment and an individual, and that the DNA of both the plant and animal can change due to their relationship. This also applies to the mind. How our individual brains and living space relate to intelligence was described in 2012 by Karl Friston of University College London in the journal *Entropy*.[150]

Friston asked how the brain can possibly exist in any steady state when confounded by so many external influences and discovered that the way we think and behave responds to outside influences in much the same way as energy flows through ecosystems or information flows through our telecommunications systems.

A steady behavioural state can only be achieved if the mind stores this information inside the brain's internal dynamics and limits the degree of 'free energy' – in this case, a metaphor for the information we receive through our senses. These dynamics can be found in any biological system that resists disorder.

The theory goes that our brains receive information from our exterior environment (where free energy is chaotic and disordered) and creates a model, akin to a reordering of information inside ourselves. At the same time, our behaviour responds to the outside environment, realigning our expectations with any changes that occur outside: we act to modify the environment to bring it back in line, rather like the dugong foraging on grass to maintain its nutrient intake at high levels.

Spend a few minutes thinking about the patterns you deliberately create in your life. Do you maintain a tidy living space? Arrange cushions on a sofa? Visit the café every Sunday morning? Bake a cake with evenly spaced cherry topping and neatly slice it into equal-sized triangles? You probably work nine to five, so you can communicate easily with colleagues and plan meetings with minimum effort. Whether you paint and draw, work in a business or run a household, how much are you tied to the primeval urge to create patterns of stability around you?

You do this every day, instinctively, without even knowing it. If you put a jigsaw on a table, how long before someone assembles it? Jigsaws are far more prone to chaos than a deck of cards, yet place one in a room with an animal like us, and it will not be long before order is created. What impact do you have on the chaos around you, and what effect do the structures you create have on your life? How connected do you now feel with entropy processes in your world, and where do you think these urges come from?

In rebuilding the world around us, our brains can reach a steady state where our internal model and behaviour matches the outside world reasonably closely. Then we are able to exist, respond and survive in our surroundings with reasonable certainty and efficiency. We correspond mentally with new information supplied by our environment day to day, which flows through us, in an entropic form. We can even feel this happening.

Think about your last holiday in a country you hadn't visited before. Everything is new. Your eyes feel wide open, you are overwhelmed with the smells, sounds and sights of an unfamiliar place. Your brain is actively building its model, a not altogether unpleasant sensation because it's happening at a normal pace, but one that could still be distracting if you were trying to hunt in a forest while avoiding predators or trying to remember the location of that particular fruit same time last year. (We're not equipped to survive when we're placed randomly into different parts of the world.)

When we travel, we are enjoying the sensation of an increase in our brain's grey matter activity, which might even hark back to emotions we felt as children. As kids, everything was new and our brains were busy creating the models that would determine our survival later in life. If we spend childhood overwhelmed by digital misinformation, we risk building chaotic brains, out of sync with the natural world we might need to survive. It's a critical area of research that is only just in its early stages. The worlds of social media and the impending 'metaverse' do not connect to ecosystems and are therefore out of touch with our animality. There is no way our survival as a species can be achieved by this virtual technology.

As adults we reminisce about feeling like a child because the sensations were new and exciting. Consider the simple action of driving along a high street where you've lived for many years. Chances are you might overlook the subtle rebranding of a shop in a different colour or altered parking restrictions – you might not be able to recall anything at all, other than the fact you passed through. Musicians and sportspeople know this as 'muscle memory'. A sports player has less time than it takes for electrical signals to reach their brain to react to a ball being hurled at them at 100 kilometres per hour. The player has learnt a response based on practice that enables them to predict in advance how to react, to have the best chance of hitting the ball. The player isn't playing the ball; they are playing their best guess at where the ball will be.

Similarly, your mind uses a previously saved version of a high street, a model of this part of your world. It would be maddening to have to process this afresh every time. When you come to park your car, you might not notice that parking restrictions have changed. That's why council has to put up a big sign telling you. After you notice, you might recheck later in another suburb, because your brain now tells you there is a heightened risk of the policy changing elsewhere. If you avoid a fine, your brain has altered, your behaviour has adapted to the new condition and the environment has changed (by virtue of changed parking activity). You've also saved energy.

This is how an animal brain minimises variational free energy in any ecosystem. You infer things about the world so you can function inside it and stay mentally stable, absorb maximum energy and help efficiently balance your ecosystem's stability.

This word 'infer' is important, as our ability to make educated assumptions about what might happen is a survival instinct. Our brains don't seek to gather huge amounts of data or try to prove everything before we make choices, because that would be folly. The constant online news infodemic we're subjected to via our phones, computers, twenty-four-hour news television and radio is an example of a chaotic exterior information system we have constructed. It has become so disordered of late that it is harming our mental health and our ability to make decisions and think clearly. We've become so overwhelmed by trying to understand a constantly changing narrative about the whole world that we can no longer behave efficiently.

It comes right back to the point about stress in animals like koalas and the way we interact with patterns of nature. Chaos is the difference between a beautiful piece of artwork and a mess. It's the difference between a fully functioning ecosystem and an untidy piece of vegetation regrowth. It's been shown that exposure to mid-range complexity fractal patterns like clouds or forests massively reduces stress levels.[151] We can survive and be healthy because we know what to expect, because the patterns of nature are repetitive and hard-coded into our brains. They are stable, more likely and therefore more predictable. Not all these patterns are external to us; they also flow through our entire physical and psychological sensory system.

Hibernating bears don't watch the news or try to calculate when to emerge. They are pre-programmed by chemical reactions in their brain's hypothalamus to climb out in spring, a set number of days after winter sets in. Likewise, your brain triggers the creation of melatonin when it gets dark, so you naturally feel sleepy at night and then wake up every morning around dawn when the sun rises.

In an unsullied ecosystem, individual intelligence is inbuilt inertia that keeps most animals from doing unpredictable things because that would lead to quicker extinction. The currency of information and our ability to interpret the world around us – to live by its simple preformed rules – is what makes or breaks a species. If we allow greed and selfishness, combined with arbitrary technological adaptations, to justify our sacrifice of animals, it runs counter to nature's laws and breaks these patterns. We're not only dealing with a conversation between humans, but we are also dealing with breakdown of cooperation between all animals on a planetary level. Those animals are delivering the information to us and, to survive, we need to respect and relearn their ecological language so we can decipher the codes to our own future wellbeing.

Disease, fevers and pest control

As you go down the food chain smaller organisms become more abundant, and when you add up the weight of every animal on Earth, three-quarters would be bacteria; perhaps surprising for an animal that weighs only one trillionth of a gram. Viruses are often ten to one hundred times more abundant than bacteria, and both types of organism fulfil important functions, even inside your body's ecosystem. Your gut bacteria are essential for digestion, and viruses balance their abundance, though we barely know how this works as there has been very little work done on 'good' viruses. What we do know is that viruses limit the potentially negative consequence of overpopulating bacteria, like a natural pest control, and this is happening at a micro level across the entire planet, from the deep sea to the atmosphere and throughout our bodies.

Tardigrades or water bears are microscopic animals that can absorb pieces of genes from archaea, bacteria and viruses. Their genetic makeup is fluid and adapts fast through a process known as horizontal gene transfer. Tardigrades can survive extreme temperatures, even short periods in outer space, and under conditions of extreme cell stress such as ice or heat, the animals' cell membranes and DNA break down into pieces. When the animal rehydrates and its cells reform, it mixes with the fractured genes from adjacent microbes. About a fifth of their DNA comes from these other animals, and it's thought that foreign genes may be more resilient and could help explain how the species survived all five mass extinctions.[152] It's not so strange when you consider our body is packed with microorganisms and human cells are full of DNA from bacteria: the mitochondria that we couldn't even draw breath without.

Have you ever walked in a desert and felt the sand crunch beneath your feet, looked down and seen tessellated flakes that curl up at the side? These are biocrusts and are a fungal-bacteria community described by scientists as the 'living skin' of deserts.[153] They bind the sand surface, reduce erosion, capture carbon and nitrogen and, vitally, help retain surface water. Their destruction through intensive agriculture and desert wars have contributed to a huge increase in the frequency of dust storms. Behind the scenes, the decline to extinction of animals like Bactrian camels in Mongolia or scimitar-horned oryx in Africa, and their replacement with hard-hooved feral goats, has affected the fragile nutrient-cycling processes that created and maintained these systems. Almost ninety per cent of the Sahara Desert no longer has its megafauna.[154] Storms carry huge quantities of free-flying cyanobacteria, as many as ten billion in every gram of dust, the kinds that create toxic algal blooms, as well as fungal spores and viruses. There is increasing concern among scientists that we are exposing entire continents to a wide range of microbial health threats.[155]

Most diseases are what we call 'zoonotic', meaning they are passed to us via animals. That's hardly surprising since we are animals and more similar and dependent on wildlife-driven ecosystems than we have realised. An increasing body of knowledge shows that the relationship between the predators and scavengers that occupy our ecosystem is responsible for some of the worst epidemics in recent history and that decline in numbers of top predators increases this risk of disease in humans.[156]

In India and Africa, use of the anti-inflammatory drug diclofenac to treat livestock has resulted in an incredibly rapid ninety per cent decline in vulture populations, leading to an increase in feral dogs carrying and infecting people with rabies.

For obvious reasons, as we degrade habitats, illegally harvest wildlife and mix them with domestic animals in markets, we increase our exposure to diseases like coronavirus or Ebola. When authorities issue bounties on wildlife, it's often ill-informed, as removing even more animals from the system is a short-term solution that makes the long-term risk even greater. The most species-rich ecosystems are the safest when it comes to disease.[157]

And hay fever sufferers should need little persuading about the health impacts of losing animals from ecosystems, except there seems to be no recognition of the subject. Pollen is male plant sperm and, as in animals, is created in huge excess. One storm in northern Europe in 1991 deposited 50,000 tonnes of material, each square centimetre containing up to 1,170 pollen grains, enough to turn snow yellow. The pollen from recently introduced pine trees dominates ocean sediment off New Zealand and has altered food chains in the deep sea.[158] The lifetime pollen production of a single beech tree has been estimated at 20.5 billion pollen grains.[159] The quantity circulating in our atmosphere defies explanation. When it comes to natural particulates, pollen is one of the main constituents of air that enters your lungs when you breathe. Dogs, cats, horses and other animals can also get hay fever just like us.

But pollen is also protein and is consumed by most insects, from bees and ants to microscopic springtails, of which there can be 8,000 for every cubic metre of soil. Herbivores also would have eaten grass pollen in huge quantities and deposited it into soil where it became nutrient. Insect populations are in global freefall through the use of insecticides, herbicides and other poisons, as well as light pollution.

Almost fifty per cent of beetles, bees and grasshoppers have disappeared in just ten years,[160] and climate change is increasing the length of the growing season worldwide. It only takes a tiny reduction in insect abundance to create an unfathomable surplus of pollen. Earth's vegetation cover today is greater than it was a few decades ago. A warmer, damper Earth promotes more growth. All up, it's the perfect storm, and hay fever sufferers bear the brunt.

When we disturb ecosystems by changing the pyramidal abundance of wildlife (even in our bodies when we kill gut fauna), we break these pre-existing life support structures. The diseases and fevers we incur are just pest invasion on a micro scale. Contentious as it may

Pangolins are the most illegally trafficked animals in the world. They also carry coronavirus. Viruses must serve an important role in animal and therefore forest ecology. Pandemics arise when we break these subtle and complex relationships, leading to destruction of the animal-led processes that stabilise ecosystems and our lives.

seem, killing locusts during a plague could be the worst thing to do as it pushes available energy further down the food chain where it will give advantage to a new undetected plague, this time of microorganisms or a virus that's released into crops or even human populations.

Similarly, killing the vectors of disease transmission rather than reintroducing predators is likely to make things worse. For example, the transmission of tuberculosis between wild animals and cattle has caused the UK government to cull more than 100,000 wild badgers. Being one of the UK's remaining examples of mammal megafauna, this will have had untold impact on the ecosystem integrity of an already fragile farming system that's facing imminent widescale loss of soil fertility. It may also trigger new problems. For instance, liver flukes are a rather horrible parasite that infect cattle via freshwater snails. Who knows whether the eradication of badgers, or any other animals in intensively farmed areas, will increase that or other similar risks? Badgers no longer have any natural predators, and golden eagles, once widespread, are now only found in the far north of England and Scotland.[161] Meanwhile, the killing of birds of prey on UK farmland remains a major concern for conservation groups. In order to tackle tuberculosis, it could be far easier to reintroduce predators. After all, what's the alternative?

A study published in *Nature* in 2019 used a combination of field data and a theoretical model to look at the animal impact of wolves on the prevalence of tuberculosis in wild boar.[162] In the short-term scenario wolf numbers were allowed to increase, and this stabilised wild boar populations, reducing disease prevalence by five times over fourteen years and almost wiping it out in thirty years.

As with the amplification and concentration of nutrients by animals, we hugely underestimate the scale and intensity of animal impact on disease control and how simple, cost-free and useful an alternative nature-based approach can be for our health. Relatively small numbers of predators can have a huge impact on disease and pest reduction. Meanwhile, our attempts to control disease through killing animals almost always ends up in even more ecological damage.

In the 1970s, after DDT pesticide was banned, bird of prey numbers in the UK countryside rapidly increased. The chemical is a bio-accumulator, a toxic mix that has a soil half-life of two to fifteen years and an aquatic half-life of 150 years. That's to say, 100 kilograms of DDT takes about eighty years to reach one per cent in soil and 1,200 years in water.

DDT is absorbed into the root systems of plants to be eaten by its target, aphids, a farm pest that reduces crop yield. Aphids consume a tiny amount, but pigeons and songbirds were eating large numbers of aphids and concentrating larger doses of DDT in their own body tissues. When birds of prey ate the pigeons and songbirds, they were consuming an even larger amount, non-lethal, but enough to suppress their cell's ability to make calcium, so they laid thin-shelled eggs that broke under the birds' weight during incubation. Sparrowhawks and peregrine falcons almost went extinct by crushing their own eggs.[163]

After DDT was banned, UK raptor populations recovered rapidly, but then this led to conflict between farmers and the Royal Society for the Protection of Birds. When the first Birds of Conservation Concern data came out in 1996, it suggested that ninety per cent declines in some common farmland songbirds including the skylark and corn bunting was caused by pesticide use killing the songbird's insect prey, critical during the breeding season. Faced with this inconvenient truth, farmers began to suggest that the decline was due to recovering bird of prey populations. But this was a poor assumption.

Before China's sparrow war of 1958 when tree sparrows were hunted to virtual extinction in three days, Chairman Mao presumed sparrows only ate grain, therefore crop yield would rise in their absence. The birds were integral to the farmland ecology and, by eating insects, were protecting the Chinese from locust infestations. The sparrows were saving millions of human lives each year.

According to a review by Bauer and Hoye, locusts can multiply into swarms capable of consuming in one day enough vegetation to feed 400,000 people for a year.[70] In 1874, there were locust plagues in Kansas so large they blocked out the sun, and it's estimated that a single swarm contained 27 million tonnes of insects, taking five days to pass overhead. Insects make up most of prairie chicken diet, grasshoppers/locusts being about a quarter,[164] with each bird occupying between one to two hectares and moving an average of about 430 metres every three days, day in, day out.[165] Before European settlement, a pair of birds would have fed continuously, suppressing the emergent locusts at a sustainable level, feeding on the hatchlings before they could become a winged menace. Wild prairie chickens and a suite of other prairie birds used to be abundant, but by the time land had been settled and grasslands 'improved' for agriculture, many of these birds faced extinction and remain dependent on tiny wildlife refuges.

Like Mao, farmers also are overlooking the interdependence of all animals and their collective role in ecosystem stability when they blame birds of prey for causing songbird declines. It's a biologically implausible argument, because predator and prey cannot exist without one another. Species richness is higher in systems with predators,[166] and the only long-term solution to world agricultural decline is to rebuild wild bird and animal populations because animals have an equal role to play in our food security.

Meanwhile, our pest problems are not as we see them. Urban pigeons and seagulls are exploiting the chaos and surplus energy we've caused, even in the form of discarded chips and sandwich crusts. It's nature's way of restabilising things we've damaged; wildlife is stepping in to protect the systems that provide our life support and are crumbling under our mismanagement. Pests are gathering up surplus energy and beginning the process of rebuilding ecosystems. We need to be careful when using pesticides that we are not making problems worse for ourselves.

During the COVID-19 epidemic, there were reports of rat infestations in homes from Sydney to London. Because people were dining in, there was less waste in bins around towns, so rats were raiding homes instead. Rat infestations, like locust swarms, are a consequence of our ecological footprint and capitalise on an abundance of free energy. If our response is to poison the rats, we won't ever fix the problem; rats will continue to come back or maybe we'll end up with a cockroach problem, on top of contaminated water from rat poison. Rat poison is now killing birds of prey that would have fed on the rats[167] (bioaccumulating in the same way as DDT), which increases the risk of disease transmission by rats. It's a vicious circle we need to break if we're to be healthy. Wouldn't it just be simpler and more cost-effective to get our own waste management under control and rebuild an ecosystem that is balanced with our needs and those of other wild animals? One where predators and prey are harmonised and disease minimised naturally.

Food security and clean water

Wildlife transfers and amplifies nutrient processes, creating rich soil that is slowly released into the environment in just the right quantity to avoid becoming pollution. By cultivating plant diversity, animals also apply pressure on individual plants to store the maximum amount of energy-giving nutrients to survive. This in turn has created ecosystems packed with food, containing concentrated amounts of vitamins and trace elements, allowing an abundance and diversity of larger animals to exist, including humans. An abundance and diversity of wildlife, alongside agricultural production, is key to our own food security.

Every gardener knows you need worms to grow tomatoes and the occasional fresh load of manure, which comes from animals. Anyone who has grown their own also knows they taste better, but why? No surprise, there is a link between energy chaos and the nutrient value and taste of food we eat.

The humble tomato, grown organically, can be thirty-five per cent smaller by weight at maturity but pack a mean punch when it comes to nutrients. The stress imposed on tomatoes from growing in an organic (wilder) setting makes vitamin C at concentrations over fifty per cent higher and phenolic content almost 140 per cent higher,[168] which, in association, create natural antioxidants and protect our bodies against the ravages of free oxygen molecules, which contribute to aging.

Despite their smaller size, the tomatoes are suppressing energy chaos far more efficiently than happens in modern farming practice because they are exposed to stress caused by animals grazing on them.

Modern farming also causes a loss of omega-3 fatty acids from meat such as chicken, and replaces it with less energy-rich and unhealthy fats. Intensive feeding and lack of exercise has turned chicken meat from red to white, which means when it's sold on a cost per kilo basis, you're buying energy in the form of fat, whereas smaller organic chicken is packed with omega-3. Our bodies can't produce this essential protein, which is vital for neurodevelopment in children and even helps prevent Alzheimer's disease. A team from the Institute of Brain Chemistry and Human Nutrition at London Metropolitan University found the amount of omega-3 in chicken meat had declined nearly threefold since the 1970s, all due to intensive agriculture.[169] Non-organic chicken farming contains less ordered energy as the wildlife-driven processes that create maximum nutrient concentration patterns for natural human food haven't been allowed to occur.

Human beings live at about halfway up the trophic pyramid,[170] somewhere between the top carnivores and the plants. At this level, we need a system that supplies more concentrated sources of nutrient, and it is animals that are the mechanism. They transfer, amplify and concentrate this energy, centralising our food availability. Megafauna do this for us on a landscape scale and insects on a vegetation scale. And because we are omnivores (eating both plants and animals), we need the animals above and around us, as much as the insect herbivores below. The ecosystem needs all the animals in proportion to maintain its stable structure.

While we commonly think of animals as visitors in their habitat, that's wrong. Even we know supermarkets wouldn't exist unless animals like us built them, because it takes humans to both shop and stock shelves for shops to be viable. Why would we think the same doesn't go for wildlife and ecosystems? Animals engineer ecosystems. Take humans away and no-one will build supermarkets. Take animals away and there are no ecosystems either. Animals build and maintain the ecosystems that deliver our food. As far as human survival goes, animals might as well be the ecosystem, as it collapses without them.

A friend told me about a development threatening a coastal estuary and wetland in Australia where the developer had indicated that a massive decline in waterbirds may represent an opportunity, because the 'carrying capacity' of the wetland would be larger as a consequence. Their logic was that fewer birds meant more space for more birds. That's only logical if you think birds are only wetland customers, but that's not the case at all. Animals build the ecosystem too.

Estuaries are covered with a nutritious, energy-giving biofilm made of diatoms, microorganisms that are rich in fatty acids and excrete a biological glue. These sticky films mix with the surface up to a few centimetres deep and hold it together.[171] Birds such as eastern curlew, red-necked stint, curlew sandpiper, great knot and bar-tailed godwits migrate tens of thousands of kilometres from the Arctic to feed in these wetlands, and the smallest and most numerous, the stints and sandpipers, consume diatoms directly using feathery tongues. Each season they arrive in vast mercurial flocks, settling predictably at every tide for months of the year. They follow an invisible map that leads them to fan out across the estuary, synchronised to the ebbing and flowing of energy.

We don't know exactly how important biofilms are, but they could be among the most productive ecosystems on Earth. Very little, if any, work has been done on the value of shorebirds to nutrient flow in estuaries, or on their importance in amplifying and transporting nutrients between tides. Given their vast numbers and omnipresence, the birds are clearly a major player, but if you search the scientific literature you'll find an abundance of studies on how shorebirds are

---

Tapirs have an intense effect on forest ecology, but their populations have fallen dramatically due to hunting pressure and habitat loss. They maintain the integrity of forests by ensuring waste is returned to the soil where it can drive biological cycles. Soil nutrients quickly disappear in their absence.

dependent on estuaries but nothing on how estuaries are dependent on shorebirds.

Each bird, all day, is consuming, moving and re-depositing waste into the system, and they migrate on an enormous global scale as well. The magnitude at which animals and birds tend the land and sea is nothing short of extraordinary.

Wild pigs and Brazilian tapirs in the rainforests of South America have been shown to massively enhance forest nutrient processes.[172] Without these larger animals, ammonium (a source of nitrogen) would be ninety-five per cent less available and the rate of nitrate turnover would also be far lower. The study found they were moving nutrients into places that would otherwise have been quite nutrient-poor, and without them the rate of nutrient loss exceeded the rate of natural replenishment. If you take the animals out, the fertility of the whole forest becomes unsustainable.

Don't forget, though, that it is the absence of surplus nutrients that makes a system stable, where the animals are absorbing everything into the food chain to maximum efficiency, so nothing seeps out as pollution. A single Australian lyrebird moves 350 tonnes of soil each year.[173] As a consequence, Melbourne city-dwellers can quench their thirst with fresh mineral water coming out of their taps at home. Crystal-clear fresh water, therefore, becomes the natural outcome of animal impact, and that's also critical to human survival. Ecosystem integrity, food security and clean water all go hand in hand.

Every conspicuously sized animal on Earth is following a daily routine of transferring, amplifying and concentrating nutrients in a predictable way, which leads to patches of fertility where the processes of smaller animals absorb this into biological systems to create rich soil and fisheries. The link with human food security is so strong that there are well-documented cases of humans starving from the consequences of killing birds.

As mentioned earlier, the most infamous of these was in 1958, when Chairman Mao as part of the Great Leap Forward policy identified tree sparrows, alongside rats, mosquitos and flies, as four great pests of the regime, and all across China sparrows were chased by people on rooftops, tired out until they fell from the sky, shot, poisoned, netted, captured in traps or glue. In Beijing alone, three million people mobilised to kill almost a million birds. Across China it's thought hundreds of millions, maybe as many as a billion tree sparrows perished.

Mao's justification for the cull was that sparrows ate grain and throughout Beijing, loudspeakers told people that 'fifty million sparrows will eat as much as will feed three million people for a year. Therefore, we must eliminate the sparrow.'[174]

In the following two years, China was plagued by an unprecedented locust infestation, collapsing grain production and, according to Chinese officials, causing the starvation and deaths of 15 million people. (Unofficially, there may have been at least twice as many.) The largest human starvation event on Earth was a consequence of a number of failed agricultural policies, and the sparrow killings were a final affront.

Particularly during the breeding season, even traditionally grain-feeding birds switch to insects like locusts, as they are greater in protein and vital for the development of young. China's tree sparrows, now almost extinct, had spent the breeding season grazing on juvenile locusts when they were most abundant, turning to lower-energy grains and seeds only at other times of the year. Simply killing a large number of small birds made the ecosystem uninhabitable for humans.

Wholesale extermination of species is not unprecedented. One of the most famous bird extinctions after the dodo was the US passenger pigeon, a super-abundant North American continental migrant that Simon Pokagon, last chief of the Pottawatomie, described as 'like some great river' flowing in flocks lasting for hours on end.[175]

Passenger pigeons would descend to nest and feed in their thousands on oaks, chestnuts and beech forests, nesting in mega-colonies. There were billions of birds in the late 1870s, but it took fewer than fifty years to be hunted to extinction. The last individual died in Cincinnati Zoo in 1914.

Genetic studies have shown passenger pigeon populations were at least as abundant for 20,000 years before any human ancestors reached the North American continent.[176] The birds' feeding behaviour would boost seed growth through selected grazing because a pigeon's beak wasn't large enough for the biggest acorns, so only the strongest seeds reached the ground. Canopy disturbance would reduce competition between trees and open up gaps to let light into the forest floor, meaning better oak tree germination and increased diversity of other species, which benefited a wide range of other plants and animals.

Australia's koalas might have similar impact. Eight million were killed for the fur trade with their pelts shipped to London, the United States and Canada between 1888 and 1927.[177] In 2015 there were estimated to be 90,000 koalas left, and the catastrophic bushfires in

2019–2020 wiped out three-quarters of animals remaining in New South Wales. The population continues to decline at an alarming rate, and today there are fewer than one per cent of pre-European settlement numbers. A single koala occupies a territory of about one hectare and eats about 230 kilograms of leaves each year. Before Europeans arrived, this was just over two per cent of the area's entire annual leaf production over about a tenth of the roughly one million square kilometres of eastern Australian forests.

The animals would have been supporting entire trophic pyramids of birds and insects, as well as contributing nutrients to the ground around trees and helping diversify flowers and mid-storey vegetation, and all of the above ecosystem processes would stack up to a monumental impact on soil fertility (and erosion mitigation), clean water and climate mitigation. Almost everything we rely on for a habitable country would have been significantly contributed to by koalas (notwithstanding all the other animals they share the country with).

Fire has long been considered a key driving force in US oak forest regeneration, but evidence shows that it's not enough without the passenger pigeons' massive canopy-opening processes. These days little light reaches the forest floor, and with regeneration suppressed all fire does is clear the few emerging saplings. The leaf litter that would once have been processed by animals, carbon mulched into the soils, is now released into the atmosphere and the aging forests are falling over with no hope of rebirth. The passenger pigeon, like all animals, was the stabilising entity of an entire ecosystem. Its absence increases the transfer of energy into the atmosphere, upsetting the oak forest ecosystem and Earth's climate.

The last passenger pigeon died after the last of the present-day oak tree saplings germinated. How will we ever know or be able to reverse the impact the loss of this migrant has had on these forest ecosystems? Once an abundant animal is in freefall decline to extinction and we have no way to reverse this, the consequence on human lives and livelihoods will be severe, even if we can't foresee the exact effects.

The dramatic loss of songbirds across all Earth's continents almost certainly explains recent outbreaks of locusts across northeast Africa, India and Australia. It's been calculated insectivorous birds worldwide eat between 400 and 500 million tonnes of insect prey annually.[178] Media and agricultural scientists blame loss of crops on the locusts, but they are simply responding to a surplus availability of energy, a climate ripe for breeding.

Off the African west coast of Namibia an explosion of jellyfish happened after several decades of commercial harvest of their natural prey, anchovies and sardines. The resulting massive density of jellies clogged up the water intake systems of trawlers, making it impossible to fish.[179] This 'locust effect' of booming jellyfish populations has even shut down nuclear power plants in Scotland and Sweden and the aircraft carrier USS *Ronald Reagan*.

A huge rise in the biomass of two-metre-long jumbo squid off the US west coast has scientists and fisheries experts equally concerned. The theory goes that they naturally hang out in the deep sea where oxygen is heavily depleted and predators can't spend much time. Populations of hammerhead sharks that specialise in deep-sea predation and may have fed on them have been almost completely destroyed, while simultaneous overfishing of predatory tuna has led to an eruption of squid populations that feed on the massive surplus of the tuna's natural prey. As if that wasn't enough, the free energy from agricultural pollution, like an ocean equivalent of climate change, has created such intense algal blooms that 'dead zones' are replicated extensively in shallow water all along the coast. The new conditions provide more and more habitat for these jet-propelled, fifty-kilogram eating machines and because they can breed and grow really fast, they are beginning to directly compete with the same fish that fleets have long relied on to support coastal livelihoods. This proliferation of squid and octopus is happening all over the world, and no-one knows what consequence it will have.[180]

We certainly need to be very careful with our next moves. Killing wildlife under the auspices of 'management' is like sacrificing pawns in a game of chess; only so many such moves are possible, as Chairman Mao discovered years ago.

A belief that animals are mere commodities, rather than a functioning part of ecosystems, leads to atrocious assumptions and decisions that affect our very survival. It is as ridiculous as it is dangerous to form a conclusion that's the material opposite of what we need to feed ourselves, and this gives us a clue to why and how our society has failed to protect biodiversity on a monumental level.

Today you can watch artisanal fishers in dugout canoes in Indonesia follow flocks of seabirds to find concentration patches of baitfish. Ironically, some fishers who follow frigatebirds will capture, poison or shoot them if they attempt to eat the fish themselves.[181] Off South America, fishers have been caught deliberately cutting the beaks off albatrosses when the birds get tangled in longlines and nets.[182] Farmers in East Gippsland, Australia, used to shoot flocks of ibis in their fields, until scientists pointed out the birds were actually eating chafer larvae that fed on the roots of their valuable crops. If you see patches of animals in abundance, it's safe to assume they are doing long-term good. It's always best to resist the urge to kill inconvenient wildlife as they are almost inevitably protecting you from a greater risk.

These days, industrial fishing trawlers return to biodiversity hotspots using positions stored in geographic information systems or by pinging the water column with high-frequency sonar to spot fish shoals, but they are still using traditional knowledge to home in on places where the most intact trophic pyramids exist, where the greatest concentration of energy is packed into a vibrant gathering of sea creatures. They are still directly dependent on wildlife.

Despite the technology, since about 1996, global fisheries landings have been in rapid decline.[183] While this is certainly due to overfishing, it hides a more worrying truth. The indiscriminate haulage of dolphins in nets, of albatross on longlines and an extraordinary amount of bycatch (fish that are not the commercial target) is often discarded at sea, breaking the stable pyramids that allowed companies to serve fish into the world's kitchens and restaurants for decades. Beth Fulton of Australia's Commonwealth Scientific and Industrial Research Organisation said that 'sharks are the glue that holds marine ecosystems together'. That without sharks, the house of cards falls down. There is little to no direct observation of this happening at sea, as the process is complex and there are few intact shark populations left for us to study: oceanic white-tipped sharks once abundant in the Indian Ocean are almost gone. But mathematically, it is implausible to think that oceans can function without animals in the right proportions, and sharks hold a special significance.

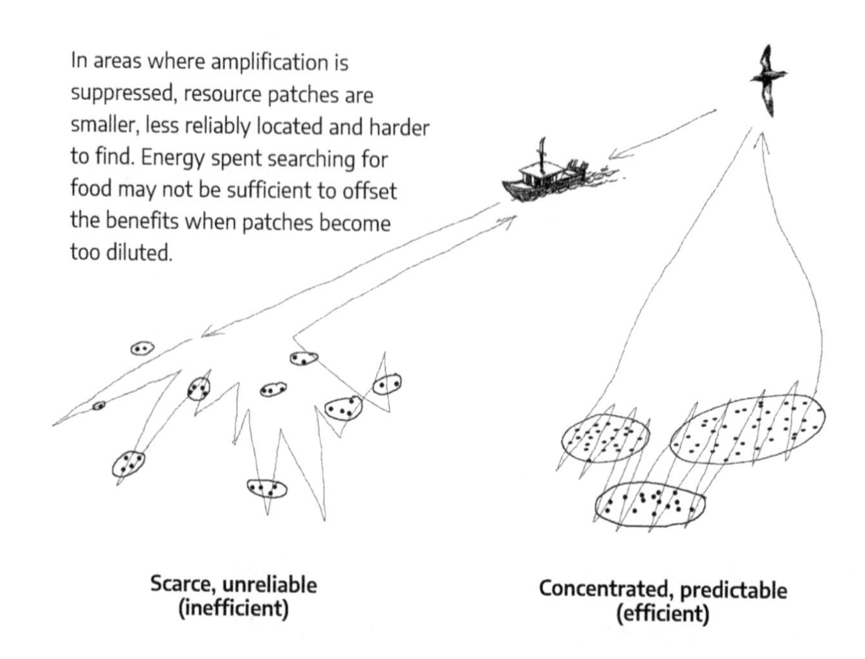

As the shapes of ecosystems collapse, the energy that was once delivered in nutritious, bite-sized pieces becomes a dilute and chaotic flood. This is rich pickings for tiny creatures, a dense, three-dimensional abundance of microorganisms, absorbing the available energy in a finger-click and spreading it out far and wide where it's no longer accessible for us. A fishing boat that leaves harbour today will find it increasingly difficult to locate economically viable fish patches and, apart from a fistful of fuel receipts, risk returning home empty-handed. Farmers have the same problem, so they have become

---

The life of every animal is a trade-off between the energy spent to find food and energy absorbed from eating it. The same is true for farming, fisheries and our daily lives. Animals help concentrate nutrients in bigger patches, and this supports entire food chains and the economies on which our entire civilisation depends.

increasingly dependent on applying large volumes of chemical fertiliser as an unnatural substitute for the loss of wildlife.

Loss of global ecosystem services due to land degradation and desertification costs up to ten trillion US dollars annually.[184] Australia regards the decline in value of farmland production to be up to nine per cent of agricultural production, meaning Australian farmers could be making an additional few billion dollars profit a year, if ecosystems were restored.[185] That's only production, though. Additional benefits to farmers would also be received as a flow-on from ecosystem services, and this could mean over a hundred billion dollars a year flowing back into the wider economy – a figure equivalent to the amount Australia paid in welfare during the pandemic. By allowing land degradation, we are effectively removing the equivalent of an entire nation's income from the economy.

Imagine the opportunity: by rebuilding wildlife we could reverse land degradation and secure health and livelihoods for everyone.

Ecologists use the words 'patchwork mosaic' to describe variation in ecosystems. Some areas are permanently food-rich and others ramp up temporarily, for example each year, or during La Niña or El Niño periods. Mobile animals are responsive to these changes, tapping into a knowledge database hard-coded into their brains, triggering behaviour that subtly matches the perturbations of a natural world that has been just stable enough for millennia to keep them reliably functioning and healthy. In doing so, abundant animals amplify the energy from plants, absorbing it inside food chains, concentrating it inside themselves and re-releasing it in clouds of bioavailable carbon, nitrogen, phosphorus and other life-giving nutrients.

This is what makes for the most incredible wildlife spectacles. When you next see a flock of birds or a plague of locusts on the news, you're watching natural laws in action, implementation of learnt behaviour in a system that responds to surplus energy, its purpose being to restore balance. It may seem indiscriminate, but it's more precise and measured than our combative use of pesticides. The key to future food security is to rethink the role of all animals in rebuilding functioning ecosystems, even if they appear to be an inconvenience.

The story untold, the one that always seems to be missing from the narrative of climate change, overfishing, deforestation, rewilding, conservation or environmental planning, is the one where animals are essential to the functioning of ecosystems and the role they play in structuring our world, making it liveable, past, present and future.

Early scientists thought that in the absence of grazing, a forest, grassland or ocean system would naturally revert to a particular state. There are innumerable 'climax' states, all quite unpredictable, especially in the presence of climate change. For example, any present vegetation system can shift irreversibly into something completely different if you change the wildlife regime. This isn't much use if you've developed agricultural techniques, food supply chains and culture all based on the status quo. Now we understand more about the role of animals in these systems, agricultural scientists and ecologists have found that in intact landscapes (still full of animals) changes are less unpredictable and less chaotic. That situation is easier to reverse.[186]

Forces that would normally drift ecosystems towards chaos are kept in check by animals, and the longer they've been present, the more stable things are. If we're to have any chance of reversing the damage we've done, we have to adopt a completely new way of thinking about animals and their value in our lives. One of the most important things wildlife does for us and all animals is to create patterns of food availability in such a predictable way that we can go out and farm, fish and hunt, knowing when and where it's best to spend our time.

Rather than judging animals too quickly for doing what comes naturally, we need to be much wiser about how we live among them.

Climate and the weather

Climate change isn't caused by carbon dioxide in the atmosphere. Climate change is the consequence of surplus energy in the form of carbon dioxide *reaching* the atmosphere. The amount of carbon on Earth hasn't changed, only the distribution of carbon into places where it's less useful for our survival. It's important to make this distinction, or else we could waste time and money only trying to tackle the gas (the symptom) and not addressing causes of ecosystem collapse.

The current crisis is caused by two separate but connected things: 1) our burning of prehistorically buried fossil fuels; and 2) the loss of animals from the carbon cycle.

Ever since Swedish scientist Svante Arrhenius first developed theories in 1896 that predicted increasing carbon dioxide levels could warm Earth's climate, we've been focusing on only one part of the equation. In the 'Science Notes and News' section of New Zealand's 1912 *Waitemata & Kaipara Gazette*, it was written:

> The furnaces of the world are now burning about 2,000,000,000 tons of coal a year. When this is burned, uniting with oxygen, it adds about 7,000,000,000 tons of carbon dioxide to the

atmosphere yearly. This tends to make the air a more effective blanket for the earth and to raise its temperature. The effect may be considerable in a few centuries.

– *Digital archives of the National Library of New Zealand, 1912*[187]

The possibility of catastrophic climate change was put in a memo to US President Jimmy Carter in 1977. By 1994, it was recognised by the world, through introduction of the United Nations Framework Convention on Climate Change with the ultimate objective 'to stabilize greenhouse gas concentrations at a level that would prevent dangerous anthropogenic (human-induced) interference with the climate system'.[188] The models created to track and inform progress in tackling climate change will become one of humankind's most important scientific achievements.

Beyond the well-established link between atmospheric carbon levels and global heating, we don't know exactly how climate change works because we don't know how much we depend on wildlife to restabilise systems, even if we stop emitting carbon today.

Biodiversity is infinitely more complex than our climate models and solutions suggest. Because animal-driven biodiversity has been omitted from most models to date, we don't yet recognise the magnitude of animal impact. We are so focused on our burning of fossil fuels that we may have created a smokescreen for a far greater threat, which is the decline in animals and the impact that is already having on destabilising the biosphere. This threatens to lead us down a dead-end alley of bluntly engineered carbon capture ideas and large-scale tree planting.

Wildlife and the structures we (and all animals) create are the mechanism we need to moderate excess energy in Earth's biosphere –

and that's how we create food, water and avoid disease. It stands to reason that the energy that forms our climate (for that is all it is, heat energy) is integrally coupled to the behaviour and abundance of animals, while the integrity of the ecosystems they form is the very fabric of our own survival because it keeps the Earth cool. The truth is that animal extinction is causing the collapse of stable climate systems, leading to huge impacts on the likelihood of our species' survival. Our burning of fossil fuels is significant, but it has distracted us from this other much bigger problem: we are undermining the biodiversity processes that animals maintain – and we are part of – that keep the planet in working order and habitable.

We're only just beginning to work out the scale and intensity of animal impact on climate systems because we're only just realising the importance of ecosystems. Twenty twenty-one marked the start of the UN Decade on Ecosystem Restoration, and the pandemic, climate change and collapsing ecosystems are behind a global push to use 'nature-based solutions', to rebuild resilience – a survival strategy humans will need if we're to maintain our way of life. It has been suggested that ecosystem restoration could account for a third of our carbon capture needs by 2030.[189]

The global conservation community is struggling to define 'nature'. We have not yet accepted the importance of animals as ecosystem engineers, nor do we understand just how much resilience we have lost after killing most of the animals on Earth already. It's hard to know how reliably we can depend on nature, when we've so little wildlife left and we're stacking so much excess carbon into the atmosphere. According to Oxfam, there isn't enough planet Earth to accommodate all the nature-based solutions to climate change that member countries at the 2021 Climate Change Conference have pledged.[190]

The question that remains is: how do ecosystems stabilise? In May 2019, a few months before I started writing this book, the late EO Wilson (he edited the book *Biodiversity*, published before the history-defining Rio Earth Summit in 1992), was asked to give a couple of lectures on ecosystems. In an interview for *Quanta Magazine* Wilson admitted that he knew little about them and that understanding what threatens their equilibrium was vital to saving the environment. It's animals. Only wildlife can stabilise ecosystems.

The complexity of biodiversity means we might never be able to describe these systems fully. It's easier to model the universe and the physical weather than it is to describe the practically infinite multitude of ecosystem interactions. Perhaps this is what has led to animals being ignored in our important planetary equations and why animal impact is largely overlooked. We can, however, make many inferences about the significance of animal impact on climate.

In 1883, oil was used in a stormy sea-rescue to reduce large waves. The crew of the 276-tonne *Grecian* bound for Portugal from Philadelphia was overloaded by a disreputable owner who, in 1881, had refused to accept a Lloyd's of London surveyor's judgement about the maximum load waterline and had been stripped from the registry. After three days of heavy seas and the *Grecian* taking on water, the crew of the petroleum ship *Martha Cobb*, by miracle chance, appeared nearby. After failing to calm the sea using petroleum oil leaked into the ship's bilges, Captain Greenbank instructed his crew to try pouring a five gallon can of fish oil into the scuppers, which slid into the sea.

After twenty minutes the breakers disappeared and a dinghy was successfully launched, rowed uphill against the gale three times, and all the crew were rescued.

There was a suggestion in the story that the fish oil had a 'magical' effect.[191] Based on accounts from the crew of the *Martha Cobb*, scientists calculated that the five gallon drum would have spread to an area of 3,600 square metres in twenty minutes[192] and another study found 340 millilitres of vegetable oil would spread to 12,000 square metres. When the supply of oil is interrupted, it evaporates but, while present, it not only suppresses waves, it *stops them growing.*

Unlike crude oil or petroleum, fish and vegetable oils have a polar structure like a magnet. One end is attracted to water, and the other end is not. These molecules spread into a single-molecule-thick blanket but not so fast that the layer tears, even in relatively choppy seas. The oils' properties, it seems, are not so magical after all. Given millions of years of co-evolution of animals and ocean ecosystems, it's not difficult to imagine a connection between these biological and physical entities. The oil produced by animals such as whales can stop waves growing, even in heavy seas. The use of oil to calm seas has long been known by European fishers.

> … in crossing a bar or in landing through surf, they press the livers of the fish, until the oil exudes and then throw them ahead of their boats. Lisbon fishers carry oil to use in crossing the bar of the Tagus in rough weather. Whalers have used oil and blubber in severe storms for the last two centuries; they usually hang large pieces of blubber on each quarter when running before a heavy sea, to prevent water coming on board
>
> – *Lieutenant W. H. Beehler, 1888*[193]

There are more unexplained accidents in shipping than any other form of transport. A third of these are due to severe weather and a quarter completely unexplained. Over 200 large cargo vessels, bigger than anything people have sailed on the ocean for centuries, were lost between 1981 and 2000,[194] and there are regular reports of 'rogue waves' hitting ships, cruise liners and even oil platforms. The most famous account is of the 200-metre-long merchant ship *München*, lost in the Atlantic Ocean in 1978. The ship itself was never found, but among the wreckage was an unlaunched lifeboat that had been hit by extreme force about 20 metres above the waterline. These waves were once thought to be seafaring myths, but modern satellite altimeters now prove the monsters are real, terrifying and more common than previously thought.

Is it possible that our extermination of ocean wildlife and interference in these processes has introduced enough surplus free energy to make these occurrences more frequent? Ocean currents and atmospheric winds are inextricably linked, and it is a question whether the sheer volume of natural oil removed from the ocean surface by the rapid extermination of most large whale species – not to mention other marine mammals, seabirds, tuna and sharks – has had a significant impact on weather and storms at sea. Scientists know water evaporates from the ocean but surprisingly little about how wind causes waves. So much so, that the University of Melbourne is building a world first: a massive wave pool called the 'Extreme Air-Sea Interaction Circuit', to investigate.

Sperm whales have been in our oceans for a few million years, and their misfortune was to have evolved spermaceti, which was valued by humans as oil for candles in the nineteenth century. A single sperm whale could yield forty-five to fifty barrels, or almost 2,000 litres.[195]

In 1993, Professor Alexey Yablokov, a courageous biologist who had been responsible for holding Russian president Boris Yeltsin to account over radiation dumps at sea in the Arctic, stood up at the Society for Marine Mammalogy's biennial conference in Texas and exposed an enormous campaign of illegal whaling from 1948, when the Soviets had killed over 275,000 sperm whales and nearly 13,000 blue whales. Both Russia and Japan, it seems, had long been falsifying records.[196] Before whaling, global numbers of sperm whales were about 1.1 million, declining by as much as eighty per cent today.[90] According to the International Whaling Convention, an estimated 362,879 blue whales were killed in the first half of the twentieth century,[197] or a reduction to just 0.07–0.29 per cent of natural levels, and there may have originally been as many as 2.5 million baleen whales in the world's oceans.[198] It's estimated 87,000,000 tonnes of baleen whale biomass were removed from marine ecosystems by whaling, or about 2.6 million large whales.

Based on studies of natural oil a litre could spread to an area of 35,000 square metres. This means whales could have been impacting twenty per cent of the Earth's ocean surface each year. Add to that the surface impact of dolphins, seabirds, predatory fish and sharks, all of which have declined substantially in the last fifty years, and it amounts to an extraordinary amount of surplus wave energy, which would otherwise have been absorbed by the activity of animals.

In the last thirty years, there has been an eight per cent increase in wave height and an overall increase in extreme waves.[199] Energy from the atmosphere creates rough seas. Friction is suppressed by oil on the surface and substantially reduces wave action, wave growth and atmospheric moisture. It's entirely plausible that eradication of natural sea-surface oil could have markedly increased large wave duration and intensity of storms. If this seems at all far-fetched, it isn't the most extraordinary impact animals have on ocean health and climate. There's the contribution seabirds make to creating continental weather systems.

After brief rainfall in the heat of summer, the stench of ammonia in seabird colonies can be overpowering. Seabird breeding islands emit more gaseous ammonia than anywhere else in the world. Studies have found they can emit as much as ninety kilograms every hour, emitted as downwind plumes after rainfall.[200] Then there are ocean algae that create a huge amount of a compound called dimethyl sulphide, which combines with atmospheric oxygen to make sulphuric acid.

When the acid mixes with the birds' ammonia, it creates atmospheric particles that seed cloud-droplets. Ammonia production is highest in the tropics where conditions tend to be warmer and wetter,[201] but authors of a 2016 paper in *Nature Communications* even found the effect to be important at Arctic seabird colonies. Their results show how cloud seed particles can grow to diameters sufficiently large to promote 'pan-Arctic cloud-droplet formation' in the summertime. In other words, in the Arctic, where ammonia emissions are relatively benign, seabird colonies are creating weather systems over the whole region. Not only that, the clouds they form reflect sunlight, maintaining the cool ground temperatures.

By protecting seabird colonies, we would be looking after rainfall systems that deliver water to our nations' farmland.

The quantity of sulphuric acid the algae can produce depends on the concentration of iron and other nutrients that whales secrete onto the sunlit water surface, but the whales also mix and stir cold water at scales never imagined before, and the consequences can mean life and death for whole societies.

In 2019, India's monsoon was much later than ever previously recorded. Higher-than-normal temperatures in Central Asia had continued to warm the Himalayas, where normally by early September the air would have been cooling, causing moisture-rich vapour to fall. This ordinarily creates a blanket of cloud on northwest winds that sweep across South-East Asia, all the way to Australia, and providing critical rainfall, on which our region's agriculture has come to depend. Instead, in 2019, the region experienced persistent winds from the southeast, drying the Australian continent and failing to deliver any moisture. By midsummer, bushfires had scoured an estimated 186,000 square kilometres of Australia, driving many animals rapidly towards extinction, collapsing the tourism industry and creating smoke plumes big enough to turn New Zealand glaciers brown and waft all the way to South America. These climate phenomena centre on the Banda Sea.

A few weeks before the bushfires I happened to be in the Banda Sea near Indonesia looking for blue whales. We were finding it difficult to locate them in areas they normally hang out in October, where the table-topped mountains of Seram cut an ominous shape on the horizon, rising over three kilometres above sea level and where, according to locals, highland headhunting tribes still live. Part of the curiosity of this region and its abundant wildlife is its small, remote human population that's allowed wildlife to prosper for millions of years.

Once winds shift northwest, blue whales often concentrate around nearby sea mounts. A year earlier, the ocean turned green and was visibly jam-packed with jellies, salps and other plankton – and there were lots of whales. This year, sustained head winds were making it uncomfortable to force our way south into the Banda Sea, and the blue whales had congregated somewhere else.

Persistent monsoon winds push warm Pacific Ocean waters south, creating a 150-metre-thick blanket of arid, nutrition-less water. These prevailing conditions mean whales have to find their way to an invisible layer beneath the sea, where there is a colder, deep-water current, which flows in the opposite direction. Spotting a weather-window, we reached the island of Banda Neira in the shadow of Gunung Api or 'fire mountain' and began seeing telltale puffs of whale blows everywhere, as dozens of blue whales had congregated to feed, giving a clue to the riches buried deep beneath the warm surface. The abnormal climate had prolonged the mixing of cool deep water in the Banda Sea – Banda was reacting to global warming; a valve against ocean over-heating had stayed on for longer to counteract the effect, and the blue whales were having a bountiful year.

Bobbing silently aboard a Zodiac in the middle of the Banda Sea, we watched blue whales emerge with an audible explosive blast from twin blowholes, clearing moisture from nostrils before taking the first of a dozen deep breaths. Each time they appear, the breaths get smaller until on the penultimate surfacing they clear their lungs with a final blast and lift their almighty tail flukes into the air. The trailing edges sport stalked barnacles that hang in the whale's slipstream. These harmless filter-feeding parasites benefit like the passengers on an aircraft, being served in-flight food each time the whales transport them into the densest patches of plankton deep below. As the muscular tail arches over, water cascades off the oily blubber like a waterfall and ends with a graceful finale, as the tail is displayed in perfect profile slipping quietly beneath the waves. Even in a choppy sea, the final muscular driving upbeat of this six-metre-wide tail flattens the surface, leaving a flat calm imprint that lasts for minutes afterwards.

In order not to disturb, we cut the engine as a blue whale passed only a few hundred metres away. The whale surfaced, paused ever so slightly and dived. The fact it even knew we were there was amazing.

Half a million blue whales were once able to survive in the world's oceans. This is the largest animal that ever lived on Earth, and no animal, let alone the biggest, can survive long in an environment that isn't stable. Human survival integrates with the survival of animals like the blue whale, which we must protect for our own sakes.

A minute later, it swam over and checked us out below the boat. Blue whales are extremely nervous, especially if anyone tries to get in the water. The largest animal that ever lived on Earth has much to fear it seems, and it's especially important to tread lightly in their presence because they live life on the very edge. Each gulp of prey uses extraordinary energy, taking in about eighty cubic metres of water.[202] When food is deep and plentiful, blue whales perform strenuous ballet-like lunges, twisting and cascading up and down through clouds of plankton. In the dark they feel their way around using sensitive hairs on their lips and jaws. A highly specialised sensory organ, discovered quite recently, attaches to where their front tooth would once have been and, along with hairs on their lips, helps them coordinate their lunge-feeding capability.[203] They can also feel for cold-water upwellings and listen for their prey, sensing subtle changes in echoes, like when you walk out of an empty room into one filled with objects.

The Banda Sea blue whales eat copepods, tiny crustaceans, no bigger than a pencil-tip, that feed on algae and microscopic diatoms and are far more highly packed with energy than krill. In 1984–85, Dutch scientists conducted plankton sampling in both the upwelling and the downwelling seasons. They found copepods dominating eighty per cent of the catch in the deep basins. One in particular, *Calanoides philippinensis*, breeds once a year, and like others in its genus is an upwelling specialist, breeding really fast once this seasonal pump is turned on.[204] The Dutch scientists reported about 4,000 copepods per cubic metre of the ocean.[205]

When the whales lunge, the pleats in their enormous mouths open up, and instead of swallowing the water they press their huge tongue against the roof of their mouth, squeezing the liquid out through baleen plates before the salty seafood soup is swallowed. Copepods flourish during the southeast monsoon, which more than triples the abundance of their algae food, which, like a forest, is the basis for the whole food chain but is buried deep below the warm tropical surface.

We live in the sunlit zone, and it's where everything to do with our climate and food happens,[206] which is why we depend on blue whales and other megafauna. They amplify the impact in the right places, like gigantic food-processing factories, lifting nutrients to the surface where they become part of our life support systems. The amount of energy a whale moves each day is extraordinary. For blue whales feeding on krill, scientists have estimated they need to eat about 1,000 kilograms per dive, which in energy terms is about 3.8 million kilojoules per day[207] – that's equivalent to the average daily intake of 500 people, which means only 55,000 large baleen whales would match the energy budget for the whole human population of a country like Australia.

During the southeast monsoon, the Banda Sea becomes one of the world's most treacherous places for shipping. Rising air over the Himalayas sucks moisture towards the northwest. These winds that parade across the Banda Sea's several-hundred-mile reach contest with strong currents and persistent swells that thwart transportation to the islands even today. Yet this is the time of year when blue whales gather en masse. The genetically isolated and svelte tropical population split off from their larger Southern Ocean counterparts after the last ice age about 20,000 years ago[208] to migrate each year, as they still do today, several thousand kilometres between the southeast coast of Australia and the Banda Sea.

The 2019 bushfires in Australia were the by-product of a global system under stress where animal behaviour was helping moderate Earth's heat budget in response to climate change. Blue whales are embedded in the system and without them, the impact would have been worse.

Just the physical effects of thousands of animals swimming up and down between the cold deep water and the warm tropical surface can provide up to a third of all ocean mixing, equivalent to the gravitational pull of the moon plus all the Earth's winds combined.[209] The turbulence from fish swimming is equivalent to the mixing effect of major storms,[210] and without blue whales, fish would be far less abundant because they depend on whales to concentrate nutrients at the surface. Without iron, there can be no photosynthesis and no food chain. Whale faecal matter can contain up to 10 million times higher concentrations of this critical ingredient than typical surrounding seawater[88] and is deposited at the surface, exactly where it's needed, to interact with the sun's energy.

Ralph Chami at the International Monetary Fund, and his colleagues, identified that an end to whaling could capture as much carbon dioxide as 2 billion mature trees.[211] Mostly due to their size, blue whales epitomise the importance of animals in creating stable weather systems. The physics and chemistry of blue whales are acutely focused on locations with the most powerful planetary forces, creating an impact massively disproportionate to their abundance. Their continuous fertilisation of the sea, in the most important places, is of critical importance to global heat regulation and climate. During upwelling events, the Banda Sea's surface temperature is a remarkable three degrees cooler,[212] moderating the temperature of the Indian Ocean and influencing weather across South-East Asia, Africa and Australasia.

It was the cooling of the ocean surface that triggered the conditions that led to catastrophic bushfires in Australia. The whales, along with all other marine vertebrates, might have contributed a third of this effect.[209] The 2019 positive Indian Ocean Dipole event and persistent southeast winds meant a bumper year for blue whales that feed on the prevailing upwellings. The difference between a benign and furious bushfire season in Australia is little more than a degree change in the ocean temperature of the Banda Sea,[213] and this blue whale pump contributed to the bushfires and destruction of huge areas of farmland and forest across southeast Australia in 2019.

Animals redistribute Earth's energy and their behaviours are reliably triggered just like a river will flow downhill. They are an integral part of how ecosystems function. In this way blue whales may have contributed to more severe bushfires but they also took dangerous heat away from the atmosphere and oceans. Two years later and Australia's bushfire areas severely flooded. Without whales these fires and floods would continue to worsen. The more animals you remove, the more ecosystems become chaotic – as predicted by Einstein's second law of thermodynamics.

It's not just about blue whales. All animals in the Banda Sea contributed to the 2019 processes and similar things are happening all the time, all over the world. Blue whales are just as significant as sharks, turtles and fish. They hold up a pillar of the food pyramid and are doing their part to keep planetary systems under control.

At the back of your fridge, the pipes that flow around the coolant can get very hot. If you remove the processes that circulate the coolant, your compressor can overheat and cause a kitchen fire. You don't disable the pump to fix the problem – you replace it, so your fridge doesn't explode.

In 2019, blue whales were responding to an enormous influx of free surplus energy, which was the consequence of heating. The prolonged monsoon winds meant the whales could feed more actively, thus reducing world temperatures, by pumping harder. But that excess heat also needs somewhere to go.

As for Australia, the country happens to be on the wrong side of the cooling system, the side that gets hot when the pumps are working overtime. It means Australians have a lot more to lose than other nations.

We simply don't appreciate how much animals are part of processes that rebalance systems that we have broken. If we did, maybe we would protect them better. The blue whales went into overdrive because climate change elsewhere meant there was suddenly an abundance of free energy in the form of strong winds from the Himalayas and the whales, just like the locusts, responded the only way they knew how. Observing the behaviour of blue whales teaches us why we should think twice before killing songbirds or even locusts! If we kill blue whales, we might protect Australia's farmland, in the short term, but we would increase ocean temperatures, reduce ecosystem productivity and contribute to greater climate chaos.

We define 'pests' as any animal we think has become too common for our liking. Mostly this is a stigma with no ecological basis. Sometimes animals might get in the way of our way of life but abundant wildlife can easily be responding to a greater threat we haven't realised yet. We need to be so careful in making this assumption about any species.

Even despite huge declines in wildlife populations to date, there is still hardly a square metre of the ocean unaffected by wildlife, and the processes they drive are influencing the weather you can see outside your window right now. Not only that, everything from sharks to seabirds swim or fly along dimethyl sulphide concentration gradients in search of food – at sea you can smell it yourself if you cruise over patches of *Trichodesmium*, a type of algae. It whiffs faintly of cut grass.

The olfactory super-sense of sharks and seabirds is one of those invisible architectures, like sound, that bind these biodiversity processes to each other. If the ocean warms and algae become more abundant, how will birds and fish tell where to find the best concentrations of food? It's like shining a light in their eyes. The energy becomes too spread-out and diluted, so finding it becomes more difficult. The ecosystem's patchwork starts to break down, and the overall quilted image becomes harder to make out. This is why we need animals to transfer, amplify and concentrate energy for us.

It is impossible to disconnect animals from the effect of climate, as they are the drivers of everything that minimises atmospheric free energy. In whatever form that energy takes, whether it's natural cloud-seeding, ocean mixing, carbon sequestration or limiting the friction between wind and the sea, animals moderate excess and keep things within liveable bounds. And they do it on an unimaginable scale and with such precision and intensity that we can never replace it with technology.

PART 5-

A blueprint for human survival

How long do we have to make the change?

In September 1800, Thomas Jefferson wrote in his *Memorandum of Services* that: 'The greatest service that can be rendered any country is to add an useful plant to it's [*sic*] culture'. I wonder which world leader of tomorrow will be ambitious enough to paraphrase Jefferson with this new statement: 'The greatest service that can be rendered any country is to add a useful animal to its culture'.

It takes centuries for animals to settle into patterns and routines of behaviour sufficient to maintain a habitable world for each other. Where animals like wolves still exist, we must protect them. Everywhere else, we have to give them the time and space to rebuild. This will take a global change in attitudes towards wild animals.

At the risk of sounding alarmist, many environmental scientists predict widespread ecosystem collapse by mid-century. Whether it's food systems, climate, fisheries or freshwater, there is reasonable evidence that from about 2050 onwards, humanity is going to enter a new phase in which efforts to counteract loss of life support systems will no longer be a question of 'whether' we should do something; it will become a necessity for survival.

On the plus side, there is a lot to be positive about today; I never thought I'd see so much passionate public discourse and lobbying for change. I hardly know anyone now who isn't starting to make personal choices to live more sparingly, putting pressure on leaders and expecting more corporate accountability for biodiversity decline. We are changing the narrative quickly.

Nonetheless, our deadline is fast approaching. Below, I've listed four stages of collapse, each increasingly serious and irreversible. If we fail to start addressing ecosystem collapse immediately, then it will take longer to rebuild wildlife populations, at which point we risk a timeline for restoring habitable ecosystems of 10,000 years or more.

- We may be facing ecosystem collapse within thirty years.
- We might need 100 years to rebuild wildlife populations. (For example, this is about how long it has taken animals like red kites in the UK to return to pre-hunting numbers.)
- We may need a further 10,000 years to fully restabilise any broken ecosystem processes (This is my best guess at how long it will probably take for animals to restabilise ecosystem processes and recreate the cultural knowledge to run them).

- Recreating a habitable Earth may take 10 million years or more, if we allow more than thirty per cent of species to go extinct (which could happen in the next hundred years or so).

The last of these points is extinction, and that's the one we have to worry most about.

Arizona student Elizabeth Miller explains that, while it's been a widely held belief that the tropics are intrinsically hotspots of biodiversity, the rate at which new species evolve is highest in cold-water environments such as the Antarctic, but these species get wiped out in successive ice ages. This means a warming planet will recover more slowly from a mass extinction event.

In the last couple of hundred million years, the tropics have enjoyed long periods uninterrupted by ice ages, and the magic number of years for ecosystems to become fully saturated by animals is about 30 million.[214] Raja Ampat, in the heart of the Coral Triangle, settled geologically about 25 million years ago following the collision of two continental plates and has remained relatively unspoilt since then, which is why in my view it represents one of the best and most powerful examples on Earth of an ecosystem in almost complete working order.

Once this point is reached, the coupled ocean–climate processes become so tightly bound to the animal kingdom that all lifeforms are at maximum density and diversity, and ecosystems are at their steadiest state. As I mentioned earlier, we don't say equilibrium because there is no such thing – there is just balance. There is always the force of entropy acting on us from the outside that we can't control, like the wind that gently rocks a tree, or threatens to knock you off your bike.

When humans first appeared on Earth, it was because the world had an abundance of food and a climate that was almost perfectly suitable. Before that, more than ninety per cent of all animal species that ever lived on Earth had gone extinct already.[215]

It's hard to accurately estimate long-historic extinction rates because the fossil record and our knowledge of the number of species today is incomplete. However, if there are about 65,000 vertebrates species on Earth[59], at a very conservative rate[216] natural processes would see one species go extinct every hundred years. All else being equal, it would take almost five million years for all the world's current animals to go extinct and for evolution to recycle new ones.

The moment any species rises from the DNA pool it's taxed for the waste it emits into the world and in its urge to succeed pits itself against universal laws that lead down a path to its own extinction. No species lasts forever, and there are few long-term survivors. Higher order animals have short duration and the average species lifespan for higher vertebrates like us is 200,000 to 2 million years.

We're already about 300,000 years old (2 million years, if you consider the genus *Homo* to include all humans) and the reason why larger animals don't last as long is because we have a disproportionate impact on the world we live in – I think we can all accept that we have had a huge effect on our world. We process so much, move so much around and create so much surplus energy, we will always put ourselves at risk.

In 1994 when his book *Extinction Rates*[217] was first published, David Jablonski said that species loss was yet to equal any of the big five mass extinctions. Since then, it's all changed.

Today, based on exceptionally good recent fossil records, we know the current rate is a lot higher and accelerating.[216] We've lost over 600 known species since 1500 CE and half of those since 1900 CE when the rate had doubled. Current rates of loss have risen from one vertebrate every hundred years to between eight and a hundred times greater.[218] With just a few generations before the next mass extinction, we have very little time left to do something about this.

The need to protect wildlife for all our sakes has become more than just a philosophy. At current rates, massive ecosystem collapse due to loss of animals is predicted within as few as three of our lifetimes, and three-quarters of all species on Earth will be gone within 250 and 540 years.[218] And worryingly, humans still largely regard animals as separate to ecosystem function.

Our removal of key species – animals – from ecosystems is tantamount to pulling skilled players out of a sports team. All teams need a diversity of skills and each player has a crucial role. Ecosystems operate similarly. Resilience forms when there is diversity of players. The success of any species continues only so long as individuals of other species aren't wiped out in the process. Success is dependent on diversity both within a species' population and by surrounding it with a diversity of other species, as no individual species can singularly maintain ecosystem structures and stability. Diversity, and the need to dovetail inside animal-led processes, reveals itself as the defining factor for human and all other animal life on Earth. Again, this simple reliance on wildlife for a habitable Earth is missing from much of the global conservation narrative.

But why should we worry? Earlier we found out that the most

successful humans in history, including Indigenous peoples, successfully recreated habitable and biodiverse living conditions in a few tens of thousands of years. That was when there was an abundance of wildlife, where perhaps human civilisations could afford to alter entire landscapes, knowing the rest of the planet could absorb the effect quite quickly. We're now living on a planet completely consumed by humans where we've killed two-thirds of all living wild creatures.

As we learnt during the COVID pandemic, it takes a lot longer to ease out of a catastrophe than it does to create one. Five million people from Melbourne, Australia, took 112 days in lockdown to eradicate community transmission from just over 700 cases to zero. Taking back control from the disastrous release of free energy caused by killing wildlife is an even greater challenge.

Wildlife populations will accelerate in size once given opportunity, but as Isabella Tree writes in her book *Wilding: The Return of Nature to a British Farm*, Knepp farm's population of turtle doves took many years to rise from ones and twos, to sixteen pairs. The original population in the UK was closer to a quarter of a million. It took them twelve years to double the population from eight to sixteen, and at that rate it might take 120 years to recover the bird's population nationally – and only if everyone works together.

We face a monumental task if we are to achieve the outcomes we need to, by mid-century, to avoid the worst of ecosystem collapse. If we let mass extinction happen, it could take 30 million years to rebuild human life support systems at the scale we'd need to survive past the next few generations.

Everything we know about our universe tells us that our lives evolved in unison with wildlife and the longest-living species are those able to contribute to the greater good by working together. Animals that adapt too fast and disrupt too much cannibalise their opportunity and die out fast. Those that exist are lucky. In survival, slow and steady always wins the race.

It takes between 1 million and 10 million years for evolutionary adaptations to stick.[219] That's to say, in a very stable long-term environment (millions of years), few species entering the lottery will become Earth's winners. In most cases, animals evolve and adapt too quickly … that's right, most species go extinct quite fast. It's not their fault. Time and entropy are continuously moving forward and animals are too distracted fighting, sleeping and having sex to keep up. It's not long before the inevitable happens. Either they go extinct, evolve into a new species or are simply replaced by something less 'yesterday' and better suited to Earth's new fashion.

Animals are slaves to their ecosystem, as are we, and the relationship Earth has with its animals has stood the test of time – millions of years of time. The only animal that really needs to be thinking about building resilience is humans, and that's because we've made ourselves into the first species on Earth threatening to cause a mass extinction, and we are at grave risk of taking ourselves down too. It's time we understood the scale and magnitude of what animals do for us.

The decisions we make over the next few decades will make the difference between hundreds or millions of years of ecosystem recovery. There are a number of actions we're going to have to prioritise, starting with the need to stop killing wildlife.

Stop killing wildlife

We began to lose wild animal populations tens of thousands of years back, but it's the last fifty years we should be more worried about. In that time we have killed over sixty-eight per cent of individual wild animals (eighty-three per cent of mammals) on Earth,[2] and we are on course to a doubling of atmospheric carbon dioxide concentration by mid-century. Wildlife make ecosystems habitable. They stabilise climate, control diseases and pests, and amplify and concentrate nutrients so we have sufficient food and fresh water. We cannot replace their services artificially, and we've already lost so much of their capacity to support our life on Earth that the most urgent priority for human survival is to stop killing wildlife altogether.

Most mass extinctions occur over periods of millions of years. During the Permian mass extinction 245 million years ago, volcanic eruptions in what became known as the Siberian Traps flooded the atmosphere with three trillion tonnes of carbon,[220] acidified the oceans and raised their temperature to almost 40°C.[221] It's the warmest our planet's atmosphere has ever been, and for another five million years it was too hot for most animals to survive.[222]

This mass extinction was the fastest ever and took only 60,000 years to kill over ninety per cent of all marine life and three-quarters of land animals, along with most of the world's forests and insects. We're heading for a sixth mass extinction in as few as 240 years from now.[218] It will have taken us maybe 300 years to eradicate most animal life on Earth while adding carbon dioxide to the atmosphere at rates similar to the Siberian Traps 250 million years ago.[223]

This will be the first time since ecosystems first started to form on land when such a huge amount of free energy has been poured into the atmosphere and ocean, while simultaneously reducing the widespread regulatory processes of billions of animals. It will also be the first time a single species has caused the destruction of most life on Earth.

Long-term studies using weather radars reveal that 2.5 billion North American migratory songbirds have disappeared since 1970,[224] a decline of thirty per cent. Twice every year, up to 2.9 billion songbirds migrate between Europe and Africa with an overall decline of fifty per cent in the last half century. The capacity of animals to transport nutrients from biodiversity hotspots and spread them around the world has declined by ninety-two per cent on land and ninety-six per cent in the oceans.[225]

Yuval Noah Harari in *Sapiens*[226] surmises that climate change caused mass extinctions and that human impact up until the recent age was largely confined to land, sparing the oceans. Noah Harari isn't entirely correct. Mass extinctions have never been *caused* by climate change. Climate change has been triggered by other causes, the consequence of which have led to mass extinction. It may seem a bit pedantic to say it that way, but it's important in the context of Noah Harari's other statement that humans in the last 100,000 years were 'overwhelmingly a terrestrial menace', because that has now changed. For the first time in our history, we are now exploiting the oceans too.

Whenever catastrophic climate change occurs, it has enormous consequences for ocean life in particular, but ocean animals are also the mechanism for regulating the worst excesses in our climate. The point is that since the Devonian mass extinction our seas have been largely untouched – that is, until the last couple of hundred years of human industrialisation. Now when we threaten ocean wildlife we are further destabilising climate.

In the 1992 book *Biodiversity* edited by EO Wilson there are chapters by authors from the inaugural Biodiversity Conference in Rio. This was shortly after the term biodiversity was coined.[227] G Carleton Ray remarked that there was little recognition of the role of large predatory animals on nutrient cycling – a point repeated almost thirty years later in a report prefaced by renowned oceanographer Sylvia Earle about fish carbon services.[93] Not much has changed. We still don't recognise the powerful influence animals have on our daily lives.

As a volume, our world's seas occupy about 1.39 billion cubic kilometres, of which 97.5 per cent are ocean basins. The rate of decline in ocean wildlife should be terrifying us.

About 1.4 million tonnes, or 100 million sharks each year are removed from the world's seas.[228] No-one alive today knows what schools of hammerhead sharks would have looked like before industrial fishing. Even today they form intimidating hordes, hugging the thermoclines against steep sea mounts, each individual parading with the swagger of an Italian mobster and diving to depths of 1,000 metres, where water is cold and devoid of oxygen.[229] They used to be exquisitely adapted to survival, but the intelligence that has served them so well for millennia makes them vulnerable to fleets of over 200 Chinese vessels, reputedly harvesting them in international waters just outside the Galápagos Islands in 2020. Off the US eastern seaboard, the species has collapsed by ninety-eight per cent.[230]

During the 1700s, when Europeans first visited places like Banda Neira, the surface teemed with life, rich with schools of spawning yellowfin tuna weighing up to 200 kilograms, consuming prey from a sea abundant with life.[231] These giants of the fish world have been virtually wiped out from the world's oceans. The stature, importance and charisma of a glittering and voracious marine top predator are rather lost when it's fished from the ocean, crammed inside a tiny ring-pull can and spread in a sandwich with mayonnaise. It hardly befits a species of such pre-eminence and significance for our future. Banda's tuna stocks began to dwindle under harvest by the Japanese after WWII. By the 1970s cooperative agreements were in place, but this coincided with reduced catch rates, despite an expansion of licences to foreign-owned vessels and a rise in illegal Chinese and Taiwanese fishing vessels.[232] In recent years the Indonesian government has been forced to call the area 'fully exploited'.[233] Indonesia's fisheries minister, Susi Pudjiastuti then started to oversee the high-profile destruction of over 200 foreign-flagged fishing boats that remained fishing illegally in the region. This followed the collapse of a $4 billion industry, where in ten years 800,000 local households – some of the poorest island nations on Earth – who had earned their living from fishing lost their livelihoods.[234]

Fish are a major source of protein for Indigenous populations worldwide, and many of the communities that live near and steward the world's most important ocean biodiversity hotspots are too poor for conservation. For example, the island communities of eastern Indonesia in the Coral Triangle are among the poorest in the world. When I began working in conservation in the 1990s, it was mostly about creating protected areas, but even in those days scientists I knew at BirdLife International and WWF Madagascar were pioneering the development of alternative livelihood strategies, so people could continue to make a living while removing pressure from ecosystems. Today it's more widely acknowledged that poverty alleviation is the first step to the conservation of some of the world's most important places, the ones on which we all depend for survival (even if they exist in different countries). But it's not the creation of money that matters, it's the empowerment of people to act in their own self-interest. As the work of my friend and colleague Anissa Lawrence of TierraMar so elegantly demonstrates, the most successful conservation programs are led by local people whose investment in their own futures leads to longer-lasting protection.

In Indonesia we went diving with manta rays at a village on the western tip of the island of Batanta and were welcomed by locals who requested that we anchor further out. They had decided themselves to use a string of homemade buoys to mark the far outer edge of the manta ray habitat. They had taken it upon themselves to protect their future. Manta rays, like blue whales, increase their activity during certain weather periods. Scientists have shown their numbers increase several hundredfold during a positive Indian Ocean Dipole and El Niño,[235] causing currents to strengthen from the Pacific Ocean, driving more nutrients onto the coral reefs, spawning huge plankton blooms. To the conventional scientific thinker, manta rays are coming to feed on the plankton. To the ecosystem scientist who understands the role of entropy and chaos reduction in ecosystem stability, the rays are responding to a surplus of free energy. They are smoothing out the creases in a system that would otherwise create chaos and suffering for the people of the village, as increased nutrient loads result in decreased coral diversity and reduced overall fish abundance. Maybe there would be outbreaks of invasive crown-of-thorns starfish too, as there are on other nearby reefs.

Here again we have an example of where animals – humans and manta ray – are so integrally connected to their environment that ignoring their effect on ecosystems leads to the abject failure of measures to protect. Animals, even if we are one, are often among the last lifeforms to be considered when it comes to conservation. This isn't confined to the poorest nations either. Governments make decisions all the time to develop land without considering that local people and the wildlife they share their land with are equal drivers of sustainability.

The irony is that according to the Institute for International Economic Development, ninety-six per cent of people who work in small-scale fisheries are overwhelmingly in developing countries. Meanwhile, eighty-six per cent of fisheries subsidies globally goes to large-scale fisheries – predominantly in the private sector from developed countries.[236] We're paying the rich to undermine the poorest nations' ability to conserve our ocean future.

Either way, our destruction of ocean wildlife is having a massive impact on the resilience of Earth's systems to restabilise.

Meanwhile, vegetation cover on land is increasing fast across the world due to climate warming,[237] but we're deforesting the most wildlife-rich habitats, such as the Amazon and the Australian bush. Warmer conditions and more free energy mean more photosynthesis, but it will favour a smaller diversity of plants, and without multiple animal tenants to graze and prune the vegetation the energy distribution will become too chaotic and of no use to our farmers and fishers.

Life-giving energy that was previously distributed near the top of the pyramid has been pushed towards the base. We've released it among the bottom feeders, the lifeforms that are small and numerous. Migratory songbirds have declined by billions, so insect plagues are becoming regular on every continent. We live among relatively few types of rats, cockroaches and other animals that outcompete everything else and spread diseases that can cause global pandemics.

Collapse of insect populations is of great concern because a diversity of abundant invertebrates is critical to ecosystem integrity and

---

It can take over 200 years for forest trees to develop holes big enough to house an animal of the size of this greater glider. The forest ecosystem, however, is not just a house. The stability of ecosystems and our civilisation depends on animals like this. Deforestation is done with scant regard for wildlife, and unless we do more conservation, it is going to be much harder for us to rebuild a habitable Earth.

soil health. It's the last line of defence, since all the other larger animals and birds have also disappeared and all there is left after that are plants, worms, fungi and bacteria. They can't create nutrient patches big enough for animals of our size to eat from.

Killing wildlife is the worst thing a farmer can do, as they are critical to maintaining soil condition. It will take decades or more to recreate the soil and vegetation processes that have been lost already, to support economically and ecologically sustainable farming, to manage widespread contamination of livestock by germs and parasites.

To have fisheries in the ocean, we need seabirds, turtles, dolphins, whales and sharks to work together. Fishers can't afford to kill albatrosses on longlines, drown dolphins in nets or discard unnecessary bycatch – no-one wants that, least of all those who make a living from the Earth and connect with it every day.

The untold story of wildlife is that animals transfer, concentrate and amplify nutrients (nutrients are the molecular vehicle for energy) globally at every spatial scale. The collective intelligence we share with all other animals maintains the reliability of these systems. We've built cities, farming systems and machines, seasonal supply chains and human populations, on the promise that food will reappear at the right time and place. It's senseless to regard animals as competitors in global food production. The sooner we realise that economies are built on the resources and the certainty animals provide, the sooner we can adapt to survive.

Killing animals is never the best solution to environmental problems because we are integrally dependent on animal-driven ecosystem structures for our life support. I'm convinced that killing pests should be the absolute last resort. Our default reaction to almost any ecological imbalance is to impose our brutality on the system to elicit rapid change, which is the antithesis of how natural systems work and in most cases is likely to make matters worse.

In Melbourne's Port Phillip Bay, where I live, sea urchins are wiping out kelp beds where their natural prey, rock lobsters, have been fished almost to extinction. Among the first reaction was mass eradication of the sea urchins by divers using hammers (I'm not joking), but the bay is two thousand square kilometres in size and any scalable effort would need to be funded annually over vast areas. Anecdotal reports from 1802 suggest that 500 rock lobsters could have been fished in a single night and none of these sea urchin predators remain today.[238] Gummy sharks are also targeted by thousands of recreational fishers. Other proposals to 'manage' sea urchins include commercialising a harvest, but that is another utilitarian option that fails to prioritise the need for more animals and to give ecosystems the room to recover.

Can the world afford to spend billions of dollars worldwide, every year, to continuously kill animals when we know this will create new and even more widespread problems? Isn't the ultimate conclusion that we end up razing all wildlife from existence, because everything eventually becomes a pest? Of course, neither of these options are practical, so surely rebuilding ecosystem structure is the only sensible way to proceed. But as Frank Biermann says, environmental policy that encompasses scientific, regulatory and cultural practice is incompatible with social–ecological systems.[7] Our old-fashioned way of thinking about, and wanting to control, nature is embedded so deeply in our behaviour that it strangles our ability to explore innovative and animal-driven solutions. Port Phillip Bay desperately needs to reintroduce urchin predators, rebuild fish stocks and conserve vast areas for rehabilitation. It won't be easy or popular among recreational fishers, but unless something drastic is done soon there won't be any fish left. Meanwhile, there are moves to kill sea urchins but how will that make things better? In Sydney people were smashing sea urchins to feed fish and the area became consumed by black algae. Removing another layer of animal biomass is like pouring fertiliser. It creates a monoculture, freeing up lots of energy and polluting the surrounding environment. This type of mistake will continue to happen until we learn the importance of animals. By creating lifeless ecosystems we risk our very survival.

And besides, how can anyone deny the simple fact that more fish means having healthier ecosystems? Commercial fisheries were shut down some time ago, and things aren't getting any better.

In one state of Australia, New South Wales, it's thought that almost half a million kangaroos are killed commercially every year, many in national parks. Even some conservationists condone killing millions of kangaroos, including red kangaroos, the country's largest remaining megafauna species, an animal that stands two metres high and can weigh eighty-five kilograms. Raymond Mjadwesch calculated that there were about 220 million kangaroos before European settlement of Australia,[239] compared to about 40 million today. Despite the declines, that's still more kangaroos than humans. How many countries in the world can boast megafauna more abundant than its human population?

Australia has a unique opportunity because it's one of the few countries in the world that still has abundant megafauna, so it was alarming to read in the *Guardian* in February 2021 an article titled 'How kangaroos could be jeopardising conservation efforts across

Australia', in which land managers expressed the intent to short-circuit and manipulate megafauna populations.

The reason they want to mass-kill kangaroos is that they are overconsuming grass in conservation areas. This is hardly a surprise when their reserves are creating ideal food conditions in areas surrounded by agricultural desert. Isolated reserves don't function, because their structure and processes are incompatible with their surroundings. Ecosystem management has to be a whole-landscape approach, or nothing at all – which is why we need a change in human values overall, especially among landowners. There is ample evidence loss of this wildlife is behind many of the environmental problems we face today, including the decline in soil fertility, food security, habitat integrity and, ultimately, climate stability.

The kangaroos are integral to recovering lost soil fertility and protecting food security because animals are the driving mechanism behind ecosystem stability – but only if they are in correct proportions and in balance with other creatures. Kangaroo habitat brings an abundance of everything else: birds, reptiles and insects that provide all the other smaller-scale transfer, amplification and concentration of nutrients. This is how and why Aboriginal land was covered in a thick friable layer of rich soil and why we cannot survive forever on a planet without wildlife.

Local overabundance of kangaroos has been blamed on an absence of the dingo, an Australian large predator that was probably introduced to Aboriginal people tens of thousands of years ago. In that time, they developed synchrony with kangaroo populations. A study in *Landscape Ecology* shows the massive impact that Australia's dingo-proof fence has had on vegetation.[240] The fence is over 5,500 kilometres long and crosses three states, but on the side with more dingos there is significantly more vegetation growth due to suppressed grazing pressure by kangaroos. This doesn't mean there are fewer kangaroos. Tiger sharks influence the behaviour of dugongs away from seagrass beds at times, allowing habitat to regenerate and come back stronger.[75] Predators like dingos also alter kangaroo behaviour. The result is greater abundance of animals and vegetation together. This increase is what drives processes that create soil, food and even water.

Many farmers dislike dingos because they threaten stock, but their absence throws the ecosystem into chaos, leading to conflict. It's not just the decline in abundance of kangaroos we should be worried about – it's the patterns they form naturally in the environment, which maintain ecosystems. Without kangaroos or dingoes, you get reduced soil fertility, which leads to declining bird and reptile populations and an increase in crop pests. This means using more pesticide and fertiliser, which further reduces ecosystem processes, and so the cycle continues to worsen until today we are faced with an existential crisis that is effectively caused by loss of animal equality in the new human-made landscape.

The soil that animals create also locks ocean moisture away where it's most useful. *The Reindeer Chronicles*[241] by Judith Schwartz tells the story about our planet's water and its association with nature. Moisture off the sea blows inland and is trapped by vegetation, locked safely away in the soil and released slowly, as plants breathe out. As we've converted our coasts to desert and cities, dust has replaced soil, and this repels moisture. Having nowhere else to go, the water cycles back out to sea building bigger and bigger clouds. Schwartz describes how the catastrophic floods in central Europe can be traced to desertification around the Mediterranean. The moisture laden air reaches bursting point and when it's blown inland, it wreaks havoc on countries like Germany. Meanwhile, farmland in Spain and Portugal, is dry and collapsed.

Our abandonment of wildlife has created the perfect storm. Animals have always helped iron out fluctuations in climate. In their absence, and in warming world, the extremes are now far greater. This makes all the difference between a warming world and one that is uninhabitable. All citizens of Earth should be supporting farmers and fishers to work with wildlife conservationists, to rebuild animal impact and preserve the integrity of land and sea. Loss of megafauna in particular will become a defining factor in our quest for human survival in years to come and, here in Australia, we have a globally significant remaining example.

Our standard approach to policy and research seems to like making things sound very complex and longwinded when the reality is restoring ecosystems is the best fix. The money that is marked for killing, monitoring or harebrained eco-engineering solutions could be used instead to experiment with innovative rewilding, because the longer ecosystems are without large animals, the harder that becomes. It's far easier and less costly to rebuild systemic, self-regulating, wildlife-driven structures than to take the financial risk and uncertainty of mass eradication of another step in the trophic pyramid.

Protect our intelligence

What if I told you that killing animals makes us less intelligent? It's a bold statement, so let me explain.

Animals balance Earth's energy budget, trading a finite amount of nutrient with plants so the sun's energy, which is tightly bound into nutrients, becomes concentrated and delivered for consumption in the right quantities, at the right time and place. Killing wild animals isn't an intelligent thing to do, as it reduces how efficiently we can find and deliver food.

What if intelligence is ultimately defined by how well an animal can survive? The sperm whale that can't hear the supertanker creeping up behind it isn't stupid. Similarly, if you're dropped at 2,000 metres under the sea to be asphyxiated and crushed to death, it doesn't make you dumber than the whale. As Bernd Würsig states, you can't rate marine mammal intelligence based on human communication or the fact they don't have hands with opposable thumbs.[242]

We are each adapted very differently in the way we connect to the world, and we're only as intelligent as we need to be to live on the Earth the way we know how.

A classical measure of human intelligence, the IQ (intelligence quotient), pits your ability to problem-solve against other people, but isn't ecosystem-relevant. Our existence is driven as much by pressures from outside ourselves as it is from inside our own minds. As a population, the information we need to make competent survival choices flows into us from the work that animals did to create ecosystem patterns.

It stands to reason that because our knowledge of where and when to expect things comes from the actions of animals, our intelligence is also an extension of the intelligences of all the animals around us. Animals borrow off each other all the time. Behaviour, language and the way we gather and use information are all extensions of the patterns that animals create, and we need to make sense of them to have a habitable world.

Humans have never survived through study and research, only through experiment, repetition and adaptation. Making mistakes is our greatest weakness but also our path to success. For early human cultures in Australia, the Americas and South-East Asia it wasn't so much what they 'learnt' as what they 'knew' that mattered. Aboriginal people didn't learn that what they were about to do would shape the continent for tens of thousands of years. They adapted to survive, on a discrete local level, so even languages diversified, and they could tell stories to support their own culture, reflecting their environment and how to survive.

The diversity of human languages in New Guinea follows similar patterns to animal diversity.[243] Mountains and rivers provide natural boundaries between tribes, which, over thousands of generations, have formed their own culture. When they did come into contact with each other, there may have been posturing with spears or shouting, but for the most part it would have made sense to avoid conflict. This isolation is, after all, the reason they developed different languages in the first place. The concept of language and music among Aboriginal Australians connects strongly to the landscape and identities of different groups and is thought to have contributed to the diversification of their culture and a largely peaceful coexistence. Today, traditional language diversity is declining at the same rate as wildlife.[134]

Language is the basis for preserving the combined intelligence of bloodlines, protecting the cultural knowledge necessary for your mob's survival. Even today, the tribes of New Guinea and Australia have some of the most diverse dialects of any nations on Earth. Natural selection prefers diversity because it allows populations to adapt and persist. It's one of the reasons Aboriginal culture did so well.

We draw on the combined intelligence of billions of animals worldwide. If other animals didn't know how to communicate, develop their own cultures and know where to find things, they wouldn't be able to transfer, amplify and concentrate nutrients just where we need them. This collective knowledge library is read by all animals to forage and find food globally, which gives us stable climate, clean water, fertile floodplains on which to grow crops and rich oceans to fish from. It's the basis of biodiversity, and it's the reason why fishers decide to head in a particular direction from port or farmers originally settled on fertile land. It was all on the direction of animal-led processes.

Altogether, wildlife creates a library of information, a building, shelves and floors to store everything inside, right down to writing and updating new editions, as the information to survive slowly changes. Our species was granted a library card 300,000 years ago and we use it all the time, to decide where to fish next and when to harvest crops.

When we kill wildlife, we destroy this filing system – the connectivity of ecosystems – so the knowledge we previously stored inside our brain, the information we imagined was useful, becomes redundant. Information chaos ensues, and it disrupts our ability to make survival choices of our own – just like the way our farmers can no longer predict when the next rainfall will come, because climate change has randomised weather patterns and made them more severe. Climate change, remember, is a historically final stage in global ecosystem collapse.

By killing animals or disrupting their ability to survive, life for us becomes like walking into a dark room after someone has unexpectedly placed a chair in the doorway. Except we're the ones responsible for moving the furniture.

Off Sri Lanka, a thriving and largely unregulated blue whale–watching industry has forced animals offshore, away from traditional feeding areas, directly into the path of supertankers.[244] We shouldn't be undermining the survival of blue whales for tourism and simultaneously altering their ability to deliver nutrients to traditional feeding areas, which will cause decline of local fisheries. Imagine how furious a librarian would get if you moved hundreds of books to different places, so no-one else can find them anymore.

Children born in 2090 might end up saying our generation was rather unintelligent not to have taken wildlife conservation more seriously. Yet the ability of humans to problem-solve hasn't changed in thousands of years. Take for example the Plimpton 322 tablet, an elaborately etched stone slab mathematicians have pored over for years. The tablet represents a unique mathematical approach to triangulation that hasn't been seen for 3,000 years and would have allowed Babylonian engineers to design complex architecture. It proves that the problem-solving capacity and computational sophistication of different human cultures over the ages show an equivalent level of genius.

We haven't become more or less able to problem-solve over time, but what we will call our eco-IQ has declined of late, as we've destroyed animal populations. We are draining the pool of intelligence, the information we need to survive, not by becoming more stupid but by acting more stupid.

Despite harbouring feelings of superiority over animals, our behaviour is actually making us less intelligent than the wildlife we are killing. It's funny really. We are more likely to go extinct faster than an animal that maintains ecosystem integrity. Who's the most intelligent now?

Cooperate with other animals and each other

If we learn to cooperate with our animal brethren we can survive longer and live better. So what is a successful species?

Is it one of the twenty that make up the three-quarters of seabirds maintaining the planet's ocean-nutrient processes? Is it the horseshoe crab with its fossils found 445 million years ago, one of the only species to survive the Ordovician mass extinction?[245] Is it the humble wheat, which, as Noah Harari says, was absent from North America 10,000 years ago and today dominates the great plains?[226] Is it humans, with their religion, culture, language and society, who have risen to over 7.7 billion individuals and now outnumber most species on Earth, making up six per cent of all the individual large animals?[246] Is it the Brazilian termites who built the 4,000-year-old colony the size of Britain with its 200 million mounds comprising ten cubic kilometres of soil and equivalent to several thousand great pyramids of Giza?[44] Or maybe the coral polyps of Australia's Great Barrier Reef that form the largest biological structure on Earth?

It could be the tardigrades or water bears, microscopic animals about half a millimetre long that live everywhere from mountaintops over 6,000 metres high to 4,000 metres below the sea. Thousands are living in your garden, gutters or rooftop, nestled among leaf litter or moss. Their reputation for resilience has led to many rather unpleasant experiments where species have been subjected to extreme temperatures, including -272°C, just one degree above absolute zero, the temperature at which natural particles lose all vibrational momentum – effectively the temperature when life can no longer exist. Perhaps it's those early bacteria that formed a symbiosis and whose genes skip extinctions and pass down the matrilines of every animal on Earth today.

We aren't well-equipped to answer the question 'Which is the most successful species?' because like other animals we don't have a clear purpose or role in this world. Religions have their perspectives, but nature is less embracing. Our results as individuals are as close as we come to understand what it means to be successful on Earth. Do we have a nice job? Are we well liked? Do we have children? Our culture imposes expectations on its members to behave a certain way, but none of that matters, as on a societal level the only thing that would seem to count for us is that our species persists for as long as humanly possible. For that outcome, the most immutable law is that we avoid a fight against nature, at all costs.

In 1976, Richard Dawkins published *The Selfish Gene*[247] and reframed the concept of evolution as our individual striving for genetic longevity. Dawkins explained how we come to make decisions that improve the chance of replicating our chromosomes through being kind to relatives, or exploiting the charity of others for our own ends. It was the first time anyone had popularised the view that being a species, or even an individual, was not the underlying driver for our behaviour or evolution. Have you ever wondered how a population of animals can survive when all the decisions are made by independently thinking and acting individuals? Dawkins's idea helped explain this.

Sacrificing yourself to save others seems contradictory unless you are doing it for a higher purpose, in this case, to protect your gene-flow. You might dive in front of a bus to save your children, but you're less likely to act that altruistically for a stranger. What you're really protecting is your contribution to the environment's stable protein infrastructure. You are part of a lineage that was built on entropy flow and patterns that you and all other animals formed, connected in such a way that they enmesh planet Earth. Your behaviour and physical nature was aligned with your environment long ago, so within you is the ability to read your outside world and respond to it the only way you know how.

One of those instincts, for most people, is to run away from a fight when you know you've a real chance of getting hurt. John Maynard Smith and George R Price in 1973 explained how avoiding conflict complements the population and broadly speaking represents the most evolutionarily stable strategy.[248] An evolutionarily stable strategy is an individual behavioural trait, rendered across a whole group, that serves to maintain its population. Smith and Price were among the first to apply game theory using the logic of decision-making to reveal optimal behaviour. Game theory is literally a game of chance, where you set up scenarios and use them to identify how things will behave.

One of the most well-known games is called prisoner's dilemma, and if you've ever watched a TV crime series you will get it straight away. Two guilty prisoners are being interrogated in separate cells, and the only way the authorities can get a conviction is to get one to testify against the other. If they both keep quiet, they both get one year in prison. If they both testify against each other, they each get two years, but if one betrays the other, one goes free and the other gets three years. Knowing this, the police tell the prisoner that his mate has accused him and he should do the same. By getting both prisoners to accuse each other, the police can get both thrown in jail – a combined total of four years (the maximum result they can achieve).

From an individual's perspective, it might make sense to accuse your friend, especially if they are not related to you, but the problem is they can do the same. The best cooperative strategy is for both prisoners to stay quiet, but in human circles that rarely happens. Humans are really bad at playing prisoner's dilemma!

In 1981, American political researcher Robert Axelrod and evolutionary biologist William Donald Hamilton published 'The Evolution of Cooperation', which became one of the decade's most widely referred-to papers in political science.[249] They ran a tournament inviting participants to submit computer-based strategies, simulating the game many times over. It's no coincidence the Showtime series *Billions* pays homage with 'Bobby' Axelrod as a wealthy investor obsessed with a tit-for-tat contest with another alpha male, the US Attorney for the southern district. The real Axelrod revealed 'tit-for-tat' as the most stable strategy. This is where an individual cooperates on the first move and then does whatever an opponent did after that. If an opponent decides to testify against you, you testify against them. If they protect you, you do the same. In a fictional police drama, the inspector tells the prisoner he's been accused by his associate and now the best thing for him to do is to point the finger straight back.

But because the first choice is either protect or testify, there are two outcomes and, as Dawkins explains, this means there are also two stable alternatives in the 'tit-for-tat' scenario. This is apparently why our society always seems to converge on two-party politics. The least-complex way of describing party motives, the one requiring minimum information, is to call out politicians as 'left' and 'right' leaning, labour or conservative, Democrat or Republican.

In the Axelrod game theory trials, a population dominated by individuals who always testified against each other ended up beating all other strategies, even though it resulted in a metaphorical more years in prison rather than one.

Why are humans so bad at cooperation when, in nature, this would not be an evolutionarily stable strategy? What is the difference? It's simple.

Life is a zero-sum game in which all parties have equal chance of gain or loss. 'Zero-sum' means the players have equal worth, or let's say, everyone dies in the end! When you're playing the game today, against someone you know, it's short-term and you aren't going to die (hopefully). It is only when the game is iterated millions upon millions of times in nature, where death or extinction are *always* the end result, that the tit-for-tat process eventually yields. Like the ancestral islanders of Nauru who collect and protect seabirds, you can choose to kill your neighbour's frigatebirds and to appear more powerful, but if everyone continued that way eventually your whole society would starve. The most likely behaviours to survive don't have to be the most dominant, as ecosystems are dynamic and moving ahead all of the time. Nature constantly selects for new and better ways of doing things, and that is how populations can last.

Political parties that shun cooperation, fail to protect wildlife and degrade ecosystems are contributing to the demise of the human species because they are imposing personal values in discordance with the natural laws that animals routinely and relentlessly enact for us on a planetary scale and have done for millions of years. The test case for this is the existence of humans in the first place, because without cooperation, without the last few tens of millions of years of relative stability, we would not be where we are today. This is why conservation is essential and why protecting the processes that allow animals to reproduce, survive and migrate are among the most important challenges we face.

We awarded ourselves the freshly engraved trophy for the Anthropocene epoch of our own making, but we haven't won yet. The only way we will is through cooperation with other animals and wildlife. It is why, when voting, it would be wise to choose parties that are multi-partisan and have leaders who avoid unnecessary conflict and have a heightened awareness of the importance of social diversity and environmental justice.

Even the most ferocious-looking and highly evolved animals are ill-equipped to kill each other. Despite a reputation for fearsome battles and having huge horns on their heads, wild sheep and goats rarely exit a fight with more than a dent in their ego. Antelope sport long, dagger-sharp horns set so far back on their heads and at such an angle that injury to a rival is almost impossible. Wild bighorn sheep from the Rocky Mountains of North America fiercely contest territory, butting heads with enormous horns that can take up a tenth of their body weight. Most animal fights are an elaborate display of bravado because escalating to a point of danger is too risky.

Blackbuck

The male's dark colour fades after rutting but retains the distinct white eye-patch

In nature, armistice leads to diversification quicker than fighting, and that's the basis of adaptation and survival. Diversity of species, culture, creativity and cooperative behaviour are the keys to resisting the breakdown of ecosystems into chaos. These are the richest, most stable ecosystem structures that can support the most life and big-bodied animals like us.

Birdsong increases biodiversity by minimising conflict between individuals. By being able to advertise their presence rather than fight each other, birds can more effectively create territories that fill all the available space. There are many other strategies animals use to communicate territorial boundaries and avoid fights, without having to necessarily make a sound. Strutting chest-out with big horns is one. Cape gannets from neighbouring colonies feed at different times and

---

Blackbuck are equipped with weapons that could be used to inflict harm, but injuries are rare. Horns point backwards and are mostly designed for sparring. Evolution has selected for non-combative alternatives to actual fighting because cooperation always wins out in the long term.

in different places, avoiding the risk of competing with each other for food.[250] Tigers back their hind legs up onto trees, stretching their backside above shoulder height, before emitting a squirt of heavily scented urine. Fox scats have a familiar acerbic smell that's detectable in small urban reserves where they come out of their dens to forage at night. Koalas in the Australian bush discharge a pungent mist onto the forest floor that radiates in the heat of the day, creating a wall of smell. Animals use a wide variety of sensory strategies to construct boundaries detectable by their peers, as a way to mostly avoid conflict with each other.

So how can evolution and diversification happen if there is no conflict? Smith and Price asked what happens when the only tactic is to outlast another and not die. How does an animal know how long to remain in a benign conflict, and how does this strategy become evolutionarily stable for the population?

The Red Queen hypothesis by Leigh Van Valen in 1973 uses a quote from the character in Lewis Carroll's *Alice in Wonderland*, who said, 'Now here, you see, it takes all the running you can do, to keep in the same place'. The theory goes that species from similar groups with similar ecology have a constant probability of extinction per unit of time but that they must evolve continuously and as fast as possible to survive. In other words, when it comes to extinction, human beings are no more or less likely to survive than any other species of mammal,[251] which means we all have to constantly adapt side by side.

If you are the owner of a new strategy, and it is one that fits into the ecosystem without upsetting the balance, your strategy can only win if the pay-off for you is greater than for a contestant using a different strategy against you. But if the two pay-offs are roughly equal, then your opponent's strategy will also succeed because, over time, they will meet others with the same strategy and form a subpopulation. This is like the two prisoners who refuse to testify against each other and go on to live a happy life without any regret or malice. Or it's like two political parties converging on ideas until the left and the right don't seem to really differ that much. Sound familiar?

Scientists recently observed this process in action in the Galápagos. A large cactus finch from a nearby island flew onto Isla Daphne Major, where medium ground finches were resident. The immigrant bred with the locals and the offspring were fertile, producing generations of birds with larger beaks and different songs. The new subpopulation was different enough that they segregated and continued to breed with each other.[252] A series of choices and some simple genetics, combined with an ecosystem, resulted in the diversification of new species traits. Two species became three.

Because one way of behaving can never be completely and utterly dominant, neither can an evolutionarily stable strategy be both uniform and completely permanent either. It's just not possible for one strategy to steal the stage forever because there will always be an understudy waiting in the wings, an animal of very different behaviour, who reads the same lines.

The point is, constant adaptation by animals is the ecosystem's way of responding to minor perturbations in the planet's outside behaviour, the way it responds to solar and cosmic forces. You being able to adapt your behaviour every day helps stabilise the world around you; your species does the same overall, along with groups of animals that stabilise ecosystems and whole ecosystems that stabilise the planet. It's just another pyramid, but this time, it's made up of behaviours that maximise productivity and minimise waste.

We live in the animal kingdom, where the most stable ecosystem structures favour diversification and adaptation. Thanks to wildlife, ecosystems will always settle in that direction, even though entropy forces are trying to push everything back towards chaos. The only way that can happen is through mutual cooperation. It's the same in politics. The further a political party moves to the right or left, the less they cooperate with other factions and interests, the more precarious they become until eventually they will collapse.

Reducing habitat area, increasing urban noise and wiping out small but genetically diverse populations on the fringes of urban encroachment all contribute to a reduced ecosystem resilience because it stops animals finding new ways of looking after our living environment – and degradation of our own ecosystems creates conflict within our own species too. This disruption removes barriers for peaceful reconciliation between animals, which leads to reduced diversity through increasing conflict and creates an energy monopoly more thinly spread and poorer for it. Cooperation and diversification are the winning strategy for any species that wants to play the long game because that earns us the knowledge to read the rulebook.

Social media companies have become synonymous with the concept of 'disruption', which is like knocking down millions of trees. It hurts us economically and emotionally. The internet promised to be the saviour of small business, but what it's done is given the advantage to a few large companies, those that can afford to spread themselves out thinly over huge areas – like species of microorganisms, they can exploit vast dispersed wealth for success.

Most players in life, as in ecosystems, have little control over environmental outcomes and put their hopes in the reliability of their surroundings to support them. The staff that stack vegetables in the supermarket cannot influence global financial markets or how much rain fell on the crops that year. They work consistent hours and do what their employer asks, in the hope that the system they work under has a fairly consistent structure, function and process that leads to a stable salary. Continuously disrupting ecosystems – whether natural or human-made – without a plan is not a good strategy for survival. Disrupting patterns artificially is similar to trees falling in a forest and, up to a point, it creates new opportunities for grazing animals to feed on fresh leaves of fast-growing and nutritious new plants. But throw a stone into a pond and you might at first scatter fish towards your hook and line, but they become more nervous and eventually swim away altogether if you keep doing it.

If individual interests take over, it breaks the predictability and reliability of the underlying patterns. If the rules of engagement become too uncertain and challenging, because the exterior environment has altered too quickly or become chaotic, animals stop knowing what to do, and this disconnection hastens a species' demise. This is when fighting occurs within and between species of animals, and that's a sign that someone is destined for extinction.

Another way of looking at this is in terms of equality. We can't survive on this world without animals. The inability to be able to survive without another – isn't that the ultimate definition of equality?

It's not about equal rights, it's about respect and empathy, because without an equitable valuing of wildlife we end up making our own world less habitable. This is what a zero-sum game means. If we don't respect and protect wildlife we all suffer.

Value wildlife and humans equally

It was 1864 when US president Abraham Lincoln signed an act of Congress paving the way to the 1872 creation of Yellowstone, the world's first national park. It was another ninety years later when Rachel Carson published the book *Silent Spring*, about the impact of notorious organochlorine (DDT) pesticides, which was credited to have launched a global environment movement. By 1969 the US had enacted the world's first environmental impact assessment legislation, fifty years after extinction of the passenger pigeon and about 13,000 years after the continent's sabre-toothed cats and mammoths went extinct.[253]

The same time Carson was writing her book, ecologist Garrett Hardin was working on a paper published in *Science* in 1968, titled 'The Tragedy of the Commons'.[254] Both these authors were to inspire a significant change in human values that flowed across the entire world. Hardin was also an extreme white nationalist with unsavoury views about minorities, but his idea of the tragedy of the commons dates back to an 1883 essay by British economist William Forster Lloyd, who described the unregulated effects of grazing on common land (land that anyone can use). Forster Lloyd surmised that a person who puts all their own cattle on land at the expense of others gains a value that is then deducted in equal measure from all the other people who may have benefited.

Hardin took this a step further and said that if a farmer adds one more cow to their herd, they receive a benefit of +1 but the negative is only a fraction of -1, because the environmental impact of that cow on common land is divided among the many locals who own the land. Hence, farmers who believe in the freedom of the commons will continuously add to their herds, until the common land is in ruin. Likewise, a farmer who applies fertiliser or pesticide to crops, kills songbirds and pollutes waterways is depriving the rest of society the value those songbirds and waterways would bring – because wildlife does not belong to anyone.

These are among the reasons that governments adopt wildlife protection regulations on behalf of society. Our policy systems are designed to encourage a more equitable and just sharing of resources. The moral necessity to protect ecosystems has been well documented for over a hundred years, and without environmental impact assessment and biodiversity conservation laws, society would have to absorb any effects of free-market exploitation of commonly owned creatures and wild places.

Yet today we prioritise conservation only in tiny areas where human consumption needs are the least; we allow common resources such as climate, fresh water and food security to decline; we fail to properly protect wildlife and wilderness; and we allow developments to go ahead in modified landscapes, where rare or endangered animals may once have roamed in abundance, and with little or no consideration of generating new functioning ecosystems.

In 2006, *The Australian* published an article titled 'Return of the nearly dead parrot: orange-belly holds up marina', in which future

Australian environment minister Greg Hunt said, 'It is ludicrous that a major project which will create hundreds of local jobs has been put on hold because one day an orange-bellied parrot may decide to fly over the area, even though they have not been seen in this location for a quarter of a century'.

Should the point that a species no longer exists negate the importance of a habitat? Clearly not. The absence of species indicates the possibly imminent collapse of the ecosystem because it was built by animals. The need to urgently rebuild wildlife populations is because we are an animal and the life support processes Earth delivers are a consequence of living among wildlife.

Wind forward fifteen years and Hunt's government was overseeing federal laws that protect Australia's Ramsar-listed Moreton Bay Marine Park, which is being assessed for a major property development. If approved it could destroy fifty hectares, including areas used by the critically endangered far eastern curlew, one of many birds that use the site to fatten up and prepare for a single ten-day, non-stop fight to wetlands in China, then on to Arctic breeding grounds. Only eleven of more than 1,700 federal environmental assessments for developments in important habitats have ever been turned down, and the odds are stacked against the bird because impact assessments are founded on impossible expectations.

In the 1980s, far eastern curlews numbered about 28,000, but now their population is fewer than 5,000[255] – an 81.4 per cent decline in thirty years.[256] Once far eastern curlews become as rare as orange-bellied parrots, they will no longer even be considered a useful indicator of value and we will no longer be able to study the impact they have on wetland function.

Take the indiscriminate shooting and poisoning of birds of prey. In Australia recently, a farmer was arrested for killing 406 wedge-tailed eagles, jailed for two weeks and fined $2,500. This number of eagles would have been occupying many thousands of square kilometres and have very clearly defined home ranges, the result of evolved connection with the ecosystem. The loss of each eagle would have significant impact on pest suppression and soil fertility across hundreds of farms, yet the farmer bore little or no cost of this loss.

I did a calculation of what might be the real cost using UN estimates of land degradation, and assuming that wedge-tailed eagles, as a top predator, are literally holding the ecosystem together. I worked out that it would take 29 years to recover 406 birds in the population and their combined territories would cover 1,456 square kilometres. Very conservatively, the cost works out at US$82 per hectare per year (compared to land value of US$2,271 per hectare). The total cost of killing 406 eagles came to $43 million, and that's only 0.7 per cent of the land's value over that period, taking into consideration depreciation. The difference between $2,500 and $43 million represents the degree of difference between what society *thinks* animals are worth and what they really *are* worth.

Why should it fall to conservationists to press charges when the impact is on national food security and the income of neighbouring farmland?

Our pitiful pecuniary measures for deliberately killing wild animals exist because we haven't yet realised that wildlife is a priceless part of any functioning ecosystem. When it comes to animals, the tragedy of the commons is alive and well. In Scotland, custodians of grouse moors kill hen harriers based on the ill-conceived idea that removing top predators increases grouse abundance. In the short-term, maybe, but it collapses the whole supporting ecosystem to create potentially irreversible loss. Japanese Taiji fishermen kill dolphins to stop them competing with commercially important tuna, when the reality is dolphins and tuna are part of interconnected ocean processes. In the case of commercial fisheries, ninety per cent are fished to the max[257] and despite some being considered 'sustainable', that can't be the case without the supporting ecosystem, which depends on overall ocean health and an abundance of wildlife. Having sustainable fisheries means having seabirds, sharks, whales and everything else too.

Even for the most intact ecosystems, we're not very good at quantifying their value to society because when they are undamaged they are the equivalent of a lightbulb that shines so faintly it lasts almost forever. The bulb seems to serve no obvious function to us until we suddenly need light. However, the moment we turn it up, the elements start to burn, chemical reactions wear down the metal and quite soon the bulb fails, creating permanent loss and waste. Our behaviour and the value we place on ecosystems are entangled with our fate, just like the bulb.

Consider a completely functioning, pristine ecosystem, untouched by humans, where animals are at their peak performance, reducing ecosystem chaos. The system is in a steady stable state and emitting no surplus energy. In conservation science we almost always measure ecosystems once they are breaking. We find it difficult to measure the value of fully functioning ecosystems or even know what they are: the moment they become relevant to us, they have become degraded, polluted or animals disappear – we have altered the system.

Likewise, if a scientist studies the short-term consequence of our behaviour, this can reveal different, outdated and often opposite results to what is happening at the population level – like in the prisoner's dilemma. The individuals can survive by being uncooperative, even if their behaviour is a dying trait for the population as a whole. Future survival behaviour often occurs on the margins. It's the dynamics of change and diversity that keep ecosystems healthy. If we went back 10,000 years to study the relationship between frigatebirds and fisheries on Nauru, we might struggle to see a connection. The relationship only formed after thousands of generations. Evolutionarily stable strategies are often so subtle, they don't present a measurable opportunity in the short term. It is simply not possible to describe or understand the long-term consequences of animal impact by measuring what happens today.

Every day, there are hearings – both in courtrooms and in the court of public opinion – that influence the direction of public policy so that we can have a more habitable and just planet. Decisions to protect animals are rarely made without a huge, costly and open-ended commitment to research, but does the gain in information outweigh the loss of time when it finally reveals significant impacts on public health?

It took two decades for scientists to unravel complex evidence about cyanobacterial neurotoxins killing bald eagles and other animals in the US.[258] The cause? The scientists think it comes from bromide in herbicides being used to destroy pest plants. It took forty years for scientists in *The Lancet* to publish work showing that the use of DDT pesticide (which also killed birds of prey) may have been the cause of one in six premature human births and deaths of babies.[259] We already knew pesticides destroyed ecosystem structure and function and if we had addressed that problem from the start, maybe we would not have had a human health problem.

Because ecosystems are so ridiculously complex, we end up compartmentalising studies as though they exist in a vacuum and there is no outside influence … no entropy acting on the lifeforms. Any study's conclusions may be absolutely correct, but if you apply the results at scale or long-term, the factors can become arbitrary and the outcome uncertain. It's the same reason humans will more often than

---

Birds of prey, like these wedge-tailed eagles in Australia, are among Earth's biggest predators. Their loss creates an immediate impact on ecosystem processes. Killing birds of prey also kills the land and has far-reaching negative consequences for our economies.

not lose the prisoner's dilemma game but a successful species who plays the game over hundreds of thousands of years can win – because the population that behaves more cooperatively is the one that survives.

Much of our scientific decision-making is based on principles that were never designed to evaluate the function and importance of ecosystems. Modern statistics are grounded in the work of theorists like Karl Pearson who, at University College London in 1889, studied crop variation as part of the agricultural revolution, to make decisions on a farm-by-farm basis and for the improvement of yield. This inspired the application of artificial fertilisers and led to many of the environmental problems we face today. When Pearson was creating his work, Einstein hadn't completed his second law of thermodynamics and Darwin had only recently published his theories of natural selection. A hundred and forty years later and ecologists, ecological consultants and conservationists are still using conventional statistical approaches and, every day, we make arbitrary and misleading assumptions about how these results stack up.

Unfortunately, this ecologically implausible approach also favours politics over progress, because scientific proof at scale will always be a panacea. We are so driven by the need to understand and prove everything that science has become consumed by a lust for more data and exposed itself to a vastness of disordered information, meaning we struggle to make sensible decisions.

It's the same reason you can't always decide who is right and who is wrong when you're watching the news.

According to a University of California study in 2009, Americans are reading more than ever, and it can be quantified in bytes of data –

the average being about thirty-four gigabytes every day. From 1980 to 2008, the number of bytes consumed increased by 350 per cent,[260] leading to information overload, brain fog and mental illness such as depression and anxiety. Our constant access to data through our mobile phones is polluting our minds. Even our published scientific discourse doubles every nine years[261] and adorns itself with endless ecological studies compartmentalising research into smaller and smaller fragments, with little if any objectivity or purpose for practical conservation. As far back as 1965, Derek de Solla Price said of about 35,000 journals that much of the content is background noise and without strategy.[262] Though, to be fair, there are a lot of unifying studies but we aren't always aware of these.

These approaches to channelling data into the human brain are the antithesis of Shannon's information theory – Shannon being the very person who helped build the principles on which this digital information flows. No animal, including humans, processes every piece of visual and audible data all the time, as it would drive us mad. We don't need to be able to understand everything, we just need to know how to behave in an evolutionarily stable way.

When we model ecosystems, neural function or even pandemics, we are presented with highly complex systems that change over time, and to have any chance of understanding how to behave, we have to create a virtual model (like a brain does) that simplifies things – we make inferences based on what we call 'common sense', a balance of probability that leads to the most likely fifty per cent surviving.

Traditional science faces a dilemma when trying to describe these systems, as there is no right and wrong; there are only better or worse choices today. This is because the systems aren't at equilibrium, they are in a steady state, which means we remain at all times vulnerable to outside influence and we have to adapt our response continuously. We have built a scientific industry based on big data and placed an expectation on scientists to tell the future, but that's impossible. Carl Sagan said 'science is part and parcel humility'.[263] Accepting that science is not certain, that there can never be proof but that we still have to make sensible decisions, is the first step towards finding a new way to see.

It becomes clear that this obsession is a primary reason we have failed to conserve animals and, being an evolutionarily unstable strategy, it won't help save the human race either. Scientists call this a 'complex systems dilemma', in which uncertainties stack together until everything is incalculable and confusing.

The good news is that astrophysicists, conservationists, neuroscientists, epidemiologists and many others are now adopting 'complex systems science', which takes macro trends and relates these to microscale outcomes using generative models to describe how systems work. The results have proved to be extraordinarily accurate and much quicker than conventional models because it looks at the structures that are needed to maintain stability. This is much the same as how animal brains connect to ecosystems.

A common criticism of complex science theory, though, is that it has no explicit mechanism; that it is just a principle. How is it, then, that its theories can make accurate predictions?

As Karl Friston points out,[150] these types of approach have only just begun to gain consideration. Similarly, our most profound communication technology, the way our own brains work and our whole society's political and legal systems depend on maintaining order, minimising disruption and chaos. Why would we trust in those principles for everything we hold sacred but disregard the same when it comes to conservation?

Ecosystems, however small or large, are complex. John Harte of the University of California says we don't have enough knowledge to put all these into a model, so instead we tend to choose one or two and ignore others, or we study partial systems, basing models of complex systems on upfront and arbitrary choices about what drives explicit mechanisms.[264] Ecology is also complex because species are constantly being driven to extinction. As Harte points out, physicists don't have to worry about waking up to find the Higgs boson went extinct overnight.

The science is in understanding the factors that determine the shape and patterns of the outcome. Once that's understood, it's possible to identify the main mechanisms driving, for example, ecosystem stability or resilience. The most profound and obvious being the need to restore an abundance of animals at the right proportions for a quality of life. The question becomes, why spend years researching how this works, when one could spend time and money creating the conditions to create the outcome?

It's widely acknowledged that factors such as species richness, connectivity and genetic diversity confer stability on ecosystems, even in modified landscapes.[265] A scientific model of 15,848 globally distributed animal communities, including butterflies, birds, mammals and plants, was produced that could predict between eighty-three and ninety-three per cent of the observed variation in the abundance of species. In other words, we can accurately predict the range of common versus rare species in a community anywhere on Earth.[266] Similar predictions can be made about the number of species by area, spatial distributions of individuals within species, the distribution of body sizes and metabolic rates (which connects to the amount of energy animals use) and the abundance of animals with different metabolic rates – larger animals have lower metabolic rates and vice versa.

Throughout ecology there are trends repeated at all manner of scales and across species and ecosystem types, and it has been shown across many scientific disciplines that the wrong question to ask is: what is the mechanism?[13] Harte points out that the sheer volume of mechanisms mean any one of them is unlikely to be singularly strong enough to alter patterns over multiple spatial scales and that instead, each species has an equal role to play.

Evaluating ecosystems then becomes a matter of recognising the structures and what we need to do to protect them. It's about us doing what we are designed to do as animals, to recreate the environment for ourselves and all wildlife to prosper. It's about asking: how do we protect the life support mechanisms that nature provides? That is the role that science should be playing, not merely trying to measure or replicate what's already broken. Or worse, forcing nature to do what we want it to. As Judith Schwartz reveals in *The Reindeer Chronicles*,[241] there has been rapid growth in the kinds of approaches that see people trying, at least, to restore natural processes. Examples Schwartz describes, such as China's Loess Plateau, have seen dustbowls turned back into farmland. This would have been unimaginable if not for the determination of a few visionaries who believe in the power of humanity to change environments for the better. All we need now is to accept the urgency of letting wildlife take charge and trust in our animality.

It's about doing what we evolved to do 300,000 years ago and allowing Earth to restabilise itself, the consequence being systems of life support for all. Simply doing science is not going to achieve this; it's only going to inform. We've become consumed by an agenda that aims to describe how things work, rather than making them work.

The world didn't wait to sign the nuclear non-proliferation treaty until scientists had proved there would be no third world war. Herbert York and Jerome Wiesner in *National Security and the Nuclear-Test Ban*[267] wrote about how technology would play no part in disarmament, which would require a change in human values. When we discovered the hole in the ozone layer in 1985, we didn't wait to find out whether the threat of planet-wide ecosystem collapse and rampant cancers from our use of fridges and aerosol cans would be a major problem; we acted to phase them out. We are now beginning to realise the impact of our dependence on fossil fuel and doing something about it. The canary in the coalmine isn't going to be much use if it dies of starvation long before we realise we're in danger from our own toxic build-up.

Our ability to evaluate the importance of ecosystems is nothing unless we accept the equality of wildlife within landscapes. It's not just about the impact we have on them, it's also about the impact they have on us. This is what delivered conditions just right for humankind to flourish in the first place. Let's stop thinking in terms of the impacts of wildlife loss. We share in those costs, but we also share in the benefits animals bring to our environment. They bring us stability, and that is why we need their protection. We cannot use technology or science to recreate biodiversity. We can only protect wildlife and allow nature time to reconnect itself.

Before we can do anything, we need to change the narrative and realise that animals are more equal to us than we have ever imagined before.

Substitute technology for ecology

When I started my ecology degree at the University of East Anglia in 1992, the concept of 'deep ecology' was almost twenty years old. Coined by Norwegian philosopher Arne Næss, it differentiated from 'reformist' or 'shallow' ecology, both of which trade human materialistic gain and try to offset environmental losses. It was under the latter principles that I spent twenty years as an ecological consultant and, to be fair, there were many instances where our teams were involved in the recreation of lost habitat. There is nothing more gratifying than to see the return of wild animals to areas where they had previously been lost. Some 'rewilding' is possible with a focus on structure and function of wetlands and grasslands. The repatriation of great-crested newt populations into ephemeral pools and reconnecting or maintaining ancient wetland fragments was a thrill, as was the recreation of lost water vole habitat.

Over the years, however, these wins became the exception. It was becoming increasingly clear that we'd consumed too much from nature already and that our attempts to borrow more, to try to fix the problems we'd made already, was going to force us into an irreversible debt cycle with Earth. As Elizabeth Kolbert puts it in the excellent book *Under a White Sky*,[268] we are creating even greater environmental problems by trying to solve them using the same approaches that caused them in the first place.

In the latter years, and before I gave up consulting in what is affectionately called 'brown field' ecology, I found it increasingly difficult to negotiate or envisage any way to create a gain, or even guarantee no loss, of biodiversity. Too many decisions are encoded into regulations that sidestep biodiversity considerations and put wildlife at risk – back then I didn't realise this was putting human survival at risk too. Many rare species and important ecosystems are traded for the illusion of economic gain without any realisation of the critical need for wildlife for human survival.

The natural processes that animals provide can't be replicated because they are delivered in an acutely accurate way based on millions of years of trial and error – and as they go extinct, we can't even tell where the most important places are. Animals are still our only road map to understanding biodiversity. Animals precisely distribute energy on a planetary scale, to sustain the system and respond adaptively to subtle fluctuations in patterns of weather and ocean currents. To replicate conditions artificially would be impossible. There isn't enough time to gather the knowledge of how to do it. All the funding and human resources, instead, need to be put into implementing change by rebuilding wildlife populations.

As ecosystems like Australia's Great Barrier Reef begin to collapse from bleaching caused by pollution and ocean temperature rise, we are starting to witness investment in absurd engineering solutions that at best will maintain a small and low-value reservoir of species, heavily managed, while the rest of the system declines around it. Proposals range from gene manipulation, giant fans to pump cool water to the surface, cloud-seeding from vessels and ultra-thin surface films to sunscreen corals, and the dumping of millions of tonnes of crushed rock to de-acidify seawater. In the Kansas locust plagues of 1874, people were paid to invent all manner of harebrained schemes to kill the insects, even resorting to dynamite. Dave Anthony and Gareth Reynolds in the superb podcast series *The Dollop* talk about a JA King from Boulder who invented a locust vacuum cleaner and farmers using a sheet of horse-drawn iron covered in tar like a giant piece of fly-paper.[269]

In 2020 in New South Wales, Australia, farmers were given permission to aerially bomb a mouse plague using pesticide-laden drones, which can't possibly replace the work of thousands of birds of prey covering millions of hectares. And besides, wildlife suppresses mice populations before they become a problem. Once it's a plague, it's way too late. Meanwhile, indiscriminate poisoning simply kills more of the predators that would naturally control mouse numbers and increases the risk of the plague recurring later. An Australian publication from 1999 about rodent control even identifies a lack of progress despite sophisticated rodenticides and approaches. The same publication points to natural predator decline as a key driver for mouse populations getting out of control.[270] Policymakers are either unaware or won't believe that animals can have that much impact on ecosystems.

Either way, our indiscriminate efforts to counteract nature's rebalancing of ecosystems using our technology are at best desperate and at worst a sort of eco-alchemy. When you consider the scale of what we're trying to do, engineering solutions to combat climate change are frankly ludicrous, yet super-charged with investment from politicians and billionaires desperate to commercialise themselves out of a dire situation and look like heroes (if you really want to be a hero, just invest in restoring nature and wildlife populations). With ideas for giant fans on the Great Barrier Reef, we've not come far from the 'fly-paper' efforts of farmers to kill locusts in Kansas in 1874.

NASA has reported as realistic the prospect of eventually terraforming Mars using a giant magnetosphere to deflect solar radiation, creating a thicker atmosphere and liquid surface water within a lifetime.[271] Even if this is plausible, the climate chaos and absence of sustainable ecosystems and animal life for millions of years would make it virtually impossible to engineer the kind of stability needed to support an economically healthy human population. The Biosphere 2 experiment put scientists in a structure with no connection whatsoever to the outside world, dependent for food and air, on what could be produced inside. It couldn't guarantee keeping eight people alive for two years without hundreds of millions of dollars of cost blow-out due to the unimaginable complexity of a tiny self-contained system, let alone a whole planet.[272]

It was interesting to see the conclusion of Amazon Prime's third season of sci-fi series *The Expanse* when Martian terraforming fails and people living there flee instead to already-habitable planets through an alien star-gate. It will slowly dawn on people that we can't live anywhere except Earth and in any case, what makes us think we can create something better when we can't even fix what we have now?

The animals that were doing the tasks well to begin with will be gone soon, and unless we do something quickly, it could soon be too late for us to realise that we should have been listening to the conservationists all along – that the Extinction Rebellion movement really does have a point.

Our use of agricultural technology continues to be counter-effective. Cultivated land has a fraction of the biomass value of intact grassland, even though it is heavily supplemented with fertiliser. Spiders, so important in forest and grassland, are hardly represented in cropland because when we add chemicals to the environment we destroy its structure. As we lose birds of prey and songbirds, diversity declines, free energy increases and a few adventitious species benefit and we enter a vicious cycle of pest management. As we continue to expand our dependence on artificially engineered conditions, we become locked into an ever-increasing debt to the Earth, financed by our personal taxes or paid for in the increasing cost of agrochemicals that make the situation worse.

These days phosphorus is mostly dug from finite rock reserves in North Africa, and from 1961 to 2011 production to feed a growing world population rose from 45.5 megatonnes to 198 megatonnes.[273] Its low cost has led to chronic pollution as the world's arable land and pastures are indiscriminately loaded with so much waste phosphorus; it has flowed into lakes, bays, rivers and estuaries, wiping out biodiversity processes. It even threatens Australia's Great Barrier Reef.[274]

Before this, the ecosystem had reached its most likely stable state based on smaller quantities of phosphate, spread over larger areas by animals such as seabirds. Animals put the brake on overproduction, acting like valves to limit the risk of introducing too much chaotic free energy into the system at once or in the wrong places. Today coastlines and farmland face a double threat, one from the imposition of their excess polluting chemicals and the other from the decline in animals: the loss of processes that enriched the soil, waterways and ocean, on which humanity was first built and on which our future depends.

Most people that currently live on Earth have grown up in a culture that largely believed food production was dependent on using nutrients in excess. This can be traced back to the agricultural revolution after World War II. It all started in Mexico in the 1950s, when research into chemical fertilisers was used to improve wheat yields and bolster domestic food security.

The results of agricultural 'improvement' after World War II were so rapid they were adopted worldwide, and for generations we've become brainwashed into thinking using technology to control landscapes is the right and only way to survive. If you think in terms of energy and waste, it makes less sense.

Pouring nutrients into a system creates initial disruption but ultimately reduces productivity as processes fail when the structure and function of ecosystems break down due to surplus energy. We saturate soil with nutrients to such a degree that once the plants we grow to eat are farmed, we are burning the remaining soil at orders of magnitude faster than natural processes can replace it.[275] As a result of rapid cropland production, we will see the collapse of agriculture – even the UK government forewarned of this impending collapse, as reported by the *Guardian* in October 2017 in a piece titled 'UK is 30–40 years away from "eradication of soil fertility", warns Gove'.

About the history of the British and Irish countryside, Oliver Rackham wrote about depressing changes since 1945, caused by the replacement of normal landscape dynamics with simple destruction by modern agriculture and forestry.[5] Rackham was referring to fallout from 'the years that the locust hath eaten', words from the Minister for the Coordination of Defence, repeated by Winston Churchill in 1936. These words spawned a revolution in UK agriculture, a postwar reapportioning of land and the annihilation of rural landscapes and historic heritage to raise yields and recover the economy.

According to the Food and Agricultural Organization, about eleven per cent of Earth's land surface is currently in crop production, with up to thirty-six per cent considered potentially suitable.[276] When

There are places in Australia where you can truly stand and see or hear dozens of birds at once. The world's agricultural landscapes used to be like this because entire economies were built on the impact of wildlife. A return to these dynamic animal-driven systems is still superior and more cost-effective than any of our technology.

it comes to our land-based food security, these are the facts we can be certain about:

1. Increased use of fertiliser damages soil integrity leading to more rapid loss of natural solutions for soil fertility replacement, which leads to topsoil erosion.
2. Planting more vegetation on farms does not increase soil productivity, because if it did, we wouldn't need fertilisers.
3. The original soil that we used for agriculture was created entirely by animal-driven processes.

The only solution to creating viable farms in the future is restoring wildlife populations. I grew up around farmland, and it staggers me that farmers are still being convinced to waste their future on decades of broken promises from profit-driven agrochemical companies and genetic engineers. Instead, every farmer should be looking to animal impact to rebuild and preserve the integrity of our land. Anyone who advises farmers to the contrary will be contributing to the rapid demise of global food security, and we can't turn to science for yet more years of research into what is blatantly obvious. If we're prepared to ruin everything in the short term by experimenting with more and more chemicals, why not experiment with nature-based solutions instead? Things can only get better.

We should definitely be concerned about the drastic reduction of wildlife populations, the accelerated loss of soil in the absence of animal processes and evidence that plant-driven soil erosion may have contributed to mass extinctions 350 million years ago. All this adds up to reducing Earth's capacity to support people. We are essentially digging the ground out from under our feet, and we are going to need wildlife at all levels to support this foundation's reconstruction because, no matter how hard we try, we cannot moderate our own dispersal of fertiliser well enough to recreate what billions of animals did before us.

The Hope Farm project, an initiative of the UK's Royal Society for the Protection of Birds, started in 2000 and has proved it's possible to increase wildlife populations while maintaining farm profitability.[277] Simple practical measures have meant overall number of bird territories has almost tripled and there has been a more than 400 per cent increase in the populations of important pollinators including bees and butterflies.

Most importantly, the project is now focused on addressing soil degradation. Projects like this are still sold under the mantra of 'conservation of species' when they are really the key to human survival – the key to future farming. Conservation, however, cannot be achieved until there is a change in human values. Hope Farm will not create food security, in just the same way as one person refusing to carry a handgun in the US won't stop school killings – that requires a national change in values.

Conservationists are often attacked for either being an obstacle or not being able to provide a solution to a problem, but we already know what needs to be done; we just can't do it at the necessary scale or without help from everyone else. It doesn't help that the politics of conservation drives a wedge between the people who know what to do and the landowners who stand the most to gain from their wisdom. Conservationists are underpaid and under-appreciated, and it will remain that way until farmers, fishers, politicians and the public in general accept that the efforts to restore wildlife are essential for their economies and survival.

Accept there is a limit to our population

I can't write this book without talking about human overpopulation, yet it's a subject for which I have no solution. Creating more non-human animals won't fix this. Instead, I would like to reflect on a 1964 tongue-in-cheek article John Heaver Fremlin wrote in *New Scientist*, in which he forecast human population expansion on a rate of doubling every thirty-seven years. The paper remains a witty portent of the future.

In it, Fremlin wrote of the (imagined) first 260 years after the human population reached 400 billion people after effective cooperation had been reached in the application of food technology, adding that to reach this first step would require 'the complete elimination of all land wildlife, the agricultural use of roofs over cities and roads, the elimination of meat-eating and the efficient harvesting of sea food'.[278] By 450 years' time, Fremlin was predicting the need to use massive solar arrays to light up the night sky, to generate sufficient photosynthesis to feed a population eating nothing but microorganisms, all other wildlife having been removed from the oceans. Eventually, after 890 years, his imagined population faced major heat regulation problems and needed housing for about 120 people per square metre – as the author points out, 'other possible limitations than heat will doubtless have occurred to readers'.

As amusing as his insights are, the underlying notion that there is a limit to human population can't have escaped anyone's attention on Earth, yet discussions about this inescapable problem remain scarce. Ten years ago, the United Nations Environment Program published a report predicting 9.1 billion people by 2050 and that curbing meat consumption was then, as it is now, vital to avoid world hunger.[279]

No-one really knows how many people can live on Earth – it's all theoretical – but we are almost certainly beyond a sustainable number already. There is barely a patch of land left unaffected by our existence. This is why conserving oceans is so essential: nearly three-quarters of Earth's surface is covered by ocean, responsible for one and a half times more annual carbon uptake than land plants.[258] It's our last line of defence against planetary ecosystem collapse.

Restore wildlife to survive

As a society, we have a loose grasp on ecology. Ecosystems are vastly complex and cannot be fixed by engineers, only by wildlife. One of the most profound ecological oversights of our lifetime might be the failure to acknowledge that animals are essential to balancing Earth's food security, water and climate. The path to a fair climate takes us via the creation of rich soils, healthy oceans, abundant food and a better quality of human life overall.

This should act as a warning that without animals, planting trees to address climate change might remove carbon from the atmosphere but could kill the oceans instead. We may be air-breathing animals, but we cannot survive without healthy oceans, and if we don't start thinking about rewilding the land, planting trees may do more harm than good. A recent study in *Nature* even reveals how decades of tree planting in India has failed to increase forest cover or improve livelihoods.[280]

Dredging companies more used to creating artificial islands, harbours and shipping channels have been asked to re-deepen Lake Sinai in the Middle East, which has become so silted up it's a mere few metres deep in places. There are 2.5 billion tonnes of what can probably only be described as 'toxic' sediment that they think can be used to rebuild farmland across the region. There is good evidence that the Sinai was deforested by ancient civilisations thousands of years ago.

Large-scale terraforming will not create an ecosystem unless there are animals, and each time we completely alter an existing landscape we set the clock back to zero and delay its progress to recovery once more. We have to tread carefully. Why would we think planting more new forests in the desert would be the answer to our environmental problems when Earth has more tree cover today than it did thirty-five years ago?[1] *Science Daily* published a piece titled 'Study challenges ecology's "Field of Dreams" hypothesis'. The hypothesis, put simply, is if you build a habitat, the animals will come. Scientists reported that the effects of 'management' that included animal reintroduction were six times stronger than the effects of plant biodiversity.[281] If ecologists thought about ecosystems in terms of animal impact and chaos suppression, it would be easier to understand why this is the case.

Ecosystems have to be readied for wildlife before we start replanting forests, otherwise we're creating a new sink for finance, where newly engineered habitat can make pollution worse and become dependent solely on human management for years to come. And one species cannot create stable, liveable ecosystems alone. We have to introduce animals from the start, look after them and prepare ourselves for a period of messiness, while animals get things back under control.

Fields of crops or urban parks are an illusion of tidiness, because on the outside, they look uniform and 'fit' our world view. The fact that land will erupt with life the moment it is left to nature reveals how much free surplus energy there is in the system. That's the energy that causes ecosystem malfunction and chaos. It's also the same reason why we have invasive pests.

When we abandon land, animals immediately ship nutrients in, in vast quantities. The plants that begin to grow are among the first building blocks. It's like a delivery of bricks, cement and sand to a building site (and when have you ever seen a completely tidy construction site?). It's only when animals start to work with these raw ingredients that they start to resemble something liveable.

In ecosystems each animal plays a role, and their functions are partitioned. This seems rather obvious. When you consider that if all animals had exactly the same function, there could be no 'ecosystem'. That would be like running a farmers' market with farmers but no delivery personnel, no people to put up the market stalls, no stallholders or customers. Like economies, ecosystems cannot exist without functional animal diversity.

Australian coral reef scientists have revealed how nearly forty per cent of all ecosystem tasks are done by one specialist fish species out of over 6,000.[282] This is how the role of animals in ecosystems is partitioned, in exactly the same way it is in our economy. Not everyone is a hairdresser, grocer or taxi driver. There is nothing synthetic that is anywhere near as exquisitely constructed as an ecosystem that animals build, or provides as many livelihoods for all animals, including humans.

To build natural economies at scale, though, can take thousands of years, as with the neat park-like structures and thick soils that early European settlers described when they first reached Australia. Remember, the systems and processes humans exist in are the ones that wildlife create (because we are an animal). To build a home on Earth requires the diversity and abundance of animal life needed to fulfil every job in the ecosystem construction process. That includes us.

Local people are ultimately going to have to look after the land, so they also need to be able to make a living – they are, after all, one of the most conspicuous and biggest animals. It's encouraging to find that the Great Green Wall of the Sahel has moved towards locally led programs, and maybe the Sinai will do the same. Even then, there is little focus on wildlife because there is as yet little to no global recognition that animals are the critical driver for ecosystem recovery and human survival.

Nature is always a better solution than human engineering. In Australia, where eighty-five per cent of the population lives near the coast, the cost of sea defence construction, maintenance and upgrades is not economically viable.[283] Replacing natural processes has unintended consequences. Engineering solutions to nature's free support inevitably increases taxes, and this loss makes it more expensive for all of us to live in the twenty-first century.

Despite the risk of widescale financial failure, billionaires are getting in on the action. There are prizes for engineering solutions to climate change and terrifying ideas about artificial cloud-seeding, which at worst could spiral into a competition between countries and at best cause even more disruption of weather patterns than there is currently

– a process that was working fine before the collapse of global seabird colonies. Iron fertilisation in the Southern Ocean is being suggested as a way to promote the growth of photosynthesising algae in the belief this will increase carbon capture, but it will simply add more energy to a system that hasn't enough animals left to cope. We have lost almost ninety-nine per cent of blue whales, and these, among many others, are the mechanism that could allow us to subtly re-engineer systems, in the knowledge they provide a safety net for our unsystematic approach – for that is all it can ever be. We can never precisely replicate ocean iron cycles that animals did so precisely before.

We're talking about throwing massive amounts of free energy at enormously sensitive systems that drive a planet's core functionality for human survival. Why would we imagine we could be any better at doing that to the atmosphere and ocean than we have been with fertilising the land? We're entering new territory, literally, and we have no idea the damage we will do.

Planting trees on land while we allow animals to go extinct is just another source of destabilising energy and risks sacrificing our oceans to save our atmosphere. As you drive down suburban tree-lined streets, particularly in autumn, you will see vegetation gathered everywhere in gutters, piling up around storm drains and washing into our bays, rivers and estuaries. At the base of every plant, leaves are shed continuously, piling up as waste that's emitted over almost every square inch of unpaved Earth.

Physicists started questioning some of the assumptions around Darwin's theory of natural selection almost as soon as the second law of thermodynamics was published in the early 1900s, yet over a hundred years later, we're still largely ignoring the profound impact of Einstein's discovery on our approach to conservation. His simple unifying concept of entropy, which predicts that ecosystems will fall into chaos without animals, hasn't been taught upfront to university students studying ecology over the last few decades. A whole generation of conservationists seem largely unaware of how these systems connect, and this untold story is what's missing from the global dialogue on climate change and why we have not been able to justify animal conservation as part of that. Yet.

It's recently been suggested that sargassum, a type of floating seaweed, is critical to carbon sequestration.[284] Despite apparent declines in the mid twentieth century,[285] though, sargassum has increased substantially in the last ten years.[286] In 2019, the biggest seaweed blooms ever recorded swamped the tropical Atlantic, with 20 million tonnes of seaweed stretching 8,850 kilometres between the Gulf of Mexico and West Africa.[287] These dying plants are starving the ocean of oxygen, killing animal life and rotting away on beaches, destroying tourism. Why? Because of an ecosystem imbalance almost certainly caused by the collapse of entire ocean food chains.

These might seem trivial matters, but a politician will think that because you have more seaweed, that 'Nature is adjusting, we're all going to be okay'. Whereas the real problem – the lack of wildlife – is overlooked.

The world's ecosystems are already responding to increasing atmospheric carbon by naturally increasing global vegetation cover.[237] (The Earth is getting warmer, and there is more carbon dioxide in the atmosphere, like there was 350 million years ago.)

Deliberately adding more waste-producing plants to our world, without a parallel commitment to wildlife conservation, will create more problems than it solves. It's the same reason we need to be really careful about pouring pesticides on locusts. Locusts aren't the cause of crop damage; the cause is loss of songbirds. Pests are a symptom of an environment we have changed.

Most conservation is done in tiny patches of land where the biodiversity benefits of animals aren't shared by our farmers and fishers. Proving animals are essential for stable climate and food security empowers ecologists. Tree planting, for example, is *not* an ecological solution to climate change unless wildlife and, more specifically, biodiversity is protected alongside.

What we need to be doing is regrowing ecosystem structures and stocking them with abundant wildlife everywhere. This would give conservation ecologists the recognition they deserve for securing humanity's future, and they, not engineers, should be at the frontline of solving these most urgent of the world's problems.

PART 6-

The way forward

Anthropocene: the era of self-preservation

As a wildlife conservationist, you want to preserve a world rich in animals because you know this is what needs to happen, but maybe you haven't yet been able to explain why. I hope this book goes some way to helping you do this and justifying the work of all those people I know, and more, who devote their lives to the protection of wildlife all over the world. We can build a new way to see wildlife that can be used by everyone to understand how critical animals are for our world and inspire a new generation of support for animal welfare and conservation.

As prehistoric large animals declined, humans had to become more specialised to hunt smaller prey, and their brains increased in size. However, brain size has nothing to do with intelligence. Intelligence is a measure of how elegantly your species is connected to country. That is what determines your ability to survive.

By reimagining how the world works we can find the missing piece that connects conservation with the future of humanity. It's how we need to start thinking, if we're to make the right decisions for humanity's future and understand – and value – the impact animals still have on our world today.

I also hope that it will give everyone else the chance to realise we can be part of the solution as well as the problem, because that is why and how we exist. The truth is that human survival can only be guaranteed though conservation and coexistence with wild animals, because they are the source of ecosystems that create the life support structures and climate stability we all need to survive. Tread lightly on the Earth, treat animals with respect and learn to live alongside them (whatever the inconvenience) and you are doing more than your fair share for our species' survival.

Saving animals is one very simple objective that can define everything we do from now on to protect our fragile existence on Earth.

Though most of us live in cities, separated from the land, any assumption that wildlife is no longer critical to our future survival would be misguided. Peak success of *Homo sapiens* was only for a short portion of the time we've existed on Earth, while we were surrounded by abundant and diverse animal populations.

We need animals because otherwise the physical Earth is little more than a bowl full of raw unmixed ingredients. The bowl represents Earth's physical conditions: the continents, ocean basins, wind and currents, filled with the sugars that plants extract. This energy settles where it's most likely to, based on its shape. Earth's mixing bowl could have had continents arranged in different ways and we would be having the same conversations now, identifying identical processes in different places.

Unmixed energy is not enough for us to live. A mouthful of raw, unmixed ingredients is unpalatable and provides nothing substantial to eat. We have the tendency to think that animals are like the icing on the cake, but they're not; they are the bakers, because it isn't until animals combine the ingredients that they start to resemble something edible, something with the sugars concentrated in biscuit-sized pieces. Our farming and fisheries are simply mechanisms to harvest the biscuits of energy that animals cooked and distributed for us, providing the concentrated resources that allow us to extract sufficient nutrients to live, maintain Earth's climate and provide job security and welfare for all.

The kitchen, full of tools and animals that do the cooking, is the 'ecosystem'. The mixing processes are called 'biodiversity', and this is the word we all know but don't understand; the crucial component that allows animals to turn habitats into something that gives us life.

The traditional and most widely acknowledged meaning of biodiversity is defined by the 1992 United Nations Convention on Biological Diversity as 'The variability among living organisms from all sources, including, "inter alia", terrestrial, marine, and other aquatic ecosystems, and the ecological complexes of which they are part: this includes diversity within species, between species and of ecosystems'. This is another way of describing all the things that make up an ecosystem and what it does as a result of the combined functionality of all its components.

The interactions between wildlife – from soil to sea – mean everything to our species' survival. Each time you sneeze from hay fever it should serve as a reminder of how unhealthy we've made the Earth by killing animals. Our only way forward is to let wildlife rebuild the rich systems that protect us from harm.

I don't think this definition has enough purpose. It doesn't relate the function to our own survival, or the critical importance of animals in that process. I prefer to say:

Biodiversity conservation is everything animals (including humans) must do to moderate the flow of energy through ecosystems, in order to mitigate the collapse of ecosystems and provide a habitable planet for our survival.

Our most successful habitable period was when we had little free energy in our environment because all the food built on energy supply by plants was cooked into these edible chunks by animals.

When we kill wildlife, we hammer the biscuits and shatter them into crumbs. With fewer animals left, uncooked ingredients are worthless to larger creatures like us but become ideal for plagues of locusts, cockroaches, viruses and bacteria. That's not a habitable world for humans.

We've only just begun to destroy wild animal populations at breakneck speed, and our role on Earth has rapidly switched to one of self-preservation because we can no longer rely on our animal counterparts to look after our basic life support systems. Ironically, Aboriginal humans may have contributed positively to surplus energy from plants by killing megafauna, but that time long since passed. Today we have unbalanced our environment so much and so quickly that killing wildlife makes us our own greatest threat, and we've named this lonely new epoch after ourselves: the Anthropocene. We now owe it to our species to reverse the loss of wildlife for our sake and theirs. And what a wonderful thing that is to hope to achieve together.

Choose not to do to something to make a difference

The most valued of my possessions is a pair of high-quality binoculars I bought in 1996 with my first pay cheque after I left university. They cost the equivalent of about £1,000 in today's money and with a lifetime warranty have enabled me to see countless thousands of birds, mammals, whales and dolphins, landscapes and insects. They've done more to connect me with nature than any other purchase, and they don't plug into the internet, they don't need charging and they are still optically outstanding after thirty years. Go and buy yourself a decent pair of binoculars, and they'll have a bigger impact on your life and learning than almost anything else.

Then ask yourself this question. When was the last time you *didn't* do something, in order to make a difference?

Because of our animality we impose changes on our environment, but what if we could be more sparing? Remember, your choice to do or not to do something is the most powerful influence you have on the universe. Choose not to drive to the shops and instead walk or cycle. Choose not to buy that meat or fish you suspect might be contributing to ecosystem collapse. Choose not to buy that bottled water. Choose not to invest in that company that is causing deforestation. Choose not to book that business flight when you could resolve things by meeting over the phone. Choose not to put the heating on for an hour and instead put on a jumper. Choose not to support leaders who don't care about nature. Choose not to stay silent and complicit when decisions are made that kill animals and affect your future. We spend our lives fretting about what we can do to help when the reality is the greatest impact you can ever have is choosing *not to do something*. It's the ultimate power we all have to make a difference.

And spread the word that wildlife conservation is crucial for creating a habitable planet and for the survival of all animals, including our own species.

An impact statement on behalf of animals

The world we were born into couldn't exist without wildlife because animals and ecosystems are inseparable. Without wildlife, Earth cannot be habitable for human beings.

Each time we remove a wild animal from the environment, we reduce its connectivity to the landscape for its entire lifetime. Its functional activity is lost to our world thousands of times over – the processes that create clean air, fertile soil, rich fisheries and stable climate. We lose animals on a linear scale but the impact, the life support they give us, is lost at an exponential rate and cannot ever be replaced by our technology.

To alter the trajectory of our planet from one that will become uninhabitable to one where humans can survive as part of the nature that made us, we have to rebuild the wildlife populations that support us. Ecologists and conservationists need to be paid to protect animals against all odds, to work with farmers and fishers, to recreate lost species richness and the diversity of life support ecosystems on which our entire global economy is built.

In his blog under the heading 'Which charity?' author Seth Godin explains that we hire non-profit organisations when we don't know how to solve a problem, because organisations that address problems that can be solved are called businesses.

Animals solve a problem we don't know how to solve and one that science never will. It's possibly the biggest existential problem humanity has ever faced. We stand no chance of ever understanding or addressing it through our own technological means. If animals were a non-profit, providing problem-solving services, this would be their impact statement:

Animal Impact Statement

- Animals create ecosystems by building structures that are the mechanism to stabilise planetary energy at scale and avoid catastrophic climate chaos, the death of the oceans and the collapse of human society;
- Animals transfer, amplify and concentrate nutrients on a phenomenal scale, delivering resources to make farms and fisheries economically viable and provide critical and sustainable human food security; and
- Animals suppress the eruption of pandemics and pests like locust, jellyfish and squid, which plague our farms and fisheries and put lives at risk.

Ten-point plan for a change in human values

Here is my ten-point plan to begin the process of creating a global change in human values necessary to start rebuilding wildlife populations. Some of these are things you can do. Others are things you might expect your leaders or conservationists to be doing. You can do your part by being more generous to the animals around you. And you can support those who are steering society to a better outcome for all wildlife:

1. At every level of society put animals first and accept that we owe other animals the same level of respect as humans, because we are an animal and cannot exist without wildlife alongside us.
2. Teach the world how the absence of animals from our lives will almost certainly lead to rapid extinction of the human race and how declines in wildlife are already leading to imminent economic and social collapse.
3. Develop new criteria for species conservation based on animals' contribution to biodiversity (their importance in ecosystem structures and their propensity to transfer, amplify and concentrate nutrients).
4. Teach the relationship between ecosystems and wildlife in school and university courses about ecology and environmental science. This is the only biologically plausible explanation for how the world works. It justifies conservation for humanity's sake.
5. Work with governments all over the world to disassemble policy and regulations that wrongly use scarcity as the surrogate for a species' value, as this has led us to make abundant errors that risk our species' survival. For all decisions that might affect our living environment, instead ask the question, 'What is the animal

impact?' Don't allow anything to be done that would reduce the impact of animals on climate, food security and water.

6 Work with local people, farmers and fishers so they can be the first to understand the impact animals have on their livelihoods and future productivity. Give them the job of becoming leaders in wildlife conservation and sustainability, so they can protect our food security. Because unless they are empowered, we have no food or future.

7 Recognise the work conservationists are doing to save the human species by paying properly for it. Allocate domestic budgets proportionate to the importance of their work in saving global soil and ocean systems, on which everything depends, and connect them with farmers and fishers to transfer knowledge and skills.

8 Invest in the rapid and scalable rebuilding of wild animal populations everywhere. This might include, for example:

    a Introducing a margin for wildlife around every agricultural field in the world and farm this as though it is food (because it is essential for soil integrity).
    b Putting an immediate halt to deliberate or unnecessary killing of any wildlife, such as migratory songbirds.
    c Taking enormous care when using pesticides to temporarily address locust plagues and other 'pests', in case we are making matters much worse.
    d Not allowing the values of protected areas to be destroyed, by any direct or indirect means, through human development.

   e Removing obstacles to large-scale animal survival, and in particular, giving wildlife the room to move around the Earth unimpeded.

9. Do not permit any new development or disturbance of fully functioning habitats that have not already been affected by humans. This would include cutting down primary forest, mining the deep ocean or fishing in mid-ocean habitats. We cannot afford to open up new frontiers of environmental damage.
10. Encourage people to connect with wildlife sustainably, such as through tourism, and actively foster a newfound respect and commitment to animals, their welfare and their lives.

Conclusion: your role in creating a change in human values

The greatest satisfaction I receive in writing this book is knowing that the choices we make as individuals are the most powerful influence and hope we have for our future and the health of planet Earth. The greatest realisation is that animals hold back a tsunami of free energy that, released, will wipe out all of humanity. For decades I've searched for my own clues as to why wildlife conservation matters, and now I've found the answer to share with you.

A change in human values is going to come down to accepting three things:

- That we are all animals like any other;

- That every small action we take individually is among the most powerful contribution any creature can ever make; and
- That we cannot survive unless we live alongside other abundant and diverse wildlife.

When we cut down old growth trees we aren't just removing lumps of wood, we're killing hundreds of animals with quadrillions of touch-points to ecosystems both now and long into the future. When we replant a tree to replace that lost wood, it doesn't have any animals living among its branches. We claim it will grow and sequester more carbon, but we're forgetting that plant carbon becomes wasteful unless animals are present. Without animals, free energy leaks back into the system, overthrowing the acutely evolved processes that stabilised our world. The very word 'eco' comes from the ancient Greek word *oikos* and means the combination of family, household and property. We're trading a home full of furniture, smiling children and laughter for a plywood-facade mansion, like sets in the movies.

When we imagine we can engineer a technical solution to the world's ecological problems, we're forgetting that the resilience of any species against its own extinction is based on stabilised patterns of complexity formed not by being forced into submission but by yielding to patterns animals created for us over millions of years. It's not a linear process. If you throw a million marbles onto your living room floor, they'll settle into a stable structure in less than a minute. Now gather them up and try to forcibly and linearly engineer the same pattern using manual labour. Ecosystems are like an unfathomable number of marbles. We have to fit around the system wildlife made for us because trying to build it mechanically is impossible.

Abundant animals are the only mechanism that holds back the tide of our own demise, and we're squeezing them out of existence. If we think the biggest risk of climate change is a warming planet, we'd be wrong. The risk is unfettered amounts of free energy causing chaos, which cannot be mitigated except by animals. Decline in the resilience of our planet is just as much a function of lack of freezing, not warming, because it's cold conditions that create the greatest rates of speciation and fastest recovery from mass extinctions. If we removed ecosystems from Earth today, we would rapidly descend into an uninhabitable Venus-like state. By thinking in a simplistic linear manner, where heat is bad and cold is good, we're ignoring the dimension of chaos and therefore the role of animals in that part of the equation. We're looking down the wrong end of the telescope, which might explain why we think the problem is smaller and further away than we'd care to admit.

If we think a world without wildlife is unimaginable, we'd be right. Because an Earth without animals isn't the world we were born into, the one that delivers our life support and enabled our species to first exist. That world, which has rich fisheries, fertile soil, clean water and plenty to eat, is built and maintained by animals. We are coupled with the condition of ecosystems, which means we share a common future with all the other creatures that live alongside us. We cannot separate ourselves from their fate and they cannot separate from ours either.

If we think we are the only animals to have culture and society, we'd be wrong. The ability to trade information, to exchange knowledge and make informed decisions is necessary, or ecosystems break down. We're more similar to other animals than we care to admit. Everything from insects to fish, birds and mammals express a social hierarchy and culture that interconnects with the systems that support all animal life on Earth. We are not superior. In the zero-sum game of extinction, we all stand to lose the same things, and because we depend on each other for our existence, we are equal.

If we are led to believe that solutions are complex, think again. Rebuilding wildlife populations and liveable ecosystems is simple; it's society and the inertia we've created for ourselves that makes the solution complicated. Younger generations tend to have a better handle on what to do and a willingness to do it because as we get older we may rigidly adhere to a world view and ideology that blinds us. It's natural that anyone would resent being questioned after they've committed decades of personal energy to a cause they believe in, yet the rapidly shifting baseline caused by ecosystem collapse is rendering attempts to 'manage' fisheries and agriculture out of date almost as soon as they are put into practice. Things are way too complex for researchers to understand with certainty, and by the time we've described how things seem to work, the theories are often already groundless.

But as a human being, another animal that shares this world with all other creatures, you have an inbuilt ability to connect with the way ecosystems function and can understand what needs to be done now, without wasting decades of research proving the obvious. How we behave is our single most powerful influence on the universe, and behave we must. To start making a difference to our own survival we have to stop seeing wildlife as an inconvenience, or a commodity to manage. We have to stop seeing humans as the sole pilot for animal passengers on our flight through space and start managing our own behaviour, so we can live alongside animals with the degree of equity and respect we owe them for giving us ecosystems.

We have to start putting wild animals first because they are the exit strategy for our plan to rebuild our lost world of ecosystems, smashed to pieces by industrial acceleration over the last fifty years. Perhaps some of you may think it's too great a stretch to claim that the environmental problems humanity faces today can be solved by rebuilding wildlife populations. But why else do you think animals exist? What else would make sense, when you are an animal too? Our animality is why we know, deep down, that all animals are essential for a habitable Earth.

The Banda Sea in far eastern Indonesia remains the closest I've come to an untouched wilderness, where people still carve out a life on the sea, entirely dependent on the food it provides. Traditional twin-mast pinisi schooners recreate the ominous outline of 'pirate' ships on the horizon and were plying the world's oceans long before Europeans discovered the region's priceless spices. Today the vessels take us on altogether more demure tourism experiences. In our brief rise as a species on Earth, we have capitalised on the Banda Sea's services to build entire western economies and even today, just like the first European visitors, we are attracted by its natural riches.

The ecology of the Banda Sea is one chapter in the chronicle of human life on Earth with a supporting cast of wildlife that are part of the largest planetary processes, from the biggest animal that ever lived on Earth to its smallest creatures. The region's blue whales, the sea's silvery leviathans, exist in a realm we can only imagine and are only just beginning to understand, despite the best science detective work. In our quest to realise our own aspirations we often forget that the world's animals remain as much a mystery now as they ever did, and that there is still much to be learnt. It is a privilege to live anywhere on Earth; even more so to be offered a rare glimpse into the way this works and discover a profound insight into our actuality as human beings. This opportunity that animals give us to understand our own meaning creates an impression that lasts beyond when any photographic negative has faded or digital storage device has been lost or corrupted.

We now know that humans aren't just the product of Earth, we are the product of the animal community we live among, the one that calmed the chaos of free energy in our ecosystems before we evolved as a species. We know that we exist, like all animals, because we are the most likely outcome of an Earth-based system that extracts energy from the cosmos, and transfers, amplifies and concentrates it inside biological processes, without which we could never find food in adequate abundance. From supermarkets to the internet, video chat, farming and landscapes, the passage between order and chaos explains the behaviour, language, culture and impact of animals on our environment. It underpins the cause and solution to many of our world's problems and – by learning to think differently about the world, as a system of energy that has to be balanced to be equitable and habitable – we can move to a new way of thinking about nature. We can develop a new survival strategy.

When you see a bird feeding in a park, it's moving nutrients around and re-depositing them in tiny areas around its nest and favourite feeding grounds. There are 'hotspots' like this at every scale from the smallest patch of Earth to whole continents, like a billion overlapping energy-containing areas, of just the right dimension, concentration and proximity to allow animals of any size or mobility to make a living.

Animals of different species – including humans – congregate together in these places because they are mutually reliant on each other to reduce free energy. You never see one animal of one type, you see multiple species of different varieties all together, and in some places the congregations are awe-inspiring. If we believe that humans represent one of the most advanced species in the animal kingdom, the end point of a creation of any kind, this means we must accept that we are connected to these places and all the animals that live alongside us. That would seem in keeping with even the most religious doctrine.

We have to accept that there are no ecosystems without animals, and these containers for biodiversity were built because of us and other animals. We have to stop thinking about animals and ecosystems as one thing or the other and realise they are one and the same. A world without animals is like a window without a frame. If you want a window, you need both simultaneously. Animals and ecosystems evolved together, and there is no disconnecting them without leaving a gaping hole in the wall.

Has our society transcended the need to accord with natural principles for survival? I doubt it. If we learn anything from animals, from the history of our planet, the rules seem simple: avoid competition at all costs and don't destroy your living environment. The consequences of failure are absolute.

We would do well to cooperate better as a society because that rule determines our own evolutionary success. But we no longer behave like good animals.

If we cannot treat ourselves and each other with respect, how do we hope to respect the wildlife that will ensure our future? Our species' fertility rates are declining so fast that according to Professor Shanna Swan we could be functionally infertile by mid-century. Swan puts this down to chemicals used to manufacture plastics, which are now in almost everything we touch, eat and even breathe. (Microplastics are now circulating atmospherically). Ironically, we know that imprudent use of chemicals kills animals – in the case of herbicides and pesticides, it's exactly what they are for. What reasonable person wouldn't imagine they might also affect humans? The answer is someone who doesn't think people are animals too. It's almost laughable that we wait decades for research to prove what we know is a patently obvious health risk.

The wildlife that we live alongside gives us the evidence we need to know how to survive. We already place our trust in our own animality every day as it's built into our biology. It even helped us create our best technology. Why not trust the same strategies through the conservation of wildlife when we know this will secure a brighter future for all humanity?

Consistency and cooperation are fundamental strategies for diversification and adaptability that lead to the steadiest stable states of existence but are challenged each day by our politics, which run counter to these natural laws. As Dawkins[247] discussed following Axelrod's prisoner's dilemma experiment in 1981,[249] there are two steady-states we can expect to achieve in the short term at least: one where we act in self-interest and one where we cooperate. The latter is the only evolutionarily stable strategy. Our survival and future quality of life is determined by our ability to cooperate with all animals, as much in our ecosystems as in our own society. If we don't cooperate, we lose the game and go extinct faster. Competition, conflict and disruption are features of a disturbed environment, one in which there are few winners and many losers, and every past mass extinction has proved this. It's why we cannot afford to have divisive politics undermine the conservation narrative and, when we vote, we're not deciding the fate of a political party any more – we're deciding the fate of humanity.

We are fast approaching a world first, a sixth mass extinction that, for the first time, will be caused by a single species: us.

But we are also living in the most extraordinary and exciting time, a period of enlightenment like we've never known, the first time in human history in which our collective minds can comprehend the significance of our place in the universe. And we know how to do things that make a difference. We are fixing the hole in the ozone layer. We are making slow progress but beginning to adopt new standards and technology to address our carbon footprint. All over the world, countries are replanting lost forests and mangroves at accelerating rates – community-driven initiatives where local ambition can scale into a global outcome. Though replanting trees to tackle climate change might replace some of the structure, reengineering the carbon cycle depends on wildlife and people, just as building a stock exchange does not immediately make everyone in the area wealthy. For that, you need a source of traders and businesses to process the money.

Protecting wildlife and accepting its overriding importance in making our planet liveable for humans is a new idea that hasn't yet gained widespread traction because it's near impossible to prove outright. We can only infer the value of wildlife through the sheer intensity and scale of their impact on our world – or by experimenting with restoring wildlife populations. To date we've only destroyed them, so how do we know? This is the change of human values we desperately need to adopt and accept – and fast – to have hope of sustaining our efforts to preserve our own species.

We can travel to look an orangutan in the face to see the expressions and emotions of our own kind reflected in the eyes of an animal that shares ninety-seven per cent of its DNA with us. We can share knowledge through global communication networks. First published in 1768, *Encyclopaedia Britannica* was one of the western world's most authoritative single sources of world knowledge for nearly 244 years and equivalent to about one gigabyte of information. Today, five-hundred times more information than that is uploaded every minute to YouTube. Many of the theories and principles this book describes can be learnt by watching beautifully crafted video narratives that simplify the disorder of countless scientific papers and mathematical equations into easily communicated narratives. When you're ready to delve deeper, almost the entire written history of science is available online to read – a decade ago, it was difficult to research a book like this without academic access. Ten years before that, it was slow trudge through a dialup MS-DOS library database,

before climbing stairs, walking past dozens of floor-to-ceiling bookshelves and thumbing through hard-copy ring-bound journal archives, or waiting a week after ordering copies of papers to be printed and posted from elsewhere in the world.

There is a role for all of us in learning how to make a difference. We achieve an emotional and joyful response with nature because it's the framework for our behaviour and how we connect with the world. As the authors of 'A Brief History of Decision Making' in the *Harvard Business Review*[288] tell us, differing opinions and a diversity of views avoids the bias inherent in the forced unanimity of select groups. The centralised bodies that take charge of sustainable forestry, fisheries and agriculture are failing, and as Ruth DeFries describes in *What Would*

An orangutan rests in a tree in southern Kalimantan, Borneo. Orangutans are both cultivators and consumers of the forest and contribute to the structure and stability of rainforest ecosystems. Our similarity to them should remind us that we come from the same place and share the same fate as all animals. We are all connected.

Nature Do?, top-down solutions have always failed because that's not how nature works.

There is an overwhelming consensus that community-driven and localised control of common resources like fisheries, wildlife and climate are the only way to solve the world's problems. Probably the most important thing anyone can do today is stand up to institutions that erode remaining values. Local parks, roadside verges, playing fields, wildlife reserves, waterways, field edges and even gardens are among the last refuges for world wildlife. According to a recent report, only three per cent of planet Earth remains ecologically intact,[289] but at least thirty per cent is needed to start reversing ecosystem collapse. But it's not about simply making a third of the world into a nature reserve – it's about restoring thirty per cent of the natural world wherever you live too. No-one can tell you that's achievable without your help!

The type of emotion you feel for your local area and your inherent knowledge are necessary prerequisites for decision-making because watching a sunset, walking near a lake or seeing animals all translate into tangible benefits for our livelihoods. A recent study found that bird species richness correlated with household income, suggesting the value of living in natural surroundings with an additional fourteen types of birds might equate to $150 a month more income for the average family.[290] However, it's more likely because we choose to buy a home based on life support factors, which is why real estate agents know that houses on the boundary of wetland, forest and grassland sell for higher prices. The habitat provides fresh water, shelter and a place to hunt. Despite humanity's technological advancements, our animality hasn't changed much after all.

We all have a profound ability to communicate ecosystem complexity and the value of wildlife to each other, through simple facts and phrases of our own that we develop from the inherent knowledge we have as animals. We may be challenged and called out as inaccurate but that doesn't matter because we are part of a collective consciousness that is more influential and important than any organisational or individual opinion. In the book *The Dawn of Everything*[291] by David Graeber and David Wengrow the authors argue that past human societies were just as sophisticated as today. It makes perfect sense. A world rich in biodiversity can only be one where animals – even humans – have developed complex patterns of culture and communication. Societal control was simply more decentralised.

You don't have to change the world either; just influence your bit of it. It's easy to imagine that you can't make a difference unless you're a David Attenborough, Greta Thunberg or Leonardo DiCaprio but that's not true.

If anything, you're the chance for conservation scientists to be creative in thought and deed. In the endless pursuit of knowledge, maybe we overthink the obvious, when the solutions to our world's greatest problems are with local communities. Scientists can help empower you with their knowledge and in turn, they can be inspired by your inventiveness and resolve to build a better world. It's a powerful combination.

Stepping away from the confines and conflicts of a career in research and spending unadulterated time in nature was the only way I could start to make sense of these things. The way I see the natural world now is thanks to the many people who have spent time with me in the wild. It's often non-scientists who have the most valuable and unique perspectives after observing animals in action.

Research provides snippets of detail, but the big picture ideas come from a reinterpretation of complexity ... they come from the imagination. Science can't invent things. Research can, however, help us make better decisions or realise what's in our minds – such as imagining a world with more habitable ecosystems. Isabella Tree in her book *Wilding* says that predicting what will happen when we alter landscapes is like trying to guess the future of an unborn child. The biggest leaps forward in human endeavour have been created by the most inquiring minds, and science can rarely explain how something occurs until after it's been experimented. Renowned scientist and centenarian James Lovelock points this out in his book *Novacene*.[292] The greatest physicist of the nineteenth century, James Clerk Maxwell, tried and failed, at first, to explain how James Watt's steam engine governor worked. Watt's invention accelerated the industrial revolution, and he built it using his knowledge, experimentation and intuition.

People from diverse backgrounds and experiences, such as artists, musicians, comedians and indeed anyone of us who sees the world through our own lens, ask fundamental and difficult questions that society hasn't tried to answer yet, like, 'Why are animals important?' Your animality makes you pre-eminently capable of knowing that animal conservation is essential and coming up with great ideas about how to do that.

We are all entertainers, artists and scientists to some extent and can play a strong role in telling the story of how and why animals are essential for a habitable Earth. Contemporary art is the ultimate form of social debate and you find few scientists disagreeing when a joke, picture, a verse of poetry or a phrase of music distils complex subjects into a pure statement about the state of the world, because deep down we all agree and empathise with our mutual failings as much as our success. Margaret Atwood was Booker Prize–nominated for her novel *Oryx and Crake*, and in the sleeve notes talks of a moment watching a red-necked crake from the balcony of a Queensland rainforest retreat as the moment the story suddenly appeared to her. For Atwood, experiences with wildlife and conversation with scientists helped shape her vision of a near-future dystopia. For the rest of us, our imagining of a future in which we've desecrated the world's wildlife to our own peril may be less abstract in thought, but the reality also remains possible and we feel strongly about it because it's our mind's way of responding to a threat.

It seems to me that most people share the view that we need to put conservation of animals above our own interests long enough to rebuild their populations, in order to reach a new level of equity with Earth. What we haven't achieved is a level of empowerment to do something about it. I'm nonetheless heartened every day by the extent to which the public is prepared to stand up for wildlife through personal choices, because this is creating the rapid emergence of a new way to see rare creatures and wild places.

We are beginning to appreciate and value animals for what they are, not what they represent to us. The invisible elephant in the room is the need to reverse extinctions, promote habitat diversification and rebuild food systems around local organic farming and small-scale fisheries. This means more nutritious food that will be sustained in a landscape full of sharks, whales, dolphins, insects, seabirds, songbirds and birds of prey, and humans, all together. We have to know that the sparrow must exist to avoid the locust years of the future, and that the only way out of this complex ecosystem problem is through a better relationship with wildlife. The footprints from the elephant in the room are everywhere, but the real species are disappearing. We cannot give up now, just when we are becoming self-aware enough to understand what needs to be done.

Human life on Earth has always been and will continue to be dependent on wildlife because ecosystems cannot reach a steady stable state without them. Animals created the conditions for us to succeed, and civilisation is built on their foundations. Our future depends on an equitable respect for wildlife including our own kind, as it is the animal army, not ours, that guards the ramparts of fortress humankind. A world without wildlife will be unimaginable and unliveable.

Winning the human race means preserving the integrity of our planet's ecosystems and minimising energy disorder, but none of this will be possible without animals. It is a race we can only hope to win if we partner with them in our sprint to the finish line. Does our species have the stamina and intelligence to become one of the likeliest survivors? Only time will tell.

Epilogue

Animals have had millions of years to hone evolutionary skills, to become the intelligence that connects and stabilises physical, chemical and biological worlds through smell, sight, acoustics and many dozens of additional senses, only some of which we possess.

One way or the other, life is going to continue in some shape or form. In the Australian bush there are long-legged feral cats devastating local wildlife before feeding on introduced rabbits. What will these savannahs look like in ten thousand years or more? Will the cats have

---

Green turtles live for a hundred years and drag their heavy bodies onto land to lay eggs. They epitomise the slow pace and indefatigable effort and tolerance an animal needs to be the most likely to survive for millions of years. For this reason, turtles might be among the animals most likely to outlive the human race. There is still time left for us to learn from their good behaviour.

become sabre-toothed predators, chasing hippo-sized rabbits, like the three-tonne diprotodons that succumbed to hunting pressure after humans reached the continent? In the apocalypse, will zoo animals escape and seed new communities of strange and brilliant creatures?

As long as there is not too much warmth in the sun, mass extinctions will be followed by renewed diversity, because entropy drives ecosystems towards a new steady-state, equivalent but not identical to the last. If humans no longer exist, life on Earth can continue unabashedly, and within twenty to thirty million years Earth will be awash with a new and marvellous diversity of life. What an amazing world it would be to see!

The bacterial chromosomes, engineered from primitive self-replicating proteins that help us extract the energy to live, will survive on inside the bodies of new animals. Each new species and step in evolution will create new sizes, shapes, behaviours and colours, but these same basic protein units, evolved from a single origin bacterium, will continue to live in cell mitochondria – for perhaps billions of years. Having succeeded in cheating extinction and leaping between species, these, and the plant versions, could already be the universe's most successful self-replicating lifeforms.

In five billion years, when our sun finally shatters in a supernova explosion, it will shine a million times brighter and instantly release more energy than ten billion stars, scattering embers far and wide. The material from Earth might sow the universe with fresh material for new solar systems like ours. Fragments of these molecules might survive on nearby comets and end up deposited in the bedrock of new planetoids and start the process all over again.

It's a humbling thought that our own existence may be as a vehicle for these molecules, the consequence of natural laws, to resist disorder. Understanding this could be the closest we ever get to appreciating the true meaning of life. Knowing we are part of that is surely the best reason to protect the world around us.

– THE END –

Glossary

Absolute zero. The theoretical temperature at which there is no energy (heat) omitted from molecular motion. It is the temperature at which life cannot exist.

Adaptation. The way a species alters itself in response to external environmental change. An adaptation can be behavioural and thereby increase the proportion of a subset of genes in a population. Adaptations aren't always positive.

Aerial plankton. The tiny insects that make up our atmospheric biomass and drift across whole continents, being fed on by many birds.

Amino acid. The basic building blocks of life. A small number of relatively simple organic compounds that can be put together in any combination to make all components of living animals and plants.

Amplification (of nutrients and energy). How animals consume other animals and in doing so, condense and reintroduce important energy-containing nutrients into the environment, at even higher concentrations and in patches. This makes the nutrients more readily available to the next-biggest animals, and so on.

Animal impact. The term 'impact' is used to describe the role that animals have in supporting ecosystem function – like a charity's impact statement, the outcome is positive. Animal impact is a measure of the amount of free surplus energy that an animal (or population) can remove from the atmosphere and oceans, storing it inside processes, supporting the ecosystem in a steady and stable state.

Bioaccumulation. A term generally used to describe the increasing concentration of toxic compounds in the bodies of animals that eat smaller animals that contain the toxin. For example, a toxin that doesn't naturally break down and exists in the bodies of aphids will be concentrated at higher levels in the body tissues of birds that eat lots of aphids.

Bioavailable. Molecules that can be metabolised by animals. Iron, for example, is extremely abundant in nature, but as iron oxide (rust), which isn't soluble in water. Iron is nonetheless vital for all animal respiration and plant photosynthesis. We rely on microorganisms to fix the iron into forms that can be used and on animals to concentrate it in the right time and place. In this book, when we use the term 'bioavailable', we are also referring to the energy in molecules/nutrients that is contained within biological systems and therefore not 'free energy' in the atmosphere or oceans.

Biodiversity. The variability among living organisms from all sources, including, among other things, terrestrial, marine, and other aquatic ecosystems, and the ecological complexes of which they are part; this includes diversity within species, between species and of ecosystems, plus the structure, function and processes that they form.

Biodiversity hotspot. A place where there is a culmination of many ecosystem functions and processes that combine together to create higher-than-normal energy flow. Generally, these tend to be very species-rich. We tend to view hotspots as relevant to our own spatial scale, but they can occur at any spatial scale and be either much larger or smaller than we comprehend.

Biomass. The weight of living organisms. Biomass can be measured in relation to the amount of carbon, the dry weight (with all moisture removed) or living weight. In general it can be used to describe the volume of energy that is contained inside systems, as the size of animals relates to their metabolism and, therefore, how much energy they contain and pass onto other trophic levels.

Biosphere. The combination of all Earth's ecosystems, housed inside our atmosphere.

Carboniferous. A period of geological time from about 360–300 million years ago when plants became very successful and when most of our modern coal deposits were laid down. It was after the period that the Devonian mass extinction occurred, most likely driven by the success of plants, releasing sediment into the oceans in such volumes that it killed off most marine life.

Carrying capacity. The population of animals that a steady-state ecosystem can support. It's the number that results when total mortality equals total birth rate. Populations aren't evenly distributed to carrying capacity; it depends on there being both population sources and population sinks that balance each other out. This is why it can never be said that 'animals can move somewhere else'. Loss of critical habitat will always result in reduction in carrying capacity.

Chaos. In this book, the term is used to describe the consequence of removing animals from ecosystems, which leads to release of surplus energy. This change from a state of order to a state of chaos means the movement of energy from where it's useful (predictable and concentrated safely inside food chains) to where it's not (unpredictable, dilute and released into oceans and the atmosphere). An ecosystem in a chaotic state also swings unpredictably between one extreme state and another is not habitable.

Chloroplasts. Organelles found in plants that conduct photosynthesis and thereby transfer energy from sunlight into chemical energy that the plant can then use in respiration. They are the plant equivalent of mitochondria.

Chromosome. A molecule made from DNA (deoxyribonucleic acid) that contains the genetic material of an organism.

Complex science theory. The theory that, in order to understand complex systems, you can't look at specific mechanisms as there are simply too many to understand, which is most important. Instead, you have to infer a model of the character of a system of value and make predictions about how to maintain that, in order to protect the system.

Complex systems dilemma. That systems such as ecosystems are so complicated that there may be a practically infinite number of overlapping mechanisms. Scientists who try to study the mechanisms have to make arbitrary decisions about what minutiae to study and in doing so miss the bigger picture. The mechanisms inside complex systems such as ecosystems also change over time, meaning these compartmentalised results can become quickly outdated.

Cultivation grazing. How animals evolve to graze selectively between patches, to promote greater plant growth between grazing periods.

Cyanobacteria. An early form of life that still exist today and are super-abundant in our oceans. They are similar to bacteria and are not algae but are capable of photosynthesis.

Disorder (of energy). Used in the context of entropy, disorder is where energy dissipates to becomes more chaotic. For example, the release of hot air into the atmosphere results in that energy being freer to disperse. The opposite is true when energy is locked into biological processes, when it is stored inside molecules. Stability in ecosystems occurs when there is little surplus free energy, meaning most of it is consumed into processes that create order.

Disruption. The result of an action that creates a sudden change in the stability of an ecosystem or process. This tends to create a gap where there is free surplus energy and organisms will move in to fill the space. Disruption might be a tree fall, or the application of pesticide to farmland. Disruption is important to maintain dynamics in ecosystems but becomes limiting if it happens too often or at a large scale.

Disturbance. An action that can cause disruption.

DNA (deoxyribonucleic acid). The molecules that make up chromosomes and contain the blueprint for life.

Eco-IQ. A measure of the integrity of information that you rely on to process knowledge of your environment and make competent decisions about your species' survival. Your eco-IQ is an extension of the combined intelligences of all animals that you share your space with, as they create the predictable structures and concentration of resources you need (the information you rely on). Where an IQ remains relatively constant, your eco-IQ can dilute dramatically if you collapse wildlife populations. If your eco-IQ drops, your extinction risk also increases.

Ecology. The study of the interaction between animals, plants and their environment.

Ecosystem. A community of plants and animals that interact to form a steady stable state, in which the maximum diversity and abundance of species can coexist. Ecosystems are not fixed, they are dynamic. As a result of the actions of animals, ecosystems constantly adapt and change to remain habitable.

Ecosystem service. The value that an ecosystem provides to humans. For example, mangroves provide defence against coastal erosion, and healthy fish stocks feed people.

Ediacaran fauna. Some of the very earliest multicellular organisms, belonging to a period from about 635–540 million years ago.

El Niño. The warm phase of an ocean cycle that periodically sees warmer, nutrient-poor water flow west across the Pacific and reverses wind patterns leading to drought in Australasia. Opposite to La Niña.

Electron. A subatomic particle with a negative electrical charge and the main carrier of energy in solids.

Entropy. The degree of disorder or chaos in a system, most often used to describe thermodynamic energy but also the behaviour of information. All else being equal, physics determines that all matter and energy moves towards chaos, therefore biological systems are in a continual state of battling against entropic forces in order to remain stable.

Environmental impact. The consequence of an effect that elicits an actual change that has been evaluated and can be either reversible or irreversible.

Evolution. The gradual development of new species or adaptations due to modifications of the environment around them.

Evolutionarily stable strategy. Any individual behaviour that, when scaled to the population level, means that population is relatively stable and results in no net loss or gain in the species' status.

Exponential scale. A way of representing very large numbers to a base value. The most common is a logarithmic scale with base 10, where 10 = 1, 100 = 2 and so on. During COVID, we got used to exponential scales that doubled every few days. There are multiple ways to represent numbers like this, and it helps visualise mathematics where trends would otherwise be hard to see, due to the rapid scaling of numbers.

Extinction rate. Refers to the number of species that go extinct over a period of time. Often referred to in million species years. In other words, one million species year is a rate in which one extinction would occur each year for every million species. See also Species lifespan.

Extremophile. A species that lives in a particularly extreme environment. Examples would include species that live in deep-ocean hydrothermal vents, or bacteria that colonise volcanic hot springs.

Food chain. A single thread in a food web illustrating the chain of animals that eat each other. At the base of the food chain are small high-energy (fast metabolism) animals, and at the other end large low metabolism animals. An example would be whales eating krill that eat plankton that eat algae. Or lions that eat gazelles that eat grass.

Free surplus energy. The energy of a system that is emitted as waste and is not part of ecosystem processes. There is always some free surplus energy as this creates the basis for evolution whereby new species exploit gaps in the ecosystem where free energy becomes available. Surplus energy can occur as a result of disruption or disturbance. When surplus free energy reaches the point it manifests as pollution, it can contribute to ecosystem collapse by creating rapid change in the chemistry of oceans and atmosphere.

Freedom of the commons. From Garrett Hardin's paper in Science in 1968. Common resources such as animals, land, air and water are not owned by anyone. We are all free to use these resources.

Function (of an ecosystem). A subset of ecosystem processes and structures, where the ecosystem does something that provides an ecosystem service of value to people.

Game theory. A branch of mathematics that is generally concerned with human and animal behaviour that pits competitors against each other and tries to deduce outcomes based on participant decisions. It has been used extensively in evolutionary biology and political science, in particular to look at economies and also how we behave in war.

Geophony. The sound of a landscape caused by the energy such as wind or waves striking non-biological components e.g. mountains, or the interaction of energy with other physical biological structures such as grass and trees.

Great Ocean Conveyor. The movement of the entire planet's ocean water every one thousand years, which is driven by basin-wide gradients in salinity and temperature.

Great Oxidation Event. About 2.5 billion years ago when the biological activity of life in the ocean started to produce O2 leading to a rapid change in chemistry and mass extinctions.

Guano. The faeces of seabirds deposited on islands, once mined for agriculture, due to it being incredibly rich in phosphorus and nitrogen.

Hi-fi sound. In a music sense, the ability to record sound faithfully or exactly. In nature, a soundscape where noises are all heard and non-overlapping. The opposite is Lo-fi sound.

Hydrothermal vents. Biologically rich deep-ocean habitats generally found along continental fault lines where the Earth's crust is thin and where hot gases and mineral-rich water are vented out, heated by the magma chamber beneath.

Ice age. A period of reduction in Earth's temperature of between about 4–7 degrees that resulted in the rapid expansion of ice sheets and glaciation of much of the Earth's surface.

Information theory. A theory published by Shannon in 1948 that divides information into 'bits', each equivalent to a coin flip or a binary decision. The theory shows us the most efficient way to communicate by reducing the amount of information (bits) to the least necessary to communicate a message. Information theory drives the technology in our communication systems but can also be used to explain how ecosystems form a steady state, as the most stable structures are those where energy (the equivalent of information) is used in the most efficient way possible. This allows for maximum reduction of entropy by the efficient ordering of this information inside biological systems.

La Niña. The cool phase of an ocean cycle (opposite to El Niño) that periodically sees a reduction in warm water flow across the Pacific, meaning more nutrients reaching the west Pacific and a strengthening of normal wind patterns leading to more rainfall in Australasia.

Lifeform. Any complex self-replicating entity that behaves in a lifelike manner, from archaea and viruses to the biggest animals on Earth, plants and algae.

Limiting nutrients. Nutrients such as iron are in such low concentration in the ocean that they limit the scale of animal activity in the food chain. Limiting nutrients are any naturally occurring chemical that limits the productivity of ecosystems by its scarcity.

Lo-fi sound. In nature, a soundscape where noises are all overlapping and hard to discern one from another. The opposite of hi-fi.

Logarithm. See Exponential scale.

Magnetosphere. The magnetic field surrounding a planet such as Earth that deflects solar radiation.

Mass extinction. A period on Earth in which more than 75 per cent of all lifeforms went extinct. There have been five mass extinctions in the last 500 million years.

Maximum entropy production. Where an ecosystem achieves a steady stable state with the maximum possible number of species and there is very little free surplus energy because it is all consumed inside biological processes. Entropy dictates that all matter moves towards chaos, but animal life enables ecosystems to continually move in the opposite direction. Reaching a state of maximum entropy production is essential for stable ecosystems and hence for human survival.

Megafauna. The largest animals that represent the top of the trophic pyramid. These are the final building blocks in ecosystem structures for maximum entropy production. Megafauna can be measured at any spatial scale. The largest animal that has ever lived on Earth is the blue whale. In a grassland, spiders or songbirds could even be considered megafauna, but the term is generally reserved for animals larger than insects.

Metabolic rate. The rate of energy expenditure over time by an organism. Metabolic rate is generally higher for smaller organisms and lower for larger ones.

Mitochondria. An organelle found in large numbers in most animal cells that originates from a bacteria and contains its own unique chromosomes that are passed down the mother's side only and are used in analysing ancestry. Mitochondria house processes where respiration occurs, which releases energy for living.

Modelling. The process, either mathematically or in the human brain, of creating an internal version of something that we can refer to, to better understand how it functions and our place within. Our brains model the environment outside so we can behaviourally function. Models can also be used to help understand how ecosystems work.

Molecule. A selection of atoms held together by chemical bonds, such as an amino acid. A number of molecules fit together to create a compound.

Mutation. Change to the DNA or RNA structure of an organism that results in a change in its makeup. Most mutations are redundant or disadvantageous but are important because they create a certain amount of resilience against environmental change.

Natural selection. Darwin's theory of how species are formed, in which those that stand in closest competition with those undergoing beneficial modification and improvement will go extinct faster. Natural selection is by survival of the likeliest, not survival of the fittest. The fittest are only likely to survive because they happen to be most suited to the environment into which they are born. The environment is constantly changing, so these adaptations enable ecosystems to maintain a steady stable state.

Nutrient. A substance that contains the raw materials for life. At a chemical level, these are contained inside compounds that are absorbed into the body and essential energy-containing molecules are extracted, so that energy can be transformed into other chemical processes that use the energy for living.

Oceanography. The study of the physical, chemical and biological properties of the ocean.

Ordovician. A geological time period spanning from about 485–443 million years ago when life was mostly in the ocean and the first complex animals appeared.

Organelles. Tiny organs inside your cells such as mitochondria (in animals) and chloroplasts (in plants) that perform basic functions. The aforementioned examples originate as bacteria that formed a symbiosis with early lifeforms and help with essential processes such as respiration and photosynthesis.

Ozone. A molecule of oxygen that has three, instead of two, atoms. The ozone layer breaks down when exposed to sunlight, absorbing its energy and protecting us from harmful components of its radiation.

Pests. Animals that, as a result of free surplus energy, have become abundant and pose a threat to human agriculture.

Photosynthesis. The way in which plants extract energy by absorbing water and using radiation from the sun to combine it with carbon dioxide to create sugars.

Planetoid. Matter that has clumped together to become large enough to minimise destruction by collisions with other objects and which gradually absorbs more matter to become larger and larger. A precursor to a planet.

Plankton. A soup of microorganisms. Usually refers to all the zooplankton and algae in the ocean but can also be used to describe tiny insects in the atmosphere (see aerial plankton).

Pleistocene. The Pleistocene was from about 2.5 million years ago to 12,000 years ago, at the end of the last ice age. It encompasses the period when woolly mammoths occurred.

Prisoner's dilemma. A common gambling game that became a central part of a 1981 experiment in human behaviour and one of the most cited political science publications for a decade. The game involves two prisoners isolated in separate chambers given the choice to either testify against the other or cooperate. This results in different penalties based on whether one or both prisoners testify against the other, or both cooperate. The outcomes reveal fundamental biases associated with human behaviour. Biologists have gone on to study the theory and determine how it is that individual human beings generally play a poor tit-for-tat game, yet individual animals have come to mostly cooperate. The reason for cooperation in animals is that over millions of iterations, and as long as it is a zero-sum game, it does not make sense to do anything other than eventually cooperate. This teaches us a lot about extinction survival risk and the mistakes we make as a species when it comes to our own future as a population.

Process. The chains and cycles by which energy flows through an ecosystem. Processes can include the amplification or recycling of nutrients, storage of carbon, decomposition and any number of other systems that maintain ecosystem stability.

Productivity (of an ecosystem). The power of an ecosystem to process energy. The most productive ecosystems have reached a steady stable state with maximum entropy production. That's to say, the number of species has reached an optimum and the functions they fulfil have translated free surplus energy into nutrients that is either stored inside plants and animals, or is entrained within the biological cycles that transfer this between the ecosystem's components. A highly productive ecosystem will store maximum carbon, for example.

Pyrite. A common crystal of iron sulfide, FeS2. Sometimes referred to as 'fool's gold'.

Resilience. Referring to an ecosystem's ability to maintain a steady stable state. The need to build resilience is entirely anthropocentric and symptomatic of ecosystems that are damaged or declining, leading to loss of ecosystem services on which humans depend.

Respiration. A chemical reaction that, at its most basic, converts sugars using oxygen and creates wastewater and carbon dioxide. Respiration inside animal cells is more complicated and converts these molecules into adenosine triphosphate (ATP).

RNA (ribonucleic acid). A chromosomal molecule like DNA.

Second law of thermodynamics. Einstein's second law states that the total entropy of an isolated system can never decrease over time and is constant only if all processes are reversible. In other words, entropy forces energy to flow towards a state of greater chaos.

Soundscape. The characteristic of a landscape of sounds that is interpreted by animal minds and dictates their behaviour and response to other animals and features of the environment.

Soundtope hypothesis. The theory that acoustics support the presence of species and that the behaviour of animals determines the way they hear. In other words, animals evolve to use sound in conjunction with the local environment, behaving in the way they need to survive.

Species lifespan. Refers to the average number of years a species survives. It ranges from about 1 to 11 million years but depends on the species' size, with larger mammals usually lasting only about 1 million years and invertebrates lasting for 11 million years.

Species richness. The number of species within a given area.

Spermaceti. A waxy substance that changes density with pressure, found in the head of a sperm whale. The spermaceti organ is thought to aid in buoyancy as well as helping focus sonar beams, used in the species' echolocation.

Stable state ecosystem. An ecosystem where free surplus energy is minimised, where there is maximum entropy production and minimum waste. In such a system, there is expected to be relatively small fluctuations in atmospheric and other chemistry and where disruption or disturbance occurs, the resulting changes can be absorbed quickly by a succession of new plants and animals that enter to fill the gaps.

Static electricity. An imbalance in the negative and positive charges on a surface, resulting in an electrical signal. If you rub a balloon on a woollen jumper, electrons pass between one surface and the other. The electrons remain in place until they can be discharged by contact with a conductor and the weak signals can be detected by some animals such as bees.

Structure. Can refer to the physical, chemical or biological makeup of an ecosystem. Structure, whether it be through sound, light, forest, soil or animals, is the scaffolding that holds ecosystems together. Structural complexity at various spatial scales is essential for stable ecosystems.

Survival of the fittest. A term coined by English biologist and philosopher Herbert Spencer and found to be largely untrue. The term fits a world view that believes in violence as the ultimate adaptation but cooperation is the most evolutionarily stable strategy. Even then, the lifespan of a species is limited by external factors beyond any control.

Taxonomist. A scientist whose job it is to classify and name species.

Tipping point. The rapid movement of an ecosystem from one steady state to another state. Ecosystems don't rapidly move from one steady state to another steady state. Tipping points are typically reached when the amount of free energy is so significant that there is total structural collapse and the new state is simply one in which most of the energy is contained at the lower trophic levels. For instance, going from a species-rich grassland by applying fertiliser, you quickly reach a tipping point where only one or two grass species dominate, and there may be one or two abundant animals but these tend to be 'pests'. Tipping points cannot be easily reversed because it takes thousands and sometimes millions of years to rebuild the structure, as it depends on evolution and adaptation processes that cannot be replicated by human engineers.

Tragedy of the commons. How the exploitation of a common resource (e.g. land, water, animals) benefits one person but any negative effects of that exploitation are shared among the whole community. It is the title of Garrett Hardin's famous paper in Science in 1968.

Transfer (of nutrients). What sets animals apart from plants is that they can move. Some of the biggest migrations on Earth every day are the movements of insects like caterpillars from the stem of a plant to a leaf and back, before turning into butterflies and transferring the energy elsewhere. Large-scale migration of grazing animals and migratory songbirds moves nutrients too, over vast geographic areas. The movement is predictable, and this process underpins the amplification and concentration of nutrients, which creates the ecosystems on which we depend for all our global food security and maximises entropy production, which absorbs more carbon and stabilises climate.

Trophic cascade. The effect an animal has on the energy of an ecosystem and how this is connected to many other components around it. By removing a species, you can create a cascade or domino effect in which energy flow is disrupted, and it alters the dynamic of an ecosystem's species – in extreme examples, whole steps in the trophic chain can be removed.

Trophic level. Describes the amount of energy contained within one step of the food chain. Animals in one trophic level utilise about ninety per cent of the energy they absorb for living, emitting the rest as heat and waste. This means the next step up the trophic chain (e.g. the bigger animals that eat them) only have access to about ten per cent of the energy below them. At each step up the food chain, the amount of available energy declines and animals get bigger, with lower rates of metabolism.

Trophic pyramid. The gradual reduction in energy content, increase in body size and reduction in number of animals that occurs the higher you go up the food chain. At the base of the pyramid are a vast number of tiny high-metabolism creatures, and at the summit are the top predators. To be stable, the pyramid has to have creatures at all levels.

Upwelling. The process of cold, deep, nutrient-rich water being swept to the sunlit ocean surface, which allows algae and plankton to flourish.

Zero-sum game. A game where all players stand to gain and lose exactly the same. In evolution, extinction is a zero-sum game, explaining why animals have learnt to mostly cooperate, which is an evolutionarily stable strategy, while humans, playing the prisoner's dilemma, cannot seem to make cooperative choices and always seem to lose the game.

References

1. Ellis, E.C., et al., 'People have shaped most of terrestrial nature for at least 12,000 years'. *Proceedings of the National Academy of Sciences*, 2021. 118(17): p. e2023483118.
2. Song, X-P., et al., 'Global land change from 1982 to 2016'. Nature, 2018. 560(7720): p. 639 – 643.
3. Haddaway, N. and D. Leclère, 'WWF Living Planet Report 2020'. 2020.
4. Huffard, C., M.V. Erdmann, and T. Gunawan, 'Defining geographic priorities for marine biodiversity conservation in Indonesia'. 2012.
5. Mangubhai, S., et al., 'Papuan Bird's Head Seascape: Emerging threats and challenges in the global center of marine biodiversity'. Marine pollution bulletin, 2012. 64.
6. Rackham, O., 'The Illustrated History of the Countryside'. 1997: Phoenix Illustrated.
7. Ripple, W.J. and R.L. Beschta, 'Trophic cascades in Yellowstone: The first 15 years after wolf reintroduction'. Biological Conservation, 2012. 145(1): p. 205 – 213.
8. Biermann, F., 'The future of 'environmental' policy in the Anthropocene: time for a paradigm shift'. Environmental Politics, 2021. 30(1-2): p. 61 – 80.
9. Boyle, S.A., et al., 'Small mammal glucocorticoid concentrations vary with forest fragment size, trap type, and mammal taxa in the Interior Atlantic Forest'. Scientific Reports, 2021. 11(1): p. 2111.
10. Narayan, E., 'Physiological stress levels in wild koala sub-populations facing anthropogenic induced environmental trauma and disease'. Scientific Reports, 2019. 9.
11. DeFries, R., 'Nature's playbook: From termite queens to the carbon cycle, nature knows how to avoid network collapse. Human designers should pay heed'. 2021: Aeon Magazine. 16 March 2021.
12. Strona, G. and C.J.A. Bradshaw, 'Co-extinctions annihilate planetary life during extreme environmental change'. Scientific Reports, 2018. 8(1): p. 16724.
13. Burgess, M.G. and S.D. Gaines, 'The scale of life and its lessons for humanity'. Proceedings of the National Academy of Sciences, 2018. 115(25): p. 6328.
14. Harte, J., 'Maximum entropy and ecology. A theory of abundance, distribution, and energetics'. 2011.
15. Zhang, Z., et al., 'Three-dimensional mesoscale modelling of concrete composites by using random walking algorithm'. Composites Science and Technology, 2017. 149.
16. Grémillet, D., et al., 'A junk-food hypothesis for gannets feeding on fishery waste'. Proceedings. Biological sciences / The Royal Society, 2008. 275: p. 1149 – 56.
17. Stringer, A. and M. Gaywood, 'The impacts of beavers Castor spp. on biodiversity and the ecological basis for their reintroduction to Scotland, UK'. Mammal Review, 2016. In Press.
18. Estes, J.A., et al., 'Estes JA, Tinker MT, Williams TM, and Doak DF. Killer whale predation on sea otters linking oceanic and nearshore ecosystems. Science'. Science (New York, N.Y.), 1998. 282: p. 473 – 6.
19. Estes, J., et al., 'Trophic Downgrading of Planet Earth'. Science (New York, N.Y.), 2011. 333: p. 301 – 6.

20. Cox, B. and R. Ince, 'How to Build a Universe: Part I'. 2017, William Collins Books by arrangement with the BBC.
21. Algeo, T.J., S.E. Scheckler, and J.B. Maynard, 'Effects of the Middle to Late Devonian spread of vascular land plants on weathering regimes, marine biotas, and global climate'. Plants invade the land: evolutionary and environmental perspectives. Columbia University Press, New York, 2001: p. 213 – 236.
22. Janvier, P. and G. Clément, 'Muddy tetrapod origins'. Nature, 2010. 463(7277): p. 40 – 41.
23. Bar-On, Y., R. Phillips, and R. Milo, 'The biomass distribution on Earth'. *Proceedings of the National Academy of Sciences*, 2018. 115: p. 201711842.
24. Clements, R., et al., 'Limestone Karsts of Southeast Asia: Imperiled Arks of Biodiversity'. *BioScience*, 2006. 56(9): p. 733 – 742.
25. de Lasa, H., et al., 'Catalytic Steam Gasification of Biomass: Catalysts, Thermodynamics and Kinetics'. *Chemical Reviews*, 2011. 111(9): p. 5404 – 5433.
26. Rabalais, N.N., R.E. Turner, and W.J. Wiseman, 'Gulf of Mexico Hypoxia, A.K.A. "The Dead Zone"'. *Annual Review of Ecology and Systematics*, 2002. 33(1): p. 235 – 263.
27. Anderson, W.W., 'Iron fog of accretion'. *Nature Geoscience*, 2015. 8(4): p. 256 – 257.
28. Stanley, S., 'Infodynamics, a Developmental Framework for Ecology/ Economics'. *Ecology and Society*, 2003. 7.
29. England, J., 'Statistical Physics of Self-Replication'. *The Journal of chemical physics*, 2013. 139: p. 121923.
30. Lovelock, J., 'Gaia: A new look at life on earth. Oxford University Press, 1995. Pp. 148.'. *Quarterly Journal of the Royal Meteorological Society*, 1996. 122(530): p. 563 – 563.
31. Azua, A. and C. Vega-Martínez, 'The potential for detecting 'life as we don't know it' by fractal complexity analysis'. *International Journal of Astrobiology*, 2013. 12.
32. England, J., 'Every Life Is on Fire: How Thermodynamics Explains the Origins of Living Things'. 2020: Basic Books.
33. Marsh, H., A. Grech, and K. McMahon, 'Dugongs: Seagrass Community Specialists', in *Seagrasses of Australia: Structure, Ecology and Conservation*, A.W.D. Larkum, G.A. Kendrick, and P.J. Ralph, Editors. 2018, Springer International Publishing: Cham. p. 629 – 661.
34. Iongh, H.H., B.J. Wenno, and E. Meelis, 'Seagrass distribution and seasonal biomass changes in relation to dugong grazing in the Moluccas, East Indonesia'. *Aquatic Botany*, 1995. 50: p. 1 – 19.
35. Chen, C., et al., 'The 'scaly-foot gastropod': a new genus and species of hydrothermal vent-endemic gastropod (Neomphalina: Peltospiridae) from the Indian Ocean'. *Journal of Molluscan Studies*, 2015. 81(3): p. 322 – 334.
36. Chen, C., et al., 'The heart of a dragon: 3D anatomical reconstruction of the 'scaly-foot gastropod' (Mollusca: Gastropoda: Neomphalina) reveals its extraordinary circulatory system'. *Frontiers in Zoology*, 2015. 12(1): p. 13.
37. Whitfield, J., 'Survival of the Likeliest?'. *PLOS Biology*, 2007. 5(5): p. e142.
38. Sadedin, S., 'What Do People Commonly Misunderstand About Darwin's Theory Of Evolution?'. 2018: Quora via Forbes Magazine. Oct 3, 2018.
39. Rabosky, D.L., et al., 'An inverse latitudinal gradient in speciation rate for marine fishes'. *Nature*, 2018. 559(7714): p. 392 – 395.
40. Chaudhary, C., et al., 'Global warming is causing a more pronounced dip in

marine species richness around the equator'. *Proceedings of the National Academy of Sciences*, 2021. 118(15): p. e2015094118.

41. Osland, M.J., et al., 'Tropicalization of temperate ecosystems in North America: The northward range expansion of tropical organisms in response to warming winter temperatures'. *Global Change Biology*, 2021. n/a(n/a).
42. Evans, S.D., et al., 'Discovery of the oldest bilaterian from the Ediacaran of South Australia'. *Proceedings of the National Academy of Sciences*, 2020: p. 202001045.
43. Fahrenkamp-Uppenbrink, J., 'Finding the organelles' ancestors'. *Science*, 2016. 351(6274): p. 676.
44. Lisetskii, F., 'Estimates of Soil Renewal Rates: Applications for Anti Erosion Arrangement of the Agricultural Landscape'. *Geosciences*, 2019. 9(6).
45. Martin, S., et al., 'A vast 4,000-year-old spatial pattern of termite mounds'. *Current Biology*, 2018. 28: p. R1292 – R1293.
46. Vargo, E.L., 'Diversity of Termite Breeding Systems'. *Insects*, 2019. 10(2): p. 52.
47. Higgins, P. and S. Marchant, 'Handbook of Australian, New Zealand & Antarctic Birds. Volume 1 Ratites to Ducks'. 1990.
48. Harrison, P., 'Seabirds: An Identification Guide'. 1985: Houghton Mifflin.
49. Skira, I., 'Human exploitation of the short-tailed shearwater (Pujfinus tenuirostris)'. 1990, Papers and Proceedings of the Royal Society of Tasmania. p. 77 – 90.
50. Norman, F. 'Localised declines in colonies of the short-tailed shearwater: an explanation'. 2012.
51. Flinders, M., 'A voyage to Terra Australis / by Matthew Flinders'. 1989, Netley, S. Aust: South Australian Government Printer.
52. Schumann, N., P. Dann, and J. Arnould, 'The significance of northern- central Bass Strait in south-eastern Australia as habitat for burrowing seabirds'. 2014.
53. Olsen, S., 'The Fossil Record of Birds'. 1985, Academic Press: *Avian Biology*. p. 79 – 238.
54. Klomp, N. and M. Schultz, 'Short-tailed shearwaters breeding in Australia forage in Antarctic waters'. *Marine Ecology-progress Series*, 2000. 194: p. 307 – 310.
55. Broecker, W.S., 'The great ocean conveyor'. *Oceanography*, 1991. 4(2): p. 79 – 89.
56. Carey, M., et al., 'Trans-equatorial migration of Short-tailed Shearwaters revealed by geolocators'. *The Emu: official organ of the Australasian Ornithologists' Union*, 2014. 114: p. 352 – 359.
57. Brooke, M., 'The food consumption of the world's seabirds'. *Proceedings. Biological sciences / The Royal Society*, 2004. 271 Suppl 4: p. S246 – 8.
58. Paleczny, M., et al., 'Population Trend of the World's Monitored Seabirds, 1950-2010'. *PLOS ONE*, 2015. 10: p. e0129342.
59. Grosberg, R.K., G.J. Vermeij, and P.C. Wainwright, 'Biodiversity in water and on land'. *Current Biology*, 2012. 22(21): p. R900 – R903.
60. Larsen, B., E. Miller, and M. Rhodes, 'Inordinate Fondness Multiplied and Redistributed: the Number of Species on Earth and the New Pie of Life'. *Quarterly Review of Biology*, 2017. 92.
61. Sanderman, J., T. Hengl, and G.J. Fiske, 'Soil carbon debt of 12,000 years of human land use'. *Proceedings of the National Academy of Sciences*, 2017. 114(36): p. 9575.
62. Robertson, A.I., 'Plant-animal interactions and the structure and function of mangrove forest ecosystems*'. *Australian Journal of Ecology*, 1991. 16(4): p. 433-443.

63. Donato, D., et al., 'Mangroves among the most carbon-rich forests in the tropics'. *Nature Geoscience*, 2011. 4: p. 293 – 297.
64. Bochove, J.W., et al., 'The importance of mangroves to people: a call to action'. 2014.
65. Hutchison, J., M. Spalding, and P. zu Ermgassen, 'The Role of Mangroves in Fisheries Enhancement'. 2014. 54.
66. Cruz-Trinidad, A., et al., 'Linking Food Security with Coral Reefs and Fisheries in the Coral Triangle'. *Coastal Management*, 2014. 42.
67. Kusmana, C., 'Distribution and Current Status of Mangrove Forests in Indonesia'. 2014. p. 37 – 60.
68. Burrows, D., 'The role of insect leaf herbivory on the mangroves Avicennia marina and Rhizophora stylosa'. 2003.
69. Roach, M., 'Why You Should Plant Oaks. In the Garden. '. 2021: New York Times, March 31, 2021.
70. Wolton, R., 'Life in a hedge'. *British Wildlife*, 2015. 26: p. 306 – 316.
71. Bauer, S. and B. Hoye, 'Migratory Animals Couple Biodiversity and Ecosystem Functioning Worldwide'. *Science (New York, N.Y.)*, 2014. 344: p. 1242552.
72. Cederholm, C.J., et al., 'Pacific Salmon Carcasses: Essential Contributions of Nutrients and Energy for Aquatic and Terrestrial Ecosystems'. *Fisheries*, 1999. 24(10): p. 6 – 15.
73. Holdo, R., et al., 'Plant productivity and soil nitrogen as a function of grazing, migration and fire in an African savanna'. *Journal of Ecology*, 2006. 95: p. 115 – 128.
74. Burger, A.E., 'Dispersal and germination of seeds of Pisonia grandis, an Indo-Pacific tropical tree associated with insular seabird colonies'. *Journal of Tropical Ecology*, 2005. 21: p. 263 – 271.
75. Anderson, W.B. and G.A. Polis, 'Nutrient fluxes from water to land: seabirds affect plant nutrient status on Gulf of California islands'. *Oecologia*, 1999. 118(3): p. 324 – 332.
76. Nowicki, R.J., et al., 'Loss of predation risk from apex predators can exace bate marine tropicalization caused by extreme climatic events'. *Journal of Animal Ecology*, 2021. n/a(n/a).
77. Doherty, T.S., G.C. Hays, and D.A. Driscoll, 'Human disturbance causes wide spread disruption of animal movement'. *Nature Ecology & Evolution*, 2021.
78. Hu, G., et al., 'Mass seasonal bioflows of high-flying insect migrants'. *Science*, 2016. 354(6319): p. 1584.
79. Mizutani, A., J. Chahl, and M. Srinivasan, 'Motion camouflage in drago flies'. *Nature*, 2003. 423.
80. Mitchell, Forrest L., 'Dragonflies of the World. By Jill Silsby'. *The Quarterly Review of Biology*, 2002. 77(4): p. 462 – 462.
81. Morley, E. and D. Robert, 'Electric Fields Elicit Ballooning in Spiders'. *Current Biology*, 2018. 28.
82. Nyffeler, M. and K. Birkhofer, 'An estimated 400–800 million tons of prey are annually killed by the global spider community'. *The Science of Nature*, 2017. 104(3): p. 30.
83. Weimerskirch, H., et al., 'Flight performance: Frigatebirds ride high on thermals'. *Nature*, 2003. 421: p. 333 – 4.
84. Mensinger, A.F., 'THE SKIN | Bioluminescence in Fishes', in *Encyclopedia of Fish Physiology*, A.P. Farrell, Editor. 2011, Academic Press: San Diego. p. 497 – 503.
85. International, B. 'Species factsheet: F*regata ariel*. Downloaded from http://www.birdlife.org on 13/04/2020. '. Series 'Species factsheet: F*regata ariel*. Downloaded from http://www.birdlife.org on 13/04/2020.' 2020.

86. Gilburn, A., et al., 'Are neonicotinoid insecticides driving declines of widespread butterflies?'. *PeerJ*, 2015. 3: p. e1402.
87. Wing, S., et al., 'Seabirds and marine mammals redistribute bioavailable iron in the Southern Ocean'. *Marine Ecology Progress Series*, 2014. 510: p. 1 – 13.
88. Quick, N.J., et al., 'Extreme diving in mammals: first estimates of behavioural aerobic dive limits in Cuvier's beaked whales'. *The Journal of Experimental Biology*, 2020. 223(18): p. jeb222109.
89. Martin, J.H. and S.E. Fitzwater, 'Iron deficiency limits phytoplankton growth in the north-east Pacific subarctic'. *Nature*, 1988. 331(6154): p. 341 – 343.
90. Lavery, T., et al., 'Iron defecation by sperm whales stimulates carbon export in the Southern Ocean.'. *Proceedings of the Royal Society of London*, 2010.
91. Whitehead, H., 'Estimates of the current global population and historical trajectory for sperm whales'. *Marine Ecology-progress Series*, 2002. 242: p. 295 – 304.
92. Whitehead, H., 'Sperm Whales: Social Evolution in the Ocean'. 2003: University of Chicago Press.
93. Roman, J. and J.J. McCarthy, 'The Whale Pump: Marine Mammals Enhance Primary Productivity in a Coastal Basin'. *PLOS One*, 2010. 5(10): p. e13255.
94. Martin, A. and S. Lutz, 'Fish Carbon: Exploring Marine Vertebrate Carbon Services'. 2014.
95. Schmitz, O., et al., 'Animating the Carbon Cycle'. *Ecosystems*, 2014. 17.
96. Kiyono, Y. and Hastaniah, 'Growth of Eusideroxylon zwageri seedlings and silvicultural changes in logged-over and burned forests of Bukit Soeharto, East Kalimantan, Indonesia'. 2000. 34: p. 63 – 67.
97. Entuni, G. and R. Edward, 'A Preliminary Study on the Induction of Somatic Embryogenesis of Eusideroxylon zwageri Teijsm. and Binned (Borneo Ironwood) from Leaf Explants'. *International Journal of Agriculture Innovations and Research*, 2016. 4: p. 1 – 7.
98. Kurokawa, H., et al., 'The age of tropical rain-forest canopy species, Borneo Ironwood (Eusideroxylon zwageri), determined by 14C dating'. *Journal of Tropical Ecology*, 2003. 19(1): p. 1 – 7.
99. Dinerstein, E. and C.M. Wemmer, 'Fruits Rhinoceros Eat: Dispersal of Trewia Nudiflora (Euphorbiaceae) in Lowland Nepal'. *Ecology*, 1988. 69(6): p. 1768 – 1774.
100. Qie, L., et al., 'Impending Regeneration Failure of the IUCN Vulnerable Borneo Ironwood (Eusideroxylon zwageri)'. *Tropical Conservation Science*, 2019. 12: p. 1940082918823353.
101. Kretzschmar, P., et al., 'The catastrophic decline of the Sumatran rhino (Dicerorhinus sumatrensis harrissoni) in Sabah: Historic exploitation, reduced female reproductive performance and population viability'. *Global Ecology and Conservation*, 2016. 6: p. 257 – 275.
102. Kanamori, T., et al., 'Fluctuations of population density in Bornean orangutans (Pongo pygmaeus morio) related to fruit availability in the Danum Valley, Sabah, Malaysia: a 10-year record including two mast fruitings and three other peak fruitings'. *Primates*, 2016. 58.
103. Bellwood, D., A. Hoey, and J. Choat, 'Limited functional redundancy in high diversity systems: Resilience and ecosystem function on coral reefs'. *Ecology Letters*, 2003. 6: p. 281 – 285.

104. Jong, G.D.C. 'Current status of the seabird colony on Suanggi Island, Banda Sea'. 2011.
105. Weimerskirch, H., et al., 'The three-dimensional flight of red-footed boobies: Adaptations to foraging in a tropical environment?'. *Proceedings. Biological sciences / The Royal Society*, 2005. 272: p. 53 – 61.
106. Gammage, B., 'The biggest estate on earth : how Aborigines made Australia / Bill Gammage'. 2011, Crows Nest, N.S.W: Allen & Unwin.
107. Ballance, L.T., R.L. Pitman, and S.B. Reilly, 'Seabird community structure long a productivity gradient: importance of competition and energetic constraint.'. *Ecology*, 1997. 78(5): p. 1502 – 1518.
108. Otero, X., et al., 'Seabird colonies as important global drivers in the nitrogen and phosphorus cycles'. *Nature Communications*, 2018. 9.
109. Graham, N., et al., 'Seabirds enhance coral reef productivity and functioning in the absence of invasive rats'. *Nature*, 2018. 559.
110. Wolfe, K.M., et al., 'Post-mating survival in a small marsupial is associated with nutrient inputs from seabirds.'. *Ecology*, 2004. 85(6): p. 1740 – 1746.
111. Clarke, D., E. Morley, and D. Robert, 'The bee, the flower, and the electric field: electric ecology and aerial electroreception'. *Journal of comparative physiology. A, Neuroethology, sensory, neural, and behavioral physiology*, 2017. 203(9): p. 737 – 748.
112. Pinzon-Rodriguez, A., S. Bensch, and R. Muheim, 'Expression patterns of cryptochrome genes in avian retina suggest involvement of Cry4 in light-dependent magnetoreception'. *Journal of The Royal Society Interface*, 2018. 15: p. 20180058.
113. Higgins, J., 'Sentient'. 2021: Pan Macmillan.
114. Chen, Z. and J.J. Wiens, 'The origins of acoustic communication in vertebrates'. *Nature Communications*, 2020. 11(1): p. 369.
115. Radford, C., et al., 'Juvenile coral reef fish use sound to locate habitats'. *Coral Reefs*, 2011. 30: p. 295 – 305.
116. Vermeij, M.J.A., et al., 'Coral larvae move toward reef sounds'. *PLOS one*, 2010. 5(5): p. e10660.
117. George, J.C., et al., 'Observations on the Ice-Breaking and Ice Navigation Behavior of Migrating Bowhead Whales (Balaena mysticetus) near Point Barrow, Alaska, Spring 1985'. *Arctic*, 1989. 42(1): p. 24 – 30.
118. Zapetis, M. and A. Szesciorka, 'Cetacean Navigation'. 2018. p. 1 – 7.
119. Torres, L., 'A sense of scale: Foraging cetaceans' use of scale-dependent multimodal sensory systems'. *Marine Mammal Science*, 2017.
120. Farina, A. and N. Pieretti, 'The soundscape ecology: A new frontier of landscape research and its application to islands and coastal systems'. *Journal of Marine and Island Cultures*, 2012. 1.
121. Krause, B., 'The Great Animal Orchestra: Finding the Origins of Music in the World's Wild Places'. 2012.
122. Vester, H., et al., 'Quantifying group specificity of animal vocalizations without specific sender information'. *Physical Review E*, 2016. 93(2): p. 022138.
123. Planqué, R. and H. Slabbekoorn, 'Spectral Overlap in Songs and Temporal Avoidance in a Peruvian Bird Assemblage'. *Ethology*, 2008. 114: p. 262 – 271.
124. Cassidy, G. and R. MacDonald, 'The effect of background music and background noise on the task performance of introverts and extraverts'. *Psychology of Music*, 2007. 35: p. 517 – 537.

125. Carter, E. 'Consequences of ship noise for camouflage, anti-predation, and movement in crabs'. 2019.
126. Passchier-Vermeer, W. and W.F. Passchier, 'Noise exposure and public health'. *Environmental Health Perspectives*, 2000. 108(suppl 1): p. 123 – 131.
127. McMillan, B.T.M. and J.R. Saffran, 'Learning in Complex Environments: The Effects of Background Speech on Early Word Learning'. *Child Development*, 2016. 87(6): p. 1841 – 1855.
128. Erbe, C., 'Underwater noise of whale-watching boats and potential effects on killer whales (orcinus orca), based on an acoustic impact model.'. *Marine Mammal Science*, 2002. 18(2): p. 394 – 418.
129. Helble, T.A., et al., 'Lombard effect: Minke whale boing call source levels vary with natural variations in ocean noise'. *The Journal of the Acoustical Society of America*, 2020. 147(2): p. 698 – 712.
130. Stafford, K., C. Fox, and D. Clark, 'Long-range acoustic detection and localization of blue whale calls in the Northeast Pacific Ocean'. *The Journal of the Acoustical Society of America*, 1999. 104: p. 3616 – 25.
131. Tyack, P.L., 'Implications for Marine Mammals of Large-Scale Changes in the Marine Acoustic Environment'. *Journal of Mammalogy*, 2008. 89(3): p. 549 – 558.
132. Richardson, W.J., et al., 'Marine Mammals and Noise'. *Marine Mammals and Noise*, 2013: p. 1 – 576.
133. Akçay, Ç., et al., 'Song overlapping, ambient noise and territorial aggression in great tits'. *bioRxiv*, 2019: p. 808733.
134. Gorenflo, L., et al., 'Co-occurrence of linguistic and biological diversity in biodiversity hotspots and high biodiversity wilderness areas'. *Proceedings of the National Academy of Sciences of the United States of America*, 2012. 109: p. 8032 – 7.
135. Shepherd, S., et al., 'Extremely Low Frequency Electromagnetic Fields impair the Cognitive and Motor Abilities of Honey Bees'. *Scientific Reports*, 2018. 8(1): p. 7932.
136. Thielens, A., et al., 'Radio-Frequency Electromagnetic Field Exposure of Western Honey Bees'. *Scientific Reports*, 2020. 10(1): p. 461.
137. Ben-Dor, M. and R. Barkai, 'Prey Size Decline as a Unifying Ecological Selecting Agent in Pleistocene Human Evolution'. *Quaternary*, 2021. 4(1).
138. Ehrlich, P.R., A.H. Ehrlich, and J.P. Holdren, 'Ecoscience: Population, Resources, Environment'. 1977: W. H. Freeman.
139. Hocknull, S.A., et al., 'Extinction of eastern Sahul megafauna coincides with sustained environmental deterioration'. *Nature Communications*, 2020. 11(1): p. 2250.
140. University, S., 'The American Yawp: A Massively Collaborative Open U.S. History Textbook. 2020-2021 Updates. Stanford University Press Edition.'. 2021.
141. Whiten, A., 'The burgeoning reach of animal culture'. *Science*, 2021. 372(6537): p. eabe6514.
142. Jesmer, B.R., et al., 'Is ungulate migration culturally transmitted? Evidence of social learning from translocated animals'. *Science*, 2018. 361(6406): p. 1023.
143. Mann, J., et al., 'Cetacean Societies: Field Studies of Dolphins and Whales'. *Bibliovault OAI Repository, the University of Chicago Press*, 2001. 65.
144. Whitehead, H., T.D. Smith, and L. Rendell, 'Adaptation of sperm whales to open-boat whalers: rapid social learning on a large scale?'. *Biology Letters*, 2021. 17(3): p. 20210030.

145. Parfenov, V., 'Feral cows of the Chernobyl exclusion zone have organized a herd and behave like wild ancestors'. 2021: Naked Science. Via Google Translate. https://naked-science.ru/article/biology/odichavshie-korovy-chernobylskoj-zony-otchuzhdeniya organizovali-stado-i-vedut-sebya-kak-dikie-predki.
146. Morgan, J. and T. Hossain, 'The quest for QWERTY'. *American Economic Review*, 2009. 99: p. 435 – 40.
147. Ulanowicz, R., 'The Central Role of Information Theory in Ecology'. 2011.
148. Shin, J., et al., 'Scale and information-processing thresholds in Holocene social evolution'. *Nature Communications*, 2020. 11(1): p. 2394.
149. Dawkins, R. 'The extended phenotype : the gene as the unit of selection'. 1982.
150. Friston, K., 'A Free Energy Principle for Biological Systems'. *Entropy (Basel, Switzerland)*, 2012. 14: p. 2100 – 2121.
151. Taylor, R.P., 'Reduction of Physiological Stress Using Fractal Art and Architecture'. *Leonardo*, 2006. 39: p. 245 – 251.
152. Boothby, T.C., et al., 'Evidence for extensive horizontal gene transfer from the draft genome of a tardigrade'. *Proceedings of the National Academy of Sciences*, 2015. 112(52): p. 15976.
153. Pombubpa, N., et al., 'Insights into the desert living skin microbiome: geography, soil depth, and crust type affect biocrust microbial communities and networks in Mojave Desert, USA'. *bioRxiv*, 2019: p. 810002.
154. Durant, S., et al., 'Fiddling in biodiversity hotspots while deserts burn? Collapse of the Sahara's megafauna'. *Diversity and Distributions*, 2014. 20: p. n/a – n/a.
155. Powell, J., et al., 'Desert crust microorganisms, their environment, and human health'. *Journal of Arid Environments*, 2013. 112.
156. O'Bryan, C., et al., 'Conservation epidemiology of predators and scavengers to reduce zoonotic risk'. *The Lancet Planetary Health*, 2020. 4: p. E304 – E305.
157. Keesing, F. and R.S. Ostfeld, 'Impacts of biodiversity and biodiversity loss on zoonotic diseases'. *Proceedings of the National Academy of Sciences*, 2021. 118(17): p. e2023540118.
158. Leduc, D. and A.A. Rowden, 'Not to be Sneezed at: Does Pollen from Forests of Exotic Pine Affect Deep Oceanic Trench Ecosystems?'. *Ecosystems*, 2018. 21(2): p. 237 – 247.
159. Linskens, H.F., 'Mature Pollen and its Impact on Plant and Man', in *Sexual Plant Reproduction*, M. Cresti and A. Tiezzi, Editors. 1992, Springer Berlin Heidelberg: Berlin, Heidelberg. p. 203 – 217.
160. Sánchez-Bayo, F. and K. Wyckhuys, 'Worldwide decline of the entomofauna: A review of its drivers'. *Biological Conservation*, 2019. 232.
161. Evans, R., L. Otoole, and D. Whitfield, 'The history of eagles in Britain and Ireland: An ecological review of placename and documentary evidence from the last 1500 years'. *Bird Study*, 2012. 59: p. 1 – 15.
162. Tanner, E., et al., 'Wolves contribute to disease control in a multi-host system'. *Scientific Reports*, 2019. 9(1): p. 7940.
163. Crick, H.Q.P., 'Birds of prey in the UK: back from the brink. Published: January 1999'. BTO/HOT/ NT/ NTS/ RSPB/ SOC/ NERUSBG/ SRSG/ WRSG/ WWT/ WT/ WWF.
164. Sullins, D., et al., 'Identifying the diet of a declining prairie grouse using DNA metabarcoding'. *The Auk*, 2018. 135: p. 583 – 608.
165. Patten, M., C. Pruett, and D. Wolfe, 'Home range size and movements of Greater Prairie-Chickens'. *Ecology, conservation, and management of grouse. Studies In Avian Biology*, 2011. 39: p. 51 – 62.

166. Sergio, F., et al., 'Ecologically justified charisma: Preservation of top predators delivers biodiversity conservation'. *Journal of Applied Ecology*, 2006. 43: p. 1049 – 1055.
167. Borrell, B., 'Where eagles die'. *Nature*, 2011.
168. Oliveira, A.B., et al., 'The Impact of Organic Farming on Quality of Tomatoes Is Associated to Increased Oxidative Stress during Fruit Development.'. *PLOS One*, 2013. 8(2): p. e56354.
169. Wang, Y., et al., 'Modern organic and broiler chickens sold for human consumption provide more energy from fat than protein'. *Public health nutrition*, 2009. 13: p. 400 – 8.
170. Bonhommeau, S., et al., 'Eating up the world's food web and the human trophic level'. *Proceedings of the National Academy of Sciences*, 2013. 110(51): p. 20617.
171. Chen, X.D., et al., 'Stabilizing Effects of Bacterial Biofilms: EPS Penetration and Redistribution of Bed Stability Down the Sediment Profile'. *Journal of Geophysical Research: Biogeosciences*, 2017. 122(12): p. 3113 – 3125.
172. Villar, N., et al., 'Frugivory underpins the nitrogen cycle'. *Functional Ecology*, 2021. 35(2): p. 357 – 368.
173. Maisey, A.C., et al., 'Foraging by an avian ecosystem engineer extensively modifies the litter and soil layer in forest ecosystems'. *Ecological Applications*, 2021. 31(1): p. e02219.
174. Suyin, H., 'The Sparrow Shall Fall'. 1959: The New Yorker, October 10, 1959.
175. Barrow, M.V., Jr., 'A Feathered River Across the Sky: The Passenger Pigeon's Flight to Extinction. By Joel Greenberg'. *Environmental History*, 2014. 19(4): p. 747 – 749.
176. Novak, B., 'Deciphering The Ecological Impact Of The Passenger Pigeon: A Synthesis Of Paleogenetics, Paleoecology, Morphology, And Physiology'. 2016.
177. Australian Koala Foundation, 'So how many koalas were there?'. 2016: www.savethekoala.com.
178. Nyffeler, M., Ç.H. Şekercioğlu, and C.J. Whelan, 'Insectivorous birds consume an estimated 400–500 million tons of prey annually'. *The Science of Nature*, 2018. 105 (7): p. 47.
179. Lynam, C., et al., 'Jellyfish overtake fish in a heavily fished ecosystem (DOI:10.1016/j.cub.2006.06.018)'. 2006. 16: p. R492 – R493.
180. Doubleday, Z., et al., 'Global proliferation of cephalopods'. *Current Biology*, 2016. 26: p. R406 – R407.
181. Sedayu, A., A. Mariani, and M. Miarsyah, 'Improving the perception of Christmas Island Frigatebirds by local fishermen on Pulau Untung Jawa, Jakarta, using the Penyuluhan method.'. 2020, Kukila. p. 6 – 13.
182. Gianuca, D., et al., 'Intentional killing and extensive aggressive handling of albatrosses and petrels at sea in the southwestern Atlantic Ocean'. *Biological Conservation*, 2020. 252: p. 108817.
183. Pauly, D. and D. Zeller, 'Catch reconstructions reveal that global marine fisheries catches are higher than reported and declining'. *Nature Communications*, 2016. 7(1): p. 10244.
184. Mikulcak, F., 'The value of land: Prosperous lands and positive rewards through sustainable land management'. 2015: Initiative, The Economics of Land Degradation.

185. Gretton, P. and U. Salma, 'Land Degradation and the Australian Agricultural Industry. Staff information paper.'. 2016, Commonwealth of Australia 1996.
186. Cingolani, A., I. Noy-Meir, and S. Diaz, 'Grazing effects on rangeland diversity: A synthesis of contemporary models'. *Ecological Applications*, 2005. 15: p. 757 – 773.
187. Unknown, 'Coal consumption affecting climate', in *Rodney and Otamatea Times, Waitemata and Kaipara Gazette*. 1912: https://paperspast.natlib.govt.nz/newspapers/ROTWKG19120814.2.56. p. 7.
188. UN, 'What is the United Nations Framework Convention on Climate Change? Last visited, 6 November 2021'. United Nations Climate Change: https://unfccc.int/process-and-meetings/the-convention/what-is-the-unitednationsframework-convention-on-climate-change.
189. Griscom, B.W., et al., 'Natural climate solutions'. *Proceedings of the National Academy of Sciences*, 2017. 114(44): p. 11645.
190. Sen, A. and N. Dabi, 'Tightening the Net. Oxfam Briefing Paper, August 2021.'. 2021, Oxfam International.
191. Cox, C., 'Suppression of breakers in stormy seas by an oil film'. *International Journal of Maritime History*, 2015. 27: p. 528 – 536.
192. Cox, C.S., X. Zhang, and T.F. Duda, 'Suppressing breakers with polar oil films: Using an epic sea rescue to model wave energy budgets'. *Geophysical Research Letters*, 2017. 44(3): p. 1414 – 1421.
193. Beehler, W.H., 'The use of oil to still the waves'. 1888, Century Illustrated Monthly Magazine. p. 705 – 716.
194. Rosenthal, W. and S. Lehner, 'Rogue Waves: Results of the MaxWave Project'. *Journal of Offshore Mechanics and Arctic Engineering*, 2008. 130(2).
195. Vogel, M., 'The Light from the Whale. Clockworks'. 2014.
196. Brownell, R. and A. Yablokov, 'Whaling, Illegal and Pirate'. 2009. p. 1235 – 1239.
197. Branch, T.A., et al., 'Past and present distribution, densities and movements of blue whales Balaenoptera musculus in the Southern Hemisphere and northern Indian Ocean'. *Mammal Review*, 2007. 37(2): p. 116 – 175.
198. Pershing, A.J., et al., 'The impact of whaling on the ocean carbon cycle: why bigger was better'. *PloS one*, 2010. 5(8): p. e12444 – e12444.
199. Young, I. and A. Ribal, 'Multiplatform evaluation of global trends in wind speed and wave height'. *Science*, 2019. 364: p. eaav9527.
200. Blackall, T., et al., 'Ammonia emissions from seabird colonies'. *Geophysical Research Letters*, 2007. 341.
201. Riddick, S., et al., 'Measurement of ammonia emissions from tropical seabird colonies'. *Atmospheric Environment*, 2014. 89: p. 35–42.
202. Acevedo-Gutierrez, A., D. Croll, and B. Tershy, 'High costs limit dive time in the largest whales'. *The Journal of experimental biology*, 2002. 205: p. 1747 – 53.
203. Pyenson, N.D., et al., 'Discovery of a sensory organ that coordinates lunge feeding in rorqual whales'. *Nature*, 2012. 485(7399): p. 498 – 501.
204. Mulyadi, M., 'Zooplankton reseraches in Indonesian waters: A historical review'. *Coastal Marine Science*, 2012. 35: p. 202 – 207.
205. Baars, M.A., et al., 'Zooplankton abundance in the eastern Banda Sea and northern Arafura Sea during and after the upwelling season, August 1984 and February 1985'. *Netherlands Journal of Sea Research*, 1990. 25(4): p. 527 – 543.

206. Pusparini, N., et al., 'The Thermocline Layer and Chlorophyll-a Concentration Variability during Southeast Monsoon in the Banda Sea'. *IOP Conference Series: Earth and Environmental Science*, 2017. 55.
207. Goldbogen, J.A., et al., 'Mechanics, hydrodynamics and energetics of blue whale lunge feeding: efficiency dependence on krill density'. *The Journal of Experimental Biology*, 2011. 214(1): p. 131.
208. Attard, C., et al., 'Genetic diversity and structure of blue whales (Balaenoptera musculus) in Australian feeding aggregations'. *Conservation Genetics*, 2010. 11: p. 2437 – 2441.
209. Dewar, W., et al., 'Does the marine biosphere mix the ocean?'. *Journal of Marine Research*, 2006. 64.
210. Huntley, M. and M. Zhou, 'Influence of animals on turbulence in the sea'. *Marine Ecology-progress Series*, 2004. 273: p. 65 – 79.
211. Chami, R., et al., 'Nature's Solution to Climate Change: A strategy to protect whales can limit greenhouse gases and global warming'. 2019: Finance and Development. December 2019, Vol. 56, No. 4.
212. Gordon, A.L. and R.D. Susanto, 'Banda Sea surface-layer divergence'. *Ocean Dynamics*, 2001. 52(1): p. 2 – 10.
213. Hamada, J.-I., et al., 'Interannual Rainfall Variability over Northwestern Jawa and its Relation to the Indian Ocean Dipole and El Nino-Southern Oscillation Events'. *Scientific online letters on the atmosphere: SOLA*, 2012. 8: p. 69 – 72.
214. Miller, E., K. Hayashi, and D. Song, 'Explaining the ocean's richest biodiversity hotspot and global patterns of fish diversity'. *Proceedings of the Royal Society B: Biological Sciences*, 2018. 285.
215. Graham, J., B. Stearns, and S. Stearns, 'Watching, from the Edge of Extinction'. *Ecology*, 2000. 81.
216. Ehrlich, P., 'The scale of the human enterprise and biodiversity loss'. 1994.
217. Simberloff, D., 'Lawton, J. H. and May, R. M. (Eds.). Extinction Rates. 1995. Oxford University Press, Oxford. xii + 233 pp.'. *Journal of Evolutionary Biology*, 1996. 9(1): p. 124 – 126.
218. Ceballos, G., et al., 'Accelerated modern human–induced species losses: Entering the sixth mass extinction'. *Science Advances*, 2015. 1(5): p. e1400253.
219. Uyeda, J., et al., 'The million-year wait for macroevolutionary bursts'. *Proceedings of the National Academy of Sciences of the United States of America*, 2011. 108: p. 15908 – 13.
220. Retallack, G. and A. Jahren, 'Methane Release from Igneous Intrusion of Coal during Late Permian Extinction Events'. *Journal of Geology*, 2008. 116.
221. Sun, Y., et al., 'Lethally Hot Temperatures During the Early Triassic Greenhouse'. *Science (New York, N.Y.)*, 2012. 338: p. 366 – 70.
222. Burgess, S.D. and S.A. Bowring, 'High-precision geochronology confirms voluminous magmatism before, during, and after Earth's most severe extinction'. *Science Advances*, 2015. 1(7): p. e1500470.
223. Clarkson, M.O., et al., 'Ocean acidification and the Permo-Triassic mass extinction'. *Science*, 2015. 348(6231): p. 229.
224. Rosenberg, K., et al., 'Decline of the North American avifauna'. *Science*, 2019. 366: p. eaaw1313.
225. Doughty, C., et al., 'Global nutrient transport in a world of giants'. *Proceedings of the National Academy of Sciences of the United States of America*, 2015. 113.

226. Harari, Y.N., J. Purcell, and H. Watzman, 'Sapiens : a brief history of humankind'. 2015.
227. 'Biodiversity', ed. E.O. Wilson and H. University. 1988, Washington, DC: The National Academies Press. 538.
228. Worm, B., et al., 'Global catches, exploitation rates, and rebuilding options for sharks'. *Marine Policy*, 2013. 40: p. 194 – 204.
229. Jorgensen, S., A. Klimley, and A. Muhlia-Melo, 'Scalloped hammerhead shark Sphyrna lewini, utilizes deep-water, hypoxic zone in the Gulf of California'. *Journal of fish biology*, 2009. 74: p. 1682 – 7.
230. Myers, R., et al., 'Cascading Effects of the Loss of Apex Predatory Sharks from a Coastal Ocean'. *Science (New York, N.Y.)*, 2007. 315: p. 1846 – 50.
231. Gray, H., 'Spice at Any Price: The Life and Times of Frederick de Houtman 1571 1627'. 2019: Westralian Books.
232. Field, I.C., et al., 'Protein mining the world's oceans: Australasia as an example of illegal expansion-and-displacement fishing'. *Fish and Fisheries*, 2009. 10(3): p. 323 – 328.
233. Satrioajie, W., et al., 'The importance of the Banda Sea for tuna conservation area: A review of studies on the biology and the ecology of tuna'. *IOP Conference Series: Earth and Environmental Science*, 2018. 184: p. 012004.
234. Garrett, J., 'Indonesian minister who revels in destruction of illegal fishing boats creates job surge for small-scale fishers 14 December 2015.', in *ABC News online*. 2015: https://www.abc.net.au/news/2015-12-14/destruction-of-illegal-fishing-boats in-indonesia-jobs-boom/7027122
235. Beale, C., et al., 'Population dynamics of oceanic manta rays (Mobula birostris) in the Raja Ampat Archipelago, West Papua, Indonesia, and the impacts of the El Niño–Southern Oscillation on their movement ecology'. *Diversity and Distributions*, 2019.
236. Watson, M., 'Action for an ocean for all: Rethinking the blue economy to be inclusive, sustainable, fair and for everyone. 25 March 2019.'. 2019: International Institute for Environment and Development. https://www.iied.org/action-for-ocean-for-all.
237. Zhu, Z., et al., 'Greening of the Earth and its drivers'. *Nature Climate Change*, 2016. 6.
238. Nevill, J., 'Submission to inquiry into recreational fishing (including The impacts of spearfishing: notes on the effects of recreational diving on shallow marine reefs in Australia)'. 2010: Only One Planet Consulting. 22 March 2010.
239. Mjadwesch, R., '*Nomination to List the Large Macropods as Threatened Species under the NSW Threatened Species Conservation Act* 1995 MESS Bathurst'. 2011.
240. Fisher, A.G., et al., 'Remote sensing of trophic cascades: multi-temporal landsat imagery reveals vegetation change driven by the removal of an apex predator'. *Landscape Ecology*, 2021.
241. Schwartz, J.D., 'The Reindeer Chronicles: And Other Inspiring Stories of Working with Nature to Heal the Earth'. 2020: Chelsea Green Publishing.
242. Perrin, W., B. Wursig, and J.G.M. Thewissen, 'Encyclopedia of Marine Mammals'. Vol. 47. 2002. 1352.
243. Cardillo, M., L. Bromham, and S.J. Greenhill, 'Links between language diversity and species richness can be confounded by spatial autocorrelation'. *Proceedings of the Royal Society B: Biological Sciences*, 2015. 282(1809): p. 20142986.

244. Ilangakoon, A., 'Exploring anthropogenic activities that threaten endangered blue whales (Balaenoptera musculus) off Sri Lanka'. *Journal of Matine Animals and Their Ecology*, 2012. 5: p. 3 – 7.
245. Rudkin, D. and G. Young, 'Horseshoe Crabs – An Ancient Ancestry Revealed'. 2009. p. 25 – 44.
246. Tomasik, B., 'How many wild animals are there?'. 2009 (updated 2019): https://reducing-suffering.org/how-many-wild-animals-are-there/.
247. Dawkins, R., 'The selfish gene / Richard Dawkins'. 1976, New York: Oxford University Press.
248. Smith, J.M. and G.R. Price, 'The Logic of Animal Conflict'. *Nature*, 1973. 246(5427): p. 15 – 18.
249. Axelrod, R. and W.D. Hamilton, 'The evolution of cooperation'. *Science*, 1981. 211(4489): p. 1390.
250. David, G.m., et al., 'Offshore diplomacy, or how seabirds mitigate intra-specific competition: a case study based on GPS tracking of Cape gannets from neighbouring colonies'. *Marine Ecology Progress Series*, 2004. 268: p. 265-279.
251. Van Valen, L., 'A new evolutionary law'. 1973, *Evolutionary Theory*. p. 1–30.
252. Grant, P.R., 'Hybridization of Darwin's Finches on Isla Daphne Major, Galapagos'. *Philosophical Transactions: Biological Sciences*, 1993. 340(1291): p. 127 – 139.
253. Broughton, J.M. and E.M. Weitzel, 'Population reconstructions for humans and megafauna suggest mixed causes for North American Pleistocene extinctions'. *Nature Communications*, 2018. 9(1): p. 5441.
254. Hardin, G., 'The Tragedy of the Commons'. *Science*, 1968. 162(3859): p. 1243.
255. Studds, C., et al., 'Rapid population decline in migratory shorebirds relying on Yellow Sea tidal mudflats as stopover sites'. *Nature Communications*, 2017. 8.
256. Anonymous, 'Numenius madagascariensis (eastern curlew) Conservation Advice. Page 1 of 13. The Minister approved this conservation advice on 14/05/2015 and included this species in the critically endangered category, effective from 26/05/2015. http://www.environment.gov.au/biodiversity/threatened/species/pubs/847 -conservation-advice.pdf'. 2015.
257. Kituyi, M. and P. Thomson, '90% of fish stocks are used up – fisheries subsidies must stop emptying the ocean'. 2018: World Economic Forum, 13 July 2018. https://www.weforum.org/agenda/2018/07/fish-stocks-are-used-up-fisheries subsidies-must-stop/.
258. Breinlinger, S., et al., 'Hunting the eagle killer: A cyanobacterial neurotoxin causes vacuolar myelinopathy'. *Science*, 2021. 371(6536): p. eaax9050.
259. Longnecker, M.P., et al., 'Association between maternal serum concentration of the DDT metabolite DDE and preterm and small-for-gestational-age babies at birth'. *The Lancet*, 2001. 358(9276): p. 110 – 114.
260. Bohn, R. and J. Short, 'How Much Information? 2009 Report on American Consumers'. 2009.
261. Bornmann, L. and R. Mutz, 'Growth rates of modern science: A bibliometric analysis based on the number of publications and cited references: Growth Rates of

Modern Science: A Bibliometric Analysis Based on the Number of Publications and Cited References'. *Journal of the Association for Information Science and Technology*, 2014. 66.
262. de Solla Price, D.J., 'Networks of Scientific Papers'. *Science*, 1965. 149(3683): p. 510.
263. Sagan, C., 'The Demon-Haunted World: Science as a Candle in the Dark'. 2011: Random House Publishing Group.
264. Harte, J., 'Maximum entropy is a foundation for complexity science: the example of ecology'. 2017, Stanford University Complexity Symposium. November 14, 2017. https://www.youtube.com/watch?v=XElfPKCG69o&t=414s.
265. Jactel, H., E. Brockerhoff, and P. Duelli, 'A Test of the Biodiversity Stability Theory: Meta-analysis of Tree Species Diversity Effects on Insect Pest Infestations, and Re-examination of Responsible Factors'. 2005. p. 235 – 262.
266. White, E.P., K.M. Thibault, and X. Xiao, 'Characterizing species abundance distributions across taxa and ecosystems using a simple maximum entropy model'. *Ecology*, 2012. 93(8): p. 1772 – 1778.
267. Wiesner, J.B. and H.F. York, 'National Security and the Nuclear-Test Ban'. *Scientific American*, 1964. 211(4): p. 27 – 35.
268. Kolbert, E., 'Under a White Sky: The Nature of the Future'. 2021: Crown.
269. Anthony, D. and G. Reynolds, 'Year of the locust '. 2020: The Dollop (podcast). https://soundcloud.com/the-dollop/431-year-of-the-locust.
270. Singleton, G., et al., eds. *'Ecologically-based rodent management. ACIAR Monograph No. 59, 494p.'*. 1999, Australian Centre for International Agricultural Research.
271. Kaufman, M., 'How to Give Mars an Atmosphere, Maybe'. 2019: Many Worlds, https://manyworlds.space/2017/03/09/how-to-give-mars-an-atmosphere-maybe/.
272. Defries, R., 'What Would Nature Do?: A Guide for Our Uncertain Times'. 2020: Columbia University Press.
273. Scholz, R., et al., 'Sustainable use of phosphorus: A finite resource'. *The Science of the total environment*, 2013. 461.
274. MacNeil, M.A., et al., 'Water quality mediates resilience on the Great' Barrier Reef'. *Nature Ecology & Evolution*, 2019. 3(4): p. 620 – 627.
275. Amundson, R., et al., 'Soil and human security in the 21st century'. *Science*, 2015. 348(6235): p. 1261071.
276. Coulter, J., 'World Agriculture: Towards 2015/2030. An FAO Perspective. Edited by J. Bruinsma. Rome: FAO and London: Earthscan (2003), pp. 432, £35.00 Paperback. ISBN 92-5-104835-5'. *Experimental Agriculture*, 2004. 40: p. 269 – 269.
277. RSPB, 'Hope Farm Annual Review'. 2019.
278. Fremlin, J.H., 'How Many People Can the World Support?'. 1964, New Scientist. p. 285 – 287
279. Hertwich, E., et al., 'Assessing the Environmental Impacts of Consumption and Production: Priority Products and Materials'. 2010.
280. Coleman, E., et al., 'Limited effects of tree planting on forest canopy cover and rural livelihoods in Northern India'. *Nature Sustainability*, 2021: p. 1 – 8.
281. Guiden, P., et al., 'Effects of management outweigh effects of plant diversity on restored animal communities in tallgrass prairies'. *Proceedings of the National Academy of Sciences*, 2021. 118: p. e2015421118.
282. Mouillot, D., et al., 'Functional over-redundancy and high functional vulnerability in global fish faunas on tropical reefs'. *Proceedings of the National Academy of Sciences*, 2014. 111(38): p. 13757.

283. Morris, R., et al., 'Developing a nature-based coastal defence strategy for Australia'. *Australian Journal of Civil Engineering*, 2019: p. 1 – 10.
284. Jefferies, C., 'Designing High Seas Marine Protected Areas to Conserve Blue Carbon Ecosystems: A Climate-essential Development?'. 2019: Centre for International Governance Innovation. CIGI Papers No. 232 — November 2019.
285. Stoner, A.W., 'Pelagic Sargassum: Evidence for a major decrease in biomass'. *Deep Sea Research Part A. Oceanographic Research Papers*, 1983. 30(4): p. 469 – 474.
286. Gower, J. and S. King, 'The distribution of pelagic Sargassum observed with OLCI'. *International Journal of Remote Sensing*, 2020. 41(15): p. 5669 – 5679.
287. Wang, M., et al., 'The great Atlantic sargassum belt'. *Science*, 2019. 365(6448): p. 83.
288. Buchanan, L. and A. O'Connell, 'A Brief History of Decision Making'. 2006: Harvard Business Review. January 2006.
289. Plumptre, A.J., et al., 'Where Might We Find Ecologically Intact Communities?'. *Frontiers in Forests and Global Change*, 2021. 4: p. 26.
290. Methorst, J., et al., 'The importance of species diversity for human well being in Europe'. *Ecological Economics*, 2020: p. 106917.
291. Graeber, D. and D. Wengrow, 'The Dawn of Everything: A New History of Humanity'. 2021: Farrar, Straus and Giroux.
292. Lovelock, J., 'Novacene: The Coming Age of Hyperintelligence'. 2019: Penguin Books Limited.

Index

C

H

I

Q

R

S

About the author

Simon Mustoe has worked all over the world as an ecologist, expeditioner and conservationist. He's tumbled in boats amid frigid north Atlantic storms, trekked solo into Madagascar's remote dry forests, discovered unknown species of seabird in Australia's tropical ocean territories and recorded previously unseen whales in West Papua. His thirty years as a researcher, communicator, expert witness and consultant for industry, governments and conservation groups have offered many oblique views of our interaction with nature and candid examples of our failure to protect it and ourselves. Telling the story about our relationship with and dependence on wildlife is Simon's passion. He co-produced Australia's National Landscapes Nature Series, sends his online magazine Wildiaries to a quarter of a million Australians, and illustrates his own blog. Meanwhile, Simon continues to play an active role as adviser to important ecosystem restoration initiatives.

Acknowledgements

I want to thank everyone who has been an influence on my life in nature. My brothers, and parents William and Barbara Mustoe, for bringing me up in the Cotswold countryside and the local landowners who allowed me to roam freely as a child. The friends who joined me birdwatching from an early age, my teachers and lecturers at school and university and my earliest employers, who trained me to think differently about ecology. Fiona Seers and my children Sadie and Charlie supported me the most during periods of distraction and contemplation. This book is a culmination of all the experiences I have gathered, things I've learnt and conversations I've had throughout my formative years. I also want to thank everyone who shares their work, from the writers, filmmakers, podcasters and bloggers, to the whole scientific community. I couldn't have done this without access to the most extraordinary wisdom online. A few people have tolerated my ramblings as I have tested explanations of complex scientific ideas. Thank you Aaron Robinson for late nights around a fire, Anissa Lawrence for many a long phone call. In particular I have to thank Jess and Gavin Burbidge for their perpetual guidance on publication and copyright. And Helen Allison, Barbara Mustoe and Guy Healy for considered feedback on early drafts. My thanks also to any readers of Reddit and Twitter who indulged me with discussion, kept me honest and provided constructive criticism, and to people who have travelled with me or inspired me to do more. To my editors, starting with Alexandra Payne, who went beyond expectations, adding encouragement and important structural revisions. To Tim Harvey, Tony Ryan and

Tricia Dearborn for helping polish and proof the final manuscript, to Sarah Endicott for indexing and to my graphic designer Jarrett Skinner for layout and Nick Girling for cover artwork. Also to Ian Redmond and Jess Burbidge for their forensic assessment of the final manuscript and to David Casselman of Ecoflix for sponsorship. Finally, to Mike Da Silva for his counsel on marketing, without whom I would not be in a position to make this book successful. I would also like to acknowledge the traditional owners and custodians of the land on which this book was written, the people of the Kulin Nation. For that, I pay my respects to their Elders, past and present. Mostly I would like to thank all those who continue to dedicate their lives to fighting for wildlife.

THANK YOU TO MY SUPPORTERS

To those who bought the book on presale and helped support me. Special thanks to Tim Hochgrebe of Underwater Australasia. My thanks also go to Karena Joyce, Charissa Charissa, Alison O'Sullivan, Mick Barker, Maree Coldrey, Debbie Gwyther-Jones, Jared Tracey, Mark Jones, Melissa Brennan, Clare Murphy, Kahlin Wormell, Jacqueline Stafford-Neale, Maxine Parr, Wesley Roe, John Wenitong, Sarah Pye, Willemijn Passtoors, Jennie Burton, Julie Blake, Ingrid Kangas, Caterina Cavallaro, Moira Ferres, Brenda Marmion, Vanessa Willetts, Debbie Cooper, Cassandra Mardi, Debbie Kosh, Cathy Okeeffe, Sasha Herbert, Ricki Coughlan, Kathryn Dolphin, Nicki Cogley, K-M Doyle, Steve Hall, Joanne Neville, Karen Stalker, Merinda Sharp, Dianne Van Eck, Kerry Althoff, Claire Hoffman, Susan Driessen, Christine Lawley, Joel Hamilton-Foster, Cathryn Thoday, Debra Slater-Lee, Bronwyn Reid, Carole Benham, Jenny Longley, Rene Gorissen, Lynette Heweston, Shayna Gavin, Adrian Howard, Meagan Hollole, Rosemary Race, Marie Mann, Catherine Londenberg, Sheila Dorsey, Jason Edwards, Meredith Conroy, Brauton Heathwilliams, Brenda May, Robyn Lewis, Neil Rimmer, Jennifer Gilbert, Wendy Havard, Adam Mustoe, Debbie Saegenschnitter, Abby & Nick Morrison, Lori-Ann Shibish, Christine Regter, Helen Procter-Brown, Leanne Hodson, Anthony Lovell, Adrian Barratt, Rebecca Ford, Ruth Franks, Joeanne Katsikaros, Robyn Cochrane, Eben Viljoen, Sarah Reid, Daryn Bungey, Caitlin Jones, Hazel Brooks, Raylee Marston, Sally Pilgrim, David Pryce, Colin Armour, Janet McCarthy, Dayle Fulford, Sheryl Cornish, Leena Hack, Paul Collins, Paul Piercy, Christine Chong, Roslyn Kushinsky, Marcia Batton, Denise Illing, Wendy McWilliams, Christine Curran, Martyn Cutcher, Margaret Houk, Anna Calvert, Michael Phillips, Lizzie Corke, Rosemary St John, Josiane Broome, Patrick O'regan, Robert Brazell, Judy Bartlett, Aileen Strumpher, Andrea Britton, Robyn Byrne, John Corney, Sandra Moritz, Jessica Thomas, Louise Draper, Hannah Cattanach, Donna Wilson, Kate Ahmad, Joelene Mitchell, Iona Flett, Anne Coote, Sue Liu, Dominique Jacobs, Taryn Tiko, Dianne Crookes, Sammara Giles, Rachael Kane, Tanya Loos, Vanessa Mignon, David Roberts, Dane Haddon, Lorraine McCann, Sandy Gillis, Dave Moolman, Lauren Flint, Grace Keast, Linda Dennis, Jackie Berkelaar, Shara Turner, Jay Garnet, Jose Manuel N. Azevedo, Patrick King, David Richardson, Scott Baker and John Butfield.

Ingram Content Group UK Ltd.
Milton Keynes UK
UKHW011816290623
424300UK00003B/36

9 780645 453508